HOUSING
THE NEW RUSSIA

HOUSING THE NEW RUSSIA

JANE R. ZAVISCA

CORNELL UNIVERSITY PRESS
Ithaca and London

First published 2012 by Cornell University Press

First printing, Cornell Paperbacks, 2012

Printed in the United States of America

Library of Congress Cataloging-in-Publication Data

Zavisca, Jane R. (Jane Roj), 1972–
    Housing the new Russia / Jane R. Zavisca.
        p. cm.
    Includes bibliographical references and index.
    ISBN 978-0-8014-5037-2 (cloth : alk. paper)
    ISBN 978-0-8014-7737-9 (pbk. : alk. paper)
    1. Housing—Russia (Federation)   2. Housing policy—
Russia (Federation)   3. Residential real estate—Russia
(Federation)   4. Post-communism—Social aspects—
Russia (Federation)   5. Russia (Federation)—Social
conditions—1991–   I. Title.
    HD7345.2.A3Z38   2012
    363.50947—dc23   2011047164

Cornell University Press strives to use environmentally responsible suppliers and materials to the fullest extent possible in the publishing of its books. Such materials include vegetable-based, low-VOC inks and acid-free papers that are recycled, totally chlorine-free, or partly composed of nonwood fibers. For further information, visit our website at www.cornellpress.cornell.edu.

Cloth printing   10 9 8 7 6 5 4 3 2 1
Paperback printing 10 9 8 7 6 5 4 3 2 1

For my family

◪ CONTENTS

List of Figures and Tables   ix
Acknowledgments   xi
Abbreviations   xiii
Note on Translation and Russian Names   xv

Introduction: A Painful Question   1

PART I: THE DEVELOPMENT OF THE
         POST-SOVIET HOUSING REGIME

1. The Soviet Promise: A Separate
   Apartment for Every Family   23

2. Transplant Failure: The American
   Housing Model in Russia   49

3. Maternity Capitalism: Grafting
   Pronatalism onto Housing Policy   69

4. Property without Markets: Who Got
   What as Markets Failed   86

PART II: THE MEANING OF HOUSING
          IN THE NEW RUSSIA

5. Disappointed Dreams: Distributive
   Injustice in the New Housing Order   103

6. Mobility Strategies: Searching for the
   Separate Apartment   130

7. Rooms of Their Own: How Housing
   Affects Family Size   144

8. Children Are Not Capital: Ambivalence
   about Pronatalist Housing Policies   163

9. To Owe Is Not to Own: Why Russians
Reject Mortgages   175

Conclusion: A Market That Could
Not Emerge   194

Appendix: Characteristics of Interviewees
Cited in Text   202
Notes   207
Works Cited   219
Index   237

◣ FIGURES AND TABLES

FIGURES

I.1 Residential buildings in Kaluga   17

I.2 Khrushchevka exterior   17

I.3 Trends in housing construction and prices   18

1.1 Multiuse room in a Soviet apartment   31

1.2 Post-Soviet multiuse room in the Soviet style   32

2.1 Luxury apartment building in Kaluga   55

2.2 Index of housing affordability   56

2.3 New mortgage lending   59

3.1 Mortgage affordability with and without maternity capital   83

4.1 Renovated kitchens   90

4.2 Housing tenure by age   91

4.3 Housing tenure by family structure and income   96

5.1 Room shared by a couple and their child   108

5.2 Grandmother in kitchen shared with daughter-in-law   109

5.3 Room in a separate apartment   110

5.4 Detached luxury home   116

6.1 Prototypical property network   137

7.1 Children's rooms   155

7.2 Number of children by housing type and education   159

9.1 Soviet and post-Soviet apartment buildings   185

TABLES

I.1 Description of qualitative sample   15

I.2 Kaluga oblast compared to other regions of Russia   16

1.1 Correlates of housing status in the urban USSR   38

1.2 Odds of having a separate apartment in the USSR   40

4.1 Trends in housing inequality   89

4.2 Housing quality by income quintile   95

4.3 Analysis of transitions to separate apartments   98
6.1 Property rights and registration patterns   135
7.1 Analysis of birth of a second child   161
9.1 Use of consumer credit   189

 ACKNOWLEDGMENTS

The research and writing for this book were made possible by the support of a number of institutions. First I thank John Ackerman, my editor and the director of Cornell University Press, for his enthusiastic support. Thanks also to production editor Karen Laun and to the reviewers of the manuscript, whose careful readings and suggestions made this a better book. A fellowship at the Center for Advanced Study in the Behavioral Sciences for the 2006 Summer Institute on Economy and Society, directed by Neil Fligstein and Woody Powell, provided a stimulating environment for developing the project. Preliminary research was sponsored by a postdoctoral fellowship from the Eurasia Program of the Social Science Research Council, with funds provided by the State Department under the Program for Research and Training on Eastern Europe and the Independent States of the Former Soviet Union (Title VIII). Fieldwork was funded by a National Research Competition grant from the National Council for Eurasian and East European Research, also under authority of a Title VIII grant from the US Department of State. A junior sabbatical from the University of Arizona provided time off from teaching to collect qualitative data. The Russian Longitudinal Monitoring Survey (RLMS-HSE) was made available to me by the Higher School of Economics together with the Carolina Population Center of the University of North Carolina at Chapel Hill, and the Institute of Sociology of the Russian Academy of Sciences.

Although the research and writing of this book took place after I completed my PhD, my earlier educational and research experiences significantly shaped this work. Martina Morris, my undergraduate mentor, generously gave me my first international fieldwork experience and inspired me to pursue a PhD in sociology. Faculty of the Sociology Department at the University of California at Berkeley, where I earned my PhD, encouraged me to take intellectual risks in a discipline suspicious of international work as "mere" area studies. My mentors at Berkeley—Victoria Bonnell, Michael Burawoy, Neil Fligstein, and Michael Hout—taught me to frame my work to be relevant beyond Russia's borders. Victoria Bonnell generously continued to advise me beyond the PhD as I worked on this book. The Sociology Department at the University of Arizona has been my institutional base throughout this project. The department's reputation for its extraordinary support of assistant professors is well deserved. Thank you so much to my colleagues for mentoring me and believing in me.

Valuable feedback on portions of the manuscript was provided by Adele Barker, Victoria Bonnell, Cynthia Buckley, Deborah Davis, Ted Gerber, Bruce Grant, Alya Guseva, Erin Leahey, Stacey Richter, Michele Rivkin-Fish, Louise Roth, Robin Stryker, Jennifer Utrata, and Sandra Way. I presented portions of the research at academic conferences of the American Sociological Association; the Association for Slavic, East European, and Eurasian Studies; and the Society for the Advancement of Socioeconomics. I thank organizers and attendees of these talks, as well as of invited talks I gave at Indiana University, the University of Texas at Austin, and the University of Wisconsin at Madison.

A host of friends and colleagues in Russia helped me to organize and complete the fieldwork. Thanks especially to Nina, Victor, Iulia, and Aleftina. Three talented sociologists—Anna Evpatova, Elena Kuzina, and Aurika Zaets—conducted the interviews. Anastasia Smirnov took beautiful photos for the book, and Vladimir Pronichev managed the photo shoots.

Personal support was provided by friends, especially Svetlana, Melissa, Jen, Crystal, Rebecca, and Baabs. Family members near and far encouraged and tolerated me as I completed this book. Thanks especially to my parents Dolores and Frank, my partner Alon, and my son Roey.

 **Abbreviations**

Note: Some Russian organizations have an official English translation for the organization's name and/or acronym. In such cases I use the English version, including in bibliographic citations for Russian-language documents.

AHML	Agency for Home Mortgage Lending (*Agenstvo po ipotechnomy zhilishchnomu kreditovaniiu*)
ARHML	Agency for Restructuring Home Mortgage Loans (*Agenstvo po restrukturizatsii ipotechnykh zhilishchnykh kreditov*)
CPSU	Communist Party of the Soviet Union
FHA	Federal Housing Administration of the United States
FOM	Public Opinion Foundation (*Fond obshchestvennogo mneniia*)
Gosstroi	State Committee for Construction and Housing (*Komitet po stroitel'stvu i zhilishchno-kommunal'nomu khoziaistvu pri pravitel'stve Rossii*)
GSE	Government-Sponsored Enterprise
GSS-USSR	General Social Survey of the European USSR
HSRP	Housing Sector Reform Project
IUE	Institute for Urban Economics (*Institut ekonomiki goroda*)
MBS	Mortgage-backed securities
OKINB	Official Kremlin International News Broadcast
PFRF	Pension Fund of the Russian Federation (*Pensionnyi Fond Rossiiskoi Federatsii*)
PNP	Priority National Projects (*Prioritetnye natsional'nye proekty*)
RF	Russian Federation
Rosstat	Federal State Statistics Service (*Federal'naia sluzhba gosudarstvennoi statistiki*)
SDT	Second demographic transition
TFR	Total fertility rate
UNECE	United Nations Economic Commission for Europe
UNR	United Nations in Russia
USAID	United States Agency for International Development
VA	U.S. Department of Veterans Affairs

YFP   *Young Families Program (Podprogramma "Obespechenie zhil'em molodykh semei" federal'noi tselevoi programmy "Zhilishche")*

◼ Note on Translation and Russian Names

Translations from Russian are my own, unless otherwise noted. For government documents available in both Russian and English, I provide a citation and link for the English translation in notes. To improve readability, I have slightly modified some official translations based on my reading of the Russian originals.

The Library of Congress system of transliteration is used for Russian bibliographic entries. Interview respondents cited in the text were assigned pseudonyms, using common English spellings, even when these deviate from the Library of Congress system. A table of pseudonyms and other attributes of respondents is available in appendix A to assist readers with tracking respondents who are referred to multiple times throughout the book.

HOUSING
THE NEW RUSSIA

Introduction
A Painful Question

Most housing in the Soviet Union was built, distributed, and owned by the party-state. In 1992 the new Russian government signed an agreement with the United States to implement the Housing Sector Reform Project, which aimed to transform the housing sector into a market. The government privatized property rights to the occupants of socialist housing, creating the chief source of household wealth in the new economy. New financial institutions, modeled on the American mortgage system, laid the foundation for a market. The government tried to stimulate housing markets, as well as the birthrate, by giving mortgage subsidies to young families.

This market was slow to emerge during the chaotic 1990s, when credit for builders and buyers was scarce and construction nearly ceased. But in 2007 the Russian housing market appeared to take off. "Russia is on the verge of a construction boom," said First Deputy Prime Minister Dmitry Medvedev, citing optimistic projections on mortgage lending as evidence that housing would become more affordable.[1] That same year, the government introduced maternity capital, ten-thousand-dollar vouchers that could be applied toward a mortgage, for all women who gave birth to a second child.

The market could emerge, claimed Medvedev at a conference of bankers, because of "a revolution in consciousness—our citizens are learning to live on credit. And there is nothing wrong with that. It is the civilized path to

1

development, which many other states have followed. . . . The words 'credit' and 'creditor' come from the Latin 'credo'—trust. If trust will exist between the citizens of the Russian Federation and the banking system, then everything will be fine."[2] Popular media encouraged consumers to get in on the action. The glossy magazine *Your Mortgage* claimed in 2007 that "mortgage credit is affordable for the majority of Russians. In civilized countries no one waits to save for an apartment or house—everyone from millionaires to pensioners gets housing with credit."

This success story, however, mismatched Russians' experiences with housing after socialism. Why, after two decades of capitalist reform, has housing remained, in a common turn of phrase, a "painful question"? Deprivation caused by market failure provides part of the answer. As of 2009 most young Russians still could not afford to buy homes of their own. Many lived with extended family well into adulthood while waiting to inherit a privatized property in a dilapidated housing stock. But the pain is as much symbolic as material. Participants in focus groups commissioned by the government described the nation's housing situation as critical, catastrophic, and hopeless (FOM 2006b). Housing catalyzed postsocialist experiences of dislocation and injustice caused by the clash between foreign and local conceptions of ownership, property, and rights. New inequalities and constraints led to frustrated aspirations, restricted fertility, and ambivalence toward state and market.

This book traces the causes and consequences of housing market failure, which I conceptualize as "transplant effects." Comparative legal scholars argue that transplanting laws without adapting to local conditions exacerbates the "gap between formal law on the books and law in action," which in turn impedes economic development. The mechanism is cognitive: effectiveness of law "rests on knowledge and understanding of these rules and their underlying values by social actors" (Berkowitz et al. 2003, 177). I broaden the concept of transplant beyond the law to consider the entire housing regime Russia tried to import from the United States. American housing law is based on the belief that housing should be allocated by markets and financed with long-term loans, a belief that many Russians do not share.

In using the metaphor of "transplant failure" to describe housing market failure, I do not want to suggest that Russians themselves have failed or are somehow backward because a mortgage market has not flourished. Instead, I treat transplant failure as a way to elucidate the cultural underpinnings of mortgage finance where it is taken for granted. For example, Russians' reactions to mortgages, detailed in chapter 9, problematize the American belief that mortgage holders are homeowners. Mortgages historically were understood as providing the borrower with the right of possession, that is, use of the asset used to secure the loan until the loan is paid in full, at which time ownership is achieved (Carrozzo 2004, 766; Simpson 1986). The Russian belief that a mortgage does *not* confer ownership serves as a reminder that American belief that it *does* is a specific cultural and historical phenomenon, which itself requires explanation.[3]

This book also moves the study of markets in formation beyond the typical domains. The emerging subfield of economic sociology directs most analytical effort at understanding firms and organizations; studies of consumers are peripheral and tend to be classified as work on culture rather than on economy. For example, sociological studies of finance, which have burgeoned in the wake of the ongoing international financial crisis, demonstrate the social embeddedness and cultural meanings of lending, but neglect to do the same for borrowing. My analytical focus on how market failure affects consumers provides new insights on the social meaning of markets and the consequences of those meanings for social action.

The Meaning of Housing in the New Russia

The story of one family, the Zhukovas, encapsulates the housing problem in contemporary Russia. Three themes—normalcy, ownership, and justice—emerged as they described their housing conditions. I met Larisa Zhukova, a thirty-four-year-old accountant, in the city of Kaluga in 2001 while I was conducting fieldwork for a study of consumption. After getting divorced in 1997, Larisa moved with her son Kirill into her mother's two-room apartment.[4] Larisa called the apartment, built in the 1960s, a "Khrushchev slum."[5] She exclaimed, "This is not an apartment; it's a family dormitory!" Larisa, who typically arrived home from work after midnight, slept in the living room. Kirill shared the tiny bedroom with his grandmother Valentina. The room contained two narrow beds and Kirill's "music corner," which held a keyboard, guitar, and synthesizer. "It's abnormal for a sixteen-year-old boy to share a room with his grandmother," said Larisa. "But the alternatives—sharing a bedroom with me, or sleeping in the living room, which others have to walk through to get to the bedroom—are even worse."

This modest apartment held happy memories for Valentina, a retired seamstress. She recalled her joy when her deceased husband's workplace, a radio factory, gave them the apartment. "In the 1960s, before we got our apartment, we cooked on a kerosene stove. We didn't have central heat or water. I had to shop every day because we had no refrigerator. We shared a small house with two other families. But it seemed as if everything was good. We waited for an apartment; we had hope. When the factory gave us an apartment, we were so happy. Although now they call such apartments Khrushchev's slums, for us it was miraculous to have sanitation and two rooms of our own."

I revisited this family in 2009. Valentina had passed away and bequeathed her privatized apartment to Larisa. "But I can't help my son," Larisa lamented. "He got married and Zhenya, his wife, is pregnant. They understandably don't want to live here. A young family should live separately." The couple briefly lived with Zhenya's parents, who then exchanged their three-room apartment for a two-room apartment for themselves and a one-room apartment for the young couple. However, Zhenya's family retained property rights, and Kirill remained legally registered at Larisa's apartment. "This is better than living with in-laws," said Kirill. "It's tolerable for now—but what about the future? What if we want another child?"

Kirill looked into taking out a mortgage to buy a two-room apartment. He discovered that not only did he not earn enough to qualify for a loan, but even if he had, the home would be subject to a lien, an intolerable condition. "A mortgage is debt bondage. You pay for thirty years, but all that time the bank owns the home. If you suddenly can't pay, the bank will take the home away. . . . Housing problems were easier to solve in Soviet times. You got a job, you worked and waited, and eventually you received a free apartment. Now, even though I earn six hundred dollars a month, not bad for Kaluga, I'll never be able to earn an apartment. It's not fair."

To Live Normally

For Russians, to live in one's own apartment is to "live normally." This expectation emerged half a century ago. In 1960, most Soviet citizens lived in communal apartments or workers' dormitories in cities, or with extended family in rural areas. The Communist Party promised in 1961 that by 1980, "every family, including the families of young married couples, will have a fully outfitted apartment, corresponding to hygienic and cultural needs."[6] The separate apartment was celebrated in the Soviet media and inscribed in the logic of housing design and distribution. Millions of Soviet households moved to separate apartments, and others queued expecting to eventually receive one.

The party did not fulfill its promises—in 1990 one in four households was still waiting in line for a separate apartment—but it created a preference and expectation. The popular discourse on normality inverted the official discourse of socialist realism: if the party-state presented "the present through the prism of an imagined future" (Fitzpatrick 1992, 217), the discourse of normality compared the requirements for a dignified life with a reality that failed to measure up.

Market transition brought a fresh promise of quality housing for anyone willing to work hard. Yet nearly two decades after the collapse of communism, many Russians' housing conditions were anything but normal. In 2009 just one-third of urban Russians age twenty-one to forty lived in homes of their own. Half lived with extended family, while the remainder lived in hostels or rentals. By age forty, when most Russians have minor children, only half had a separate apartment.[7]

This discourse of the "normal" recurs across the former Soviet bloc. In a study of material culture in postsocialist Hungary, Krisztina Fehérváry finds this discourse described aspirations "equated with the market capitalism and the bourgeois middle classes of European states" (2002, 374). Normal spaces, she argues, were heterotopias that reflected the backwardness of socialism (376). This is not the case in Russian discourse on housing. There, the reference point for normality is as likely to be an imagined past—beliefs about the ease of acquiring a home of one's own in the Soviet period—as it is to be an idealized West.

A Home of One's Own

When Russians describe a home as their own, they typically use the word *svoi,* an adjective connoting possession and connection with the self. Although privatization created a class of legal owners, Russians rarely describe themselves as homeowners or property owners, except when talking about legal matters. As sociologist Deborah Davis notes in her studies of privatization in China, the complexity of property rights creates "bundles of meanings embedded in the institutions of family and kinship, the party-state, and the market," such that people "may draw on more than one logic of ownership" as they make sense of change (2004, 290; 2010, 467).

For Russians, long-term and inalienable usage rights are intrinsic to ownership. This disposition has socialist origins. Although the government owned housing in the Soviet period, citizens derived a sense of de facto ownership from their long-term usage rights, which could be transferred to descendants or swapped with other families. According to Gregory Andrusz, socialist housing satisfied individuals' cravings for "ontological security" (1987, 495–96). This craving, Anthony Giddens (1981) argues, is a feature of modern life, which has eroded the systems of kinship and tradition that previously provided people with their sense of place in society. Peter Saunders, writing about the United Kingdom, claims: "The desire for home ownership is primarily an expression of this need for ontological security, for a 'home of one's own' is above all else a physical . . . and permanent . . . location in the world where the individual can feel, literally and metaphorically, 'at home.' It is, in short, the individual solution to the societal problem of alienation" (1984, 223).

Legal ownership, however, is neither necessary nor sufficient to provide people with a practical sense of possession. The theory of bundled property rights provides a way to conceptualize ownership in the context of market transition. For housing to be commodified, people must acquire the right to use it, the right to derive income from it, and the right to transfer it to others (Davis 2003, 185). Although legally Russians have these rights, in practice commodification is incomplete due to limits on both supply and demand for credit. When credit is scarce, housing markets become illiquid, making it difficult to derive income or sell property. Most Russians do not equate a mortgage with ownership because the risk of foreclosure renders long-term usage rights insecure. Aversion to risk and resistance to credit, in turn, contribute to market illiquidity. Market failure, then, is a cultural as well as economic phenomenon.

Housing as a Right and a Reward

In the Soviet Union, housing was a right for citizens and a reward for socialist labor. Everyone who worked (and those who were incapable of working) was entitled to shelter, but work more valued by the regime was rewarded with better housing. Perestroika opened a public debate about the gap between the ideology of meritocratic distribution and the reality of elite privilege. Proponents of market reform asserted capitalism would connect productivity at work with comforts at home. Instead, housing reform produced a system of property without markets, in which housing is privatized but incompletely commodified and inheritance far outweighs wages in determining young people's housing chances.

Kirill, like many young Russians, senses little relationship between work and housing conditions. The lived experience of housing inequality in Russia produces an "immanent critique" (Burawoy and Lucáks 1992) of market ideology, even among those who have fared well. Oksana, who inherited a spacious three-room apartment in 2006, remained troubled: "When we were growing up, we always knew we would have a place to live. If our parents couldn't help us then the government would. Our children are the first generation born without a right to free housing. It's hard to imagine how this could be possible!"

Housing in Russia as an Analytical Lens

The central space of daily life, housing is both a basic need and an expression of lifestyle, the locus of the family and the center of the household economy. Housing, due to its expense and importance, provokes struggle over scarce resources and debate over the role of the state. Modern states have used housing policy to stimulate the economy, influence demography, and build legitimacy. Policy decisions both presuppose and construct particular models of the home and the family. The study of housing thus reveals the "social structures of the economy," as Pierre Bourdieu (2005) entitled his book on housing in France. Housing provides an unexploited analytical lens to understand market transition in Russia; in turn, studying transplant failure in Russia can shed light on how capitalist housing systems work elsewhere.

Studying Housing to Understand Russia

Housing is the market, bar none, that the state must create (Bourdieu 2005). In industrialized societies with complex divisions of labor, most people do not build their own homes. Yet housing is so expensive relative to income that private ownership is impossible without access to credit markets. Credit is, according to David Harvey, at the heart of the "state-finance nexus," in which the state enables the circulation of capital (2010, 48). This is especially true of housing credit. The American government built the secondary mortgage market in response to a series of economic crises and has subsidized homeownership through fiscal and tax policy. The illusion of a free market legitimized the American government's efforts to build markets, until the system descended into crisis in 2007.

Misrecognition of the government's role influenced how the American housing system was transplanted to Russia. After the Russian government transplanted the formal institutions for an American-style market—from laws on property rights to a copy of Fannie Mae—it slashed spending and tried to wither away. When a market failed to emerge, the government reclaimed its mandate to intervene in the housing sector in 2006. Maternity capital, the cornerstone of this policy shift, linked the failing housing market to the declining birthrate, a problem framed as a threat to national survival. These new subsidies were intended to support, not supplant, the market. The state has been trying to build something it insists it cannot and will not control. Putin summed up the government's uneasy relationship with housing markets as follows: "All the decisions we take in this sector must be both efficient from an economic point of view and... socially responsible. The state cannot allow itself to withdraw from the housing sector, despite the fact that the market will have priority. And this implies that the state must actively create a civilized market environment in this sector."[8]

Putin's promise to civilize the market affirmed the state's responsibility for the housing sector, but left undefined the state's role. Housing came to symbolize Russians' sense of abandonment by the state: "Leaking roofs and rapidly deteriorating housing stock were common metaphorical representations of the postsocialist crisis of accountability" (Shevchenko 2009, 40). Experiences with housing reinforce young Russians' ambivalence toward market reform. In 2005, when the economy was booming, 61 percent of Russians too young to have adult memories of the Soviet period were nostalgic for Soviet times (Munro 2006, 295). By 2009, when the economy was yet again in crisis, most young Russians I interviewed believed the housing system was broken and the government must fix it, not by stimulating markets, but by controlling them.

Housing is also a useful lens for understanding how market reform affects Russian families. In Bourdieu's words, the house "is inseparable from the household" and is an instrument of "the system of reproduction strategies" (2005, 20). The cultural imperative to reproduce has continued to outweigh the preference for a separate apartment—most Russians have one child no matter what their housing conditions. Yet a separate apartment remains requisite for a normal family life. Abandoned by the state and shut out of the market, young families attribute their decisions to postpone or forego having multiple children to housing constraints, which also provide a popular explanation for population decline.

Studying Russia to Understand Housing

The Russian case is useful in two respects for understanding housing beyond Russia. First, the regime of property without markets highlights how housing can become a distinct dimension of stratification, especially where inheritance is widespread. Second, market failure in Russia illuminates the cultural underpinnings of the American housing regime.

Most research on inequality ignores housing, focusing instead on occupation and wages as indicators of status in relations of production. When stratification researchers do include housing in their models, they typically treat it either as a proxy for socioeconomic status (SES) (Bollen et al. 2002) or as a fungible component of wealth (Crowder et al. 2006). Housing and income are highly correlated in most capitalist countries, making it difficult to isolate housing's effects. However, "among those who share the same relation to the means of production there may be considerable differences in ease of access to housing" (Rex 1968, 214–15). In Russia the relationship between housing and income is weak, making it easier to see housing's distinctive stratifying properties.

To reduce the multiple meanings of housing to just one of its aspects (e.g., SES or wealth) is to limit understanding of the manifold ways it matters in social life. Housing is less liquid than other forms of wealth, and so is not fully commensurable with other types of assets such as savings or stocks. Furthermore, housing holds other forms of value. First, housing is a durable good with inherent use value: it is a dwelling and not merely an investment. As such, its qualities can directly affect material well-being. Second, housing is an element of lifestyle that can confer status. Third, housing is a staging ground for family formation, reproduction, and dissolution. Conceptions of what kind of housing is necessary and desirable for family life condition how housing affects union formation, dissolution, and childbearing, as well as subjective well-being and political stances. A complete account of housing's stratifying role must consider these aspects of housing, not just its valuation as wealth.

Studying housing in Russia also yields sociological insight into the American housing system. Housing market transplant from the United States to Russia confirms Bourdieu's claim that "what is universally proposed and imposed as the norm for all rational economic practice is, in reality, the universalization of the particular characteristics of an economy embedded in a particular history and social structure—those of the United States" (2005, 226). Because the transplant failed, Russia provides a negative case that illuminates taken-for-granted elements of the American housing system. Russia inverts the meanings mortgages have had in the United States, at least until the 2008 subprime crisis. If the primary metaphor for a mortgage in Russia is "debt bondage," the equivalent metaphor in the United States is "homeownership." Whereas Russians are outraged by interest payments and uncertain ownership of a good they consider a basic right, Americans think paying interest on loans spanning decades is a normal condition of ownership.

Understanding Demand for Mortgage Credit

This book about a mortgage market that failed to emerge advances the sociology of finance. The literature on this subject has surged with the international credit crisis but still lacks an adequate theory of demand for credit. Recent work concentrates on explaining fluctuations in supply. Carruthers and Ariovich (2010), in their monograph reviewing the sociological literature on money and credit, write at length about the problem of trust in credit markets, mainly from the perspective of lenders. Information asymmetries, they argue, favor borrowers, who know more than do lenders about borrowers' capacity and commitment to repay their loans. The interesting puzzles for Carruthers and Ariovich include: how do lenders decide which borrowers they can trust to repay a loan, and why have they extended credit to increasingly less creditworthy borrowers? They do not ask, however, how consumers decide whether to take out loans, and if so according to what terms.

The lack of scholarship on this topic implies that demand for credit is easy to explain, and that unmet demand preexists and outstrips supply. This assumption is understandable in the study of American credit markets, where consumer demand for credit has been high for decades. But this was not always the case. Russia illustrates the complexity of generating demand when a credit market begins to emerge. First, information asymmetries do not necessarily favor borrowers. Russian consumers, even those who are deeply committed to paying their debts, find it difficult to predict their personal financial flows. This uncertainty stems not just from personal circumstances, but from systemic instability over the past two decades that has precipitated wage arrears, currency defaults, and bank closures that evaporated savings. Banking institutions (especially those backed by the government) may have better information than consumers do about this systemic context.

Russians' aversion to mortgages should inspire a rethinking of how credit for housing becomes legitimate. Most previous work on legitimation of credit concentrates on overcoming traditional taboos against usury and shame over indebtedness. However, Russians do not reject all forms of credit, as credit cards and installment loans have become commonplace (Guseva 2008). So why are mortgages less legitimate in Russia than credit cards, while the opposite is true in the United States?

To understand how housing credit takes on distinctive moral valences, I turn to the literature on the social meaning of money. Housing in Russia retains the status of a social right, essential for human dignity, which makes it less commensurable than other everyday goods.[9] Because of this special status, charging interest is repugnant to Russians. Theories on the social meaning of money shed light on why. Attempts to establish markets for certain kinds of goods and services like organ transplants, caring services, and life insurance have provoked cultural resistance, particularly when such markets were first being established. These things were believed to be priceless, beyond the market due to their moral worth (Zelizer 2005; Chan 2009; Healy 2006).

There are also taboos on what *kinds* of money can be used in what contexts. In Russia, the moral problem is not placing a price on housing per se (although most Russians think prices should be controlled to keep them low), but charging interest for a good that is a social right. As chapter 9 shows, Russians' moral critiques center on the proportion of interest to principal over the life of the loan. In the United States, the long-term, self-amortizing mortgage loan works to erase this moral distinction. Amortization holds monthly payments constant over the life of the loan, while the ratio of principal to interest in each payment gradually increases over time. Consistent payments over thirty years blur the distinction between interest and principal, which helps to morally "purify" interest payments. In Russia, however, mortgage interest is still cognitively foregrounded, and thus not easily purified.

Analytical Strategy

This book analyzes the microlevel effects of macrolevel change in Russia's housing regime. By regime, I mean the system for producing and distributing housing, as both a material object and a symbolic meaning. Part I of the book characterizes how Russia's housing regime developed into a system of property without markets: from the rise and fall of the Soviet system (chapter 1), to the failed attempt to transplant the American housing system (chapter 2), to the grafting of a pronatalist agenda onto housing policy (chapter 3). Chapter 4 describes new inequalities that emerged after housing was privatized but not fully commodified.

Part II analyzes the effects of housing market failure. Chapter 5 explores perceptions of inequality and injustice, which lead young Russians to reject housing markets. Their strategies for acquiring housing under the conditions of property without markets are the subject of chapter 6. Chapter 7 presents evidence that Russians, particularly those with higher education, restrict family size when they lack a separate apartment and/or a separate room for each child. Chapters 8 and 9 explain why Russians oppose mortgage subsidies for young families and mortgage loans in general. The concluding chapter argues that property without markets is unlikely to be a transitory phenomenon. If the state continues to base housing policy on American mortgage institutions, housing will remain a source of social suffering and political discontent even after the latest economic crisis eases.

I employ different types of data to achieve these various analytical goals. Archival data and secondary sources provide information about housing policy and macroeconomic trends in the housing sector. Survey data are used to test hypotheses about patterns of housing inequality and the effects of housing on fertility. Qualitative interviews elucidate how young Russians perceive the housing regime, and how these perceptions motivate their strategies for improving their housing conditions and for starting and growing families.

To my knowledge this book is the first to use housing as a lens to understand the relationship between state and society in Russia, and to use the Russian case to extend theories about the meaning of housing in capitalist societies. To make this task manageable, I limit the empirical scope of the project as follows. I focus on young, urban Russians age twenty-one to thirty-five. This is the primary age range when Russians get married, have children, and strive to form separate households. In 2009, when qualitative research for this book was conducted, this generation was too young to have received housing as adults during the Soviet period; tracking their housing trajectories reveals the post-Soviet relationship between state, family, and market. Age thirty-five is also the cutoff for official definitions of young families, affecting access to certain housing subsidies.[10] I restrict the analysis to the urban population, because population and housing dynamics in rural areas are so distinctive as to warrant separate study.

In this book, housing conditions, trajectories, and aspirations are measured in terms of the quest for a separate apartment. Getting a home of their own is the most significant housing problem that young urban Russians must solve. Other components of housing quality and lifestyle, such as design, renovation, and interior decoration, will be the subject of future extensions of this work.[11] I define a separate apartment as having secure property rights and living autonomously from the extended family, that is, by oneself or with one's partner and/or children.

This definition is better suited for the Russian context than are measures like "owner-occupied household" or "leaving the parental home," concepts that are often applied cross-nationally with little attention to validity (Newman 2008). Conventional studies often do not distinguish between homeowners and home buyers, treating everyone as owners regardless of the presence of a mortgage and the associated lien on the title. The ideal-typical "separate apartment" in Russia must not be mortgaged, because otherwise it is not truly one's own. Standard measures of owner occupation conceptualize housing tenure as a household-level variable. However, unequal property rights within households can produce differences in power, resources, and well-being. Household members who lack ownership rights (e.g., those who marry into a household) may have few prospects for obtaining housing elsewhere and, correspondingly, may experience housing insecurity and dependency. I treat the young adult as the primary unit of analysis, revealing inequalities across generations and within marriages.

In concentrating on the separate apartment, this book departs from many other cultural studies of housing in Russia, which instead highlight the communal apartment, a Soviet living arrangement in which unrelated families were forced to share apartments (Boym 1994; Utekhin 2004). Separate apartments, which by the late Soviet period predominated over communal arrangements, have attracted little attention from scholars, who tend to study the exotic instead of the familiar (Harris 2005, 613–14). In this book, the communal apartment is most relevant as a contemporary metaphor for a far more common living arrangement—the once separate apartment now inhabited, against everyone's will, by multiple generations of the same family. Finally, this book's scope is limited to people who have a stable place to live. It does not include the homeless, a difficult-to-reach population who are the subject of two excellent books (Höjdestrand 2009; Stephenson 2006).

Data Sources

For information on housing in the Soviet period, I rely mainly on secondary sources, as well as on archival research I conducted for a previous study of consumption during late socialism (Zavisca 2004). Policy analysis for the post-Soviet period is based on documents from institutions with influence over housing reform: USAID, the Urban Institute, the Institute for Urban Economics, and various government agencies such as the offices of the President and the Prime Minister of the Russian Federation, the administration of the Priority National Projects, the Agency for Home Mortgage Lending, the Ministry of Construction, and the Pension Fund of Russia.

Patterns of housing inequality, mobility, and fertility are analyzed using the Russian Longitudinal Monitoring Survey (RLMS), a national survey that has revisited the same individuals and households annually between 1994 and 2009 (except for skipped years in 1997 and 1999). Individuals and households who move have been followed to their new addresses since 1996, enabling analysis of mobility patterns. I supplement this data with the General Social Survey of the European USSR, which was collected in 1991 and was the precursor to the RLMS. The main statistical technique used in this book is event history analysis, a method that models the timing of events such as changes in housing tenure and family size. Statistical results are presented in simplified form to communicate the substantive findings; working papers with full results are available from the author on request.

Qualitative evidence is drawn from 130 in-depth interviews on housing and family life with young adults age twenty-one to thirty-five. The interviews were collected from July to December 2009 in Kaluga, a central

Russian city where I conducted dissertation research in 2001–2, and which I revisited in 2005, 2007, and 2009 for the study that led to this book. Interviews were conducted by a team of three Russian sociologists, under my supervision, using a semistructured interview schedule with mostly open-ended questions. Respondents were asked to describe their housing histories, current housing conditions, and future aspirations. They were also asked about how their families acquired housing in Soviet times and to compare the Soviet and post-Soviet housing systems. Their attitudes toward housing policy, maternity capital, and mortgages were also assessed. All interviews were audio-recorded and transcribed. I coded transcripts for varieties of discourse on housing needs, aspirations, and policies, and compared the distribution of these discourses across groups of respondents, based on their housing conditions, family structure, education, and gender. Details about interviewing and coding techniques are given in context as results are presented.

Respondents were recruited based on a quota sample that varied by housing tenure (extended family, renter, owner, mortgagor), education (with or without a higher degree), and gender. Descriptive statistics on the sample are in given in table I.1. The sample overrepresents renters and mortgage holders by design: the intention is to qualitatively compare across variables of interest, not to make statistical inferences to a population. Within categories of housing tenure, the sample was balanced between respondents with and without higher education (except mortgage holders, who were difficult to find, and among whom all but one had a college degree). Two-thirds of the sample are women, who were of primary interest because of my initial focus on the relationship between housing and fertility. Resources also sufficed for a supplemental but smaller sample of men. The distribution of housing tenure, education, and age is similar for men and women in the sample.

Limited resources made it necessary to restrict data collection to one location. Most single-city studies in post-Soviet Russia have been conducted in Moscow or St. Petersburg. A vast and diverse country, Russia has no representative locales. I selected Kaluga because it sits on the boundary between core and periphery, both geographically and economically. Kaluga is about two hundred kilometers southwest of Moscow and is the capital of its oblast (a territorial unit analogous to a US state). The city's population was 327,000 in 2009. The oblast's population stood at one million, three-quarters of whom lived in urban areas.

The city does not stand out when compared to aggregate statistics for the Central Russian region (see table I.2). The region's major industries as

Table I.1   Description of qualitative sample (N = 130)

Housing Tenure		Marital Status	
Extended family	33%	Single	34%
Rent/Dorm	30%	Married	45%
Own (no mortgage)	25%	Living together	9%
Mortgage	12%	Divorced	12%
Education		**Number of Children**	
Secondary	17%	0	38%
Tech/incomplete higher	33%	1	48%
Higher	50%	2+	14%
Age		**Employment Status**	
21–25	33%	Employed	75%
26–30	35%	Maternity leave	12%
31–35	32%	Other	13%
Gender			
Female	70%		
Male	30%		

of 2007 included those typical for central Russia: food processing, transit-related production and services, machine building and metalworking, electronics manufacturing, and wood and paper processing. Several foreign auto companies, including Volkswagen, Volvo, and Mitsubishi, opened factories in the region since 2005, leading to Kaluga's new nickname as Russia's "Little Detroit." Tax, tariff, and credit policies introduced in 2007 to promote domestic production led to a surge in industrial growth in the region in 2008 as foreign companies expanded local production. Most of the new jobs paid low wages, however, and growth of the sector stalled as the economy slowed in 2009.[12] As of 2008 the unemployment rate, wages, per capita income, and income inequality were typical of the Central Russian region, excluding Moscow, the wealthiest and most unequal region of Russia.

Kaluga has a diverse housing stock. Unlike many cities in European Russia, Kaluga was relatively undamaged during World War II, so many prewar structures remain. While picturesque, they are typically of poor quality and lack amenities. Figure I.1 shows a typical street, with prewar housing in the foreground, and a new apartment building in the background. To the right, obscured by trees, is a *khrushchevka*—the five-story apartment buildings that appeared across the Soviet Union during the mass housing campaign of the 1950s and 1960s. Figure I.2 depicts a typical khrushchevka apartment building. This Soviet-era housing remains the most common type of housing in Kaluga.

Table I.2 Kaluga oblast compared to other regions of Russia

	Kaluga Region	Central Russia (Excluding Moscow)	City of Moscow
Census Indicators, 2002			
Median age	40	40	39
Russian ethnicity	93%	93%	85%
Higher education, age 15+	16%	17%	30%
Higher education, age 25–34	21%	22%	35%
Socioeconomic indicators, 2008			
Male life expectancy (years)	60	60	68
Female life expectancy (years)	74	74	77
Births per 1,000 people	10.4	10.3	10.3
Dependency ratio ((old+young)/working age)	0.78	0.63	0.56
Unemployment rate	4.8%	4.7%	0.9%
Monthly income (rubles per capita)	11,800	13,200	34,200
Monthly wage (mean in rubles)	14,100	16,800	30,600
Monthly cost of subsistence (rubles)	6,300	6,600	9,800
Income held by top income quintile	44.7%	46.0%	57.9%
Income inequality (Gini coefficient)	0.38	0.38	0.54
Inflation in consumer prices (annual)	14.9%	13.7%	12.3%
Cars per 1,000 people	216	221	279
Housing indicators, 2008			
Living space per capita (square meters)	24.3	25.5	20.1
Condemned housing (% of housing stock)	5.3%	2.4%	2.0%
Mortgage debt as % of regional domestic product	3.5%	3.3%	2.0%

Sources: Rosstat, Central Bank of Russia.

Housing in Kaluga is very expensive relative to income, as is true throughout Russia. Most residents are shut out of both cash- and credit-based housing markets. However, the city's well-to-do population suffices to support new construction, as well as mortgage and rental sectors. Mortgage lending emerged earlier in Kaluga than in more distant provinces due to Kaluga's proximity to Moscow, the nation's financial and political capital. About fifteen banks offered mortgage loans in 2009 (down from more than twenty in 2008).

Kaluga's housing economy is closer to provincial Russia, however, than to the extremes of Moscow. Interviewees in 2009 frequently claimed that Kaluga's housing prices are second only to Moscow, a statistic repeated in local news. Available data do not support this assertion. According to figure I.3, trends in housing construction and prices in Kaluga are closer to national averages than they are to Moscow's extremes. The construction boom Kaluga experienced from 2006 to 2008 encouraged the perception that prices were extraordinary. Most other provinces in central Russia experienced similar

FIGURE I.1   Residential buildings in Kaluga. Photo by Anastasia Smirnova.

FIGURE I.2   Khrushchevka: Typical five-story apartment building from the 1960s. Photo by Anastasia Smirnova.

housing booms, although Kaluga's boom began later and was more com-
pressed and dramatic than elsewhere. Construction in all sixteen oblasts in
central Russia grew by at least 50 percent between 2002 and 2008, and rates
more than doubled in eight oblasts. Prices also surged during this period.
This boom is analogous to what happened in the Sunbelt region of the
United States during the same period: construction and prices peaked first in
California, next in Nevada, and then in Arizona as California-based investors
sought new markets.[13] The same was true of Moscow-based investment in

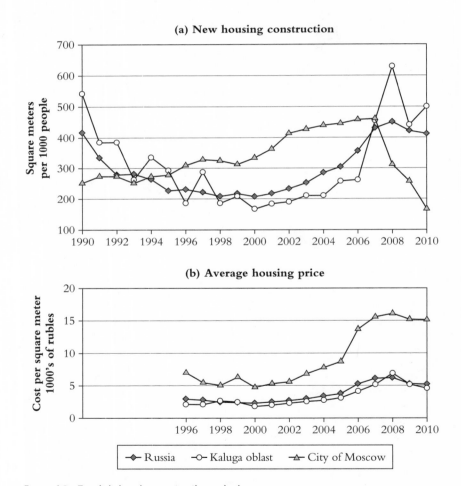

FIGURE I.3 Trends in housing construction and prices
Source: Data from Rosstat.
Note: Prices calculated as mean of average prices for new and existing housing. Adjusted for inflation using 2005
constant rubles.

surrounding regions. By 2009, construction and prices in Kaluga had recon-verged with national averages.

Fieldwork was conducted in the midst of an international financial crisis that hit Russia as well. This crisis was unforeseen when the research was planned. Nevertheless, many of the findings reported in this book can be generalized to the previous decade. I became interested in housing dur-ing 2001–2 while conducting fieldwork in Kaluga for a study of consumer inequalities. Russians repeatedly referenced housing as they interpreted their places in the new stratification order and evaluated the fairness of market transition (Zavisca 2008). Housing retains this symbolic significance today. My informants in 2001–2 also spontaneously drew the connection between housing and fertility, a key focus of this book (as well as of federal demo-graphic policy since 2006). Furthermore, as I document in chapter 9, when Russians talked about crisis in 2009, most were not talking about the most recent economic downturn or the international financial crisis. Instead, talk of crisis resembled the discourse of "permanent crisis" identified by Olga Shevchenko (2009) in her study of daily life in Moscow at the turn of the twenty-first century.

PART I

The Development of the Post-Soviet Housing Regime

 CHAPTER 1

The Soviet Promise

A Separate Apartment for Every Family

In 1957, Nikita Khrushchev issued a decree to house every Soviet family in a separate apartment within twelve years, launching "perhaps the most ambitious governmental housing program in human history" (Ruble 1993, 234). Housing the populace in separate apartments laid the groundwork for a post-Stalin social contract, which aimed to achieve social quiescence without recourse to terror (Hauslohner 1987; Cook 1993). However, the most appealing features of the separate apartment—prosperity and privacy—also made it ideologically dangerous. The party-state instructed socialist citizens on how they should live, both by disseminating propaganda and by inscribing meanings into the logics of apartment design and distribution. By the late Soviet period, the separate apartment represented an entitlement for all, a reward for work, and a place of one's own. Soviet sensibilities about housing have endured through two decades of postsocialist transformation, as subsequent chapters show. This chapter traces how the separate apartment transformed from an unrealized ideal in Stalin's time to a concrete planning norm under Khrushchev to the cornerstone of a normal life in the late Soviet period.

Housing as Power in Revolutionary Russia

When the Bolsheviks seized the Russian state in 1917, the new leadership immediately deployed housing as an instrument of power. The 1919 Party

Program recounted how the Bolsheviks consolidated control: "Striving to solve the housing question... the Soviet government completely took over all the houses owned by capitalist householders and turned them over to the town soviets; it transferred masses of workers from the slum districts in the suburbs to bourgeois houses; it turned the best of these houses over to the workers' organizations and placed the cost of maintenance of these houses upon the state" (CPSU 1961, 123). A bourgeois home, according to Lenin, was any dwelling having at least as many rooms as residents. Besides expropriating elite housing, the government nationalized factory housing when it nationalized industry. Municipal authorities also took over housing construction in large cities (Chernykh 1995).

What was this "housing question" that needed to be solved? Revolutionary idealists envisioned communal homes for communist citizens, who would leave behind the bourgeois institution of the family. More immediately, rehousing the population could advance the fledgling regime's economic and security goals. Wartime destruction and migration had exacerbated a severe shortage of urban housing. Moving the expanding working class into existing apartments gave workers a place to live without costly new construction, while dispossessing and demoralizing the prerevolutionary elite. Controlling access to housing also directed labor where the state wanted it to go, while keeping dangerous elements—hungry peasants and exiled nobility—out of major cities.

Inventing Living Space

Expropriated homes were redistributed according to the principle of "living space." The Ministry of Public Health established a so-called sanitary norm of nine square meters per person, a norm that operated as a maximum rather than a minimum in practice (Harris 2003, 36). This bureaucratic logic partitioned space as if it were "an abstract problem in geometry, not the real space of existing apartments" (Boym 1994, 125).

Allocating housing in square meters paved the way for a novel kind of housing: the "communal apartment." Strangers shared apartments, and sometimes even rooms, when workers were resettled in the homes of wealthy families, who typically retained a single room. After the shock of moving in together, collectivized residents struggled to establish a sense of normalcy. People from different class backgrounds developed symbolic strategies for preserving social distance, but also lived in conflict—over bathroom and kitchen access, pilfering, and dirt (Gerasimova 1999, 123–27).[1] This "equality in poverty" produced a new class habitus among the generation born into communal apartments

(Semenova 2004, 64–65). Nevertheless, residents strove to carve out private zones in communal spaces. Communal living, which became commonplace, never felt quite normal (Gerasimova 2002; Attwood 2004, 194).

By the 1930s most residents of cities with prerevolutionary housing stocks lived in communal apartments. Other types of collective housing developed in new settlements. Historian Steven Kotkin (1995) describes conditions in Magnitogorsk, the "socialist city of the future," which was built from scratch near an iron mine. The infrastructure of daily life lagged far behind investment in mining and steel works. Most workers suffered the Siberian climate in barracks or even tents. Sturdier brick hostels (*obshchezhitie*) were also communal: families occupied single rooms without private kitchens or bathrooms. Public dining halls and bathhouses were filthy and few, forcing people to improvise cooking facilities and do without baths.

To some historians, communal apartments were an ideological experiment gone awry, even the "cornerstone of the now disappearing Soviet civilization" (Boym 1994, 123). Likewise, hostels were to "encourage a new way of life" corresponding to "the theory on the withering away of the family under socialism" (Kotkin 1995, 193). Other historians view collective housing in the USSR as more political expedient than utopian vision (Andrusz 1984; Gerasimova 1999; Meerovich 2003). Communal apartments were far from the prototypical house-communes that idealist architects designed to free women from domestic servitude. Few of these prototypes, with their collective dining halls, laundries, and childcare, were ever realized. By the early 1930s, Soviet authorities acknowledged that the family would persist for the foreseeable future.

Housing policy served the regime's economic goals in two ways. First, communal housing was cheap. In 1929 Stalin imposed the command economy, a "deliberate decision to allocate scarce resources to armaments and capital goods and to compel the rest of the economy to manage as best it can with what remains" (Moore 1954, 37). Capital investment in housing contracted and average living space shrank by one-third within a decade, to a meager four square meters per person by 1940 (Harris 2003, 35).

Second, housing policy served to direct labor flows, since most people received housing through their jobs. Housing, a chief cause of labor shortages, was improved in priority industries to attract workers. An internal passport system further tied housing to work. Getting a job required a passport with a *propiska*, or residence permit. Would-be migrants had to secure living space before they could receive a propiska in a new city.[2] Employers who could offer living space with a propiska thus provided workers with the right to migrate, as well as housing and a job (Popov 1996).

Controlling housing also helped the regime to monitor the population. People with propiskas could be tracked, and people without them were vulnerable. A former noblewoman recalled her relief on getting residency papers: "All my papers, certificates, permits were in order; once more I felt like a human being.... In those days the absence of necessary documents made you an outcast.... You would be equally unable to find a meal or a roof, for no one . . . would let you in for the night; and after eight o'clock you would be arrested for being in the streets" (Volkonskaia 2000, 149). Collectivizing housing also facilitated surveillance. Neighbors were encouraged to inform on each other for seditious acts; doing so could free up living space, since the accused could be exiled or even executed (Kotkin 1995, 195–97; Gerasimova 1999, 122–23; Semenova 2004, 61–62).

Housing Privilege as Necessary Inequality

While most Soviet citizens crowded into communal apartments, a privileged few enjoyed private apartments. Lenin decreed that senior party officials should receive a maximum of one room per family member (for everyone else, the de facto minimum was one family per room). Party elites moved into the homes of the former nobility, appropriating their furniture and even their servants (Izmozik and Lebina 2001). Other valued persons were given extra square meters of living space, if not private apartments. A 1930 list of those entitled to more space included "the most responsible workers and employees in the State Sector who did some of their work at home, Heroes of Labour, . . . artists, writers, inventors, and registered scientific workers" (Matthews 1979, 109).

Housing inequality reinforced the regime's "hierarchy of consumption," which Stalin developed to a fatal extreme by starving the peasantry while dispensing luxury to the elite (Osokina 1997). Communism, Karl Marx had promised, would take "from each according to his ability" and give "to each according to his needs" (Marx [1875] 1977, 569). But this radiant future had to be postponed during the transitional phase of socialism. Stalin explained to a conference of prizewinning workers: "The productivity of labor is still not high enough to ensure an abundance of articles of consumption, and, as a result, society is obliged to distribute articles of consumption not in accordance with the needs of its members, but in accordance with the work they perform for society."[3]

Prizes of housing for exemplary workers were publicized in Soviet media, suggesting that quality housing was within reach for those who deserved it. For example, one prizewinner said in a speech: "I remember my childhood.

I lived in a tiny apartment. There was one bed where Mother and Father slept and a cradle for the baby, while my brother and I slept under the bed. But now I have received a good apartment, with good furniture. So my heart is rejoicing" (Slavnikova 2000, 334). Her speech echoed Stalin's slogan: "Life has become more joyous!" In fact, even model workers suffered severe privations. When the party surveyed such workers to ask what they needed, most complained about living in barracks or dorms that were crowded, cold, and far from work (Siegelbaum 1998). For them, as for most Soviet citizens, decent housing remained only a promise.

The Separate Apartment as the Radiant Future

The ideological and technological foundations for separate apartments, although not realized until the 1960s, were laid in Stalin's time (Harris 2003, chapter 2). In the early 1930s, the Party began a "Great Retreat" from cultural revolution back to a more traditional approach toward material culture and the institution of the family (Timasheff 1946; Bonnell 1993). Party leadership in 1930 suddenly deemed radical collectivization of daily life "unsound, semi-fantastical, and hence extremely harmful" due to "obstacles rooted in the economic and cultural backwardness of the country" (Andrusz 1984, 121). Architects were instructed to design separate apartments for the masses, whose cultural needs were said to be escalating (Gerasimova 1999, 114). This policy shift reflected three tendencies during the Great Retreat: to rehabilitate the family and private life; to encourage cultured conduct; and to depict living standards and lifestyles as the regime wished them to be, rather than as they were.

Stalin promised that prosperity was just around the corner. Although inequality was unavoidable, socialism would soon yield "an abundance of products and of articles of consumption of all kinds, on the basis of a prosperous and cultured life for all members of society."[4] A separate apartment symbolized the good life to come. Its meaning paralleled that of "common luxuries," such as champagne, perfume, and radios, which began to appear in shops in limited quantities (Gronow 2003).

The rehabilitation of isolated family housing also revived women's roles as wives and mothers. In 1930 the Women's Department, whose task had been to collectivize domestic labor, closed. The party-state banned abortion, rewarded large families with baby bonuses, and codified "motherhood as a Soviet woman's right and duty" in the 1936 constitution (Neary 1999, 400). Visual propaganda returned women, who had been depicted mainly as workers, to the home. Rural prosperity was symbolized by a home furnished with "accoutrements of the good life," including electric light, gramophones, sewing machines, bookshelves, soft furniture, and lace curtains (Bonnell 1993, 75–76).

If images of rural women emphasized their "achievements in both production...and reproduction" (Bonnell 1993, 75), middle-class women were to build socialism on the domestic front. At a conference of Stakhanovites' wives, the wife of a train engineer was asked, "Do you keep the apartment clean? Can your husband relax there?" She replied, "The apartment is no problem at all.... My husband doesn't have to worry or get upset about household chores—his work is the only thing he knows. When the locomotive is resting, he gets to rest, too—in a special room, where he can read and study.... This, Comrade Women, is how I helped my husband become a Stakhanovite.... I create all the right conditions at home" (Vlasovskaia 2000, 361). Wife-activists, so-called housewives to the nation, carried this domestic orientation into public spaces such as cafeterias and workers' hostels to improve hygiene and encourage cultured behavior (Neary 1999, 403, 408–10).

The ideology of "culturedness" (kul'turnost') sought to transform backward peasants into modern socialist workers (Dunham 1990, 22–23). The regime presented culturedness as a revolutionary lifestyle for the new Soviet person, although many recommended norms were adapted from Western European conceptions of civility. Neoclassical architectural styles were also repackaged as uniquely Soviet. Historian Catriona Kelly locates the distinctiveness of Soviet culturedness not in particular practices, but in the "strong emphasis on the collective significance of individual behavior" (1999, 202). Advice literature described cultured consumption as simple, useful, attractive, hygienic, and rational (Kelly 2001, chapter 4). Curtains and lampshades could transform the home into an inner sanctum for cultivating revolutionary consciousness. An article on "rational diet" instructed: "If the table is draped with a white tablecloth, the dinner tastes good and is digested perfectly. To live in a cultured way also means to eat in a cultured way" (Volkov 2000, 222). Such advice while millions of peasants starved epitomized the surreality of socialist realism, which described reality as the state wished people to imagine it, rather than as it was (Fitzpatrick 1992, 217).

Settlement patterns in new apartments belied the illusion of immanent prosperity. Architects were required to design apartments for nuclear families. However, once these supposedly separate apartments were built, they were allocated to multiple families and settled communally. A group of pragmatic architects, hoping to prevent this, turned living space norms to their advantage by designing apartments so small that a single family would fall below the sanitary norm of nine square meters per person. Although these designs were not implemented at first, they "established the basis for the layout, form, and dimensions of the small separate apartment of the Khrushchev-era mass housing campaign" (Harris 2003, 80–81).

Khrushchev's Promise: A Separate Apartment for Every Family

Housing conditions in the USSR were atrocious when Nikita Khrushchev became general secretary of the Communist Party in 1955. Little new permanent housing had been built since the USSR's founding in 1917, and World War II had damaged or destroyed one-third of the housing stock (Andrusz 1984, 19). The housing campaign launched by Khrushchev more than doubled the urban housing stock from 1955 to 1970 and rehoused 127 million people, about half of the Soviet population, in new apartments (Goskomstat 1987, 509, 516). How and why was this feat accomplished?

Prefabricated construction techniques transformed housing into an industrial sector, in which production plans were formulated according to the Soviet logic of "rational norms." These benchmarks defined how much of a given item—from eggs to shoes to housing space—an average Soviet person should consume. Since Lenin, the housing norm had been defined in square meters, without regard to the structure of either households or housing units. Under Khrushchev a new logic was overlaid onto the spatial norm: each family would be entitled to a separate apartment, just large enough to provide each family member with nine square meters of living space.

Mass housing, and the mass consumption it spearheaded, provided a new basis for security and stability after easing Stalin's terror. Plans for expensive administrative buildings and palaces of culture were suspended in favor of investment in housing (Schwartz 1965, 99). Housing's new priority also aided Khrushchev's campaign to "de-Stalinize" society. In an influential speech on construction, he accused architects of the baroque structures favored by Stalin of rushing "to build monuments to themselves" rather than useful space for society. "Carried away with architectural decorations and esthetic adornment," they had forgotten "the main thing—the cost per square meter." Ordinary people "do not want to admire silhouettes—they need a place to live!" (Khrushchev 1955).

Constructing the Separate Apartment

The astonishing rate of housing construction was made possible by maximizing quantity and minimizing cost. Architects and builders concentrated their efforts on increasing output of the key measure of productivity in the housing sector: square meters of living space. Planners did not define living space in terms of an apartment's total square meters, which was called "floor space." Instead, living space included only rooms designated for "living in," but excluded so-called auxiliary space—kitchens, bathrooms, entries, and corridors.

The sanitary norm for living space remained at nine square meters per capita. Because auxiliary space did not count toward these norms, the floor plans of the pragmatist architects of the 1930s were modified to maximize the proportion of total floor space classified as living space. Architects reduced the number of rooms per apartment while increasing their average size, thus economizing on walls. Rooms were arranged railroad-car-style, without separate entrances, to eliminate the need for corridors (Harris 2003, 113–22). Kitchens were placed next to bathrooms, and bathrooms combined with toilets, to reduce plumbing costs. Cost considerations also dictated building height, which was set at five stories, the maximum that would not require elevators (Attwood 2004, 178).[5]

Square meters of living space became a standard, commonsensical measure of housing quantity in Soviet society. The number was entered in propiskas, referenced routinely in the media, and used to calculate utility bills. Counting living space instead of rooms also led to floor plans and living arrangements that produced a different conception of "room" (komnata) in Russian than is familiar in English. Rooms were not classified by function, for example living room, bedroom, dining room, study, playroom. Soviet rooms were to serve any number of functions in daily life and were designed so that their uses might evolve as household structure changed. To this day Russians describe their apartments in terms of the number of rooms (one-room apartment, two-room apartment, etc.), not the number of bedrooms as is common in the West.

In the logic of living space, a family was entitled to nine square meters of living space per person, but each person was not entitled to a separate room. A childless couple, for example, was more likely to receive an apartment with one room of at least eighteen square meters than an apartment with two smaller rooms. A family with children was more likely to get two rooms, but a couple with one child might still be allocated a one-room apartment. When families had two or more rooms, they might choose to reserve at least one room for some subset of the household, but even then the largest or most central room usually had to serve as a living space during the day and a sleeping space at night. A parlor reserved exclusively for daytime activities was an uncommon luxury.[6]

Figures 1.1 and 1.2 depict multiuse rooms. The photo in figure 1.1, taken in 1966, shows a mechanic's family in their apartment. The bed, which converts into a sofa, served triple duty as furniture for sitting, sleeping, and playing. The family would also have eaten at the table in this room, as kitchens of this era were very small. Figure 1.2 depicts another typical room used as both a living room and a bedroom. Although the photo was taken in 2011, it retains the classic elements of the Soviet multiuse room. The beds fold into sofas for use during the day, and there is no separate living room. The décor is typical of the Brezhnev era, including the rug used as a wall hanging (and which doubles as insulation), as well as the style of the storage cabinets, light fixture, and calendar.

These new apartments were named *khrushchevkas*, after the leader who introduced them on a mass scale. Soviet authorities presented the khrush-chevka's modest design as convenient and hygienic. Yet inconvenient floor plans and shoddy construction earned this first generation of mass housing the nickname *khrushchoby*. Because planners measured housing production in square meters of living space, builders prioritized quantity over quality. Problems ranged from leaking pipes to uneven floors to kitchens too small to turn around in. Soviet media tried to transform cost cutting into a social virtue: keeping apartments small and cheap meant everyone would get one. Housing was a right for Soviet workers, readers were reminded, unlike their unfortunate counterparts in the capitalist world.[7]

Figure 1.1 Mechanic's family in a multiuse room in a Soviet apartment, 1966.
Source: Tsentral'nyi Gosudarstvennyi Arkhiv Kinofotodokumentov, SSSR, no. 185729, reprinted in Buchli (1997, 171).

FIGURE 1.2   Multiuse room shared by a parent and child in 2011. The furnishings and style have changed little since the Soviet period. Photo by Anastasia Smirnova.

Yet the low quality of housing troubled the party-state as well as residents. Khrushchev turned living standards into a Cold War battleground when he promised to "catch up with and overtake" the United States. During the so-called Kitchen Debate at the American National Exhibition in Moscow in 1959, Khrushchev said to Nixon of the American model kitchen: "You Americans think that the Russian people will be astonished to see these things. The fact is that all our new houses have this kind of equipment." On viewing an American prototype for a remote-controlled appliance console, he quipped, "Don't you have a machine that puts food in your mouth and pushes it down?... This is not a rational approach. These are gadgets we will never adopt."[8]

By exaggerating Soviet living standards and denigrating capitalist consumerism, Khrushchev belied his anxiety about catching up with the West. On the other hand, his decision to allow the American exhibition to take place suggested he was confident that Soviet living standards would improve (Reid 2008, 863–65). Criticism in the press of low quality and long waiting lists conveyed that the party-state cared about consumers' difficulties.[9] The "electric home," promised the media, was just around the corner: fantastic new appliances would relieve women of the burden of extra housework that living as nuclear families would otherwise create (Reid 2005).

Housing conditions did improve, although Soviet women, like their Western counterparts, continued to endure the second shift at home. Design adjustments during the Brezhnev administration made apartments more comfortable. Architects enlarged kitchens to make room for a table, isolated toilets from baths, and added hallways with separate entrances for all rooms. These changes made construction more costly just as investment in housing began to fall in the 1970s. Nevertheless, 40 percent of the population moved into new apartments between 1970 and 1985 (Goskomstat 1987, 373).

These new apartments needed furniture and appliances. By 1975, three-fourths of Soviet households had radios, sewing machines, and televisions, and two-thirds had refrigerators and crude washing machines. The furniture supply also expanded: production of tables and hutches increased and matching furniture suites appeared. Production of many other goods—strollers, toys, musical instruments, decorative dishes, and cleaning products—accelerated (Zavisca 2004, chapter 3). Demand for consumer goods always outpaced supply, however, as did demand for apartments in which to house them.

Distributing the Separate Apartment

Despite the incredible pace of construction, housing was always in short supply. Demand was managed via queues: people who qualified for improved housing could sign up on waiting lists at their workplaces or through their municipalities. Queues were ordered according to two conflicting principles: social equity versus necessary inequality. Need, according to the principle of equity, should govern distribution. People in extremely crowded or dilapidated housing could jump ahead in workplace queues or join municipal queues for the neediest families. Others could join the queue at the back of the line if they met minimal criteria for need: families with insufficient living space per capita, residents of communal apartments, and households composed of more than two generations.

Distributing housing according to household structure not only accommodated need; it also rewarded reproduction. Married couples without children had little hope of living apart from extended family, and an apartment for a single adult was out of the question (Attwood 2004, 184). Having a child ensured a couple a spot on a waiting list for a separate apartment with at least one room. Multiple children entitled families to at least two rooms, and up to three rooms if siblings included boys and girls. Soviet newspapers were filled with happy accounts of young families who received two-room apartments after having a second child. Thus housing became a bargaining chip to boost a declining birthrate.

Housing distribution also advanced party-state goals in industry. The party allocated more resources for housing construction to key economic sectors and enterprises, which helped to attract workers (Andrusz 1990b). Ordering enterprise queues on a first–come, first–served basis privileged seniority and motivated workers to remain at their jobs. Delegating to enterprises the tasks of constructing and distributing housing gave enterprise managers an important form of power: they could manipulate queues to reward the most valued workers (or their most valuable connections), or withhold housing to compel undesired workers to leave (Andrusz 1990a, 558).

Allocating housing through work subordinated equity to expediency. If household needs had been the authorities' paramount concern, municipal queues would have predominated. To justify the link between housing and work, Soviet leaders invoked the discourse on necessary inequality. Khrushchev argued that, although shelter was a basic right, high-quality housing was a right for work: "In building and allocating housing, we must not simply think: because a man is alive, give him a good apartment. It's necessary to look at what he is doing and what he is giving to society. In our socialist society, every person must contribute something to the general welfare and carry a certain load. Only then does he receive the right to enjoy the fruits of society's labor."[10] Likewise, Brezhnev advocated a direct dependence between worker productivity on the one hand, and wages and benefits on the other. Such inequalities would characterize what Brezhnev called "developed socialism," a long period during which the party–state would continue to construct communism (Evans 1977).

In practice, however, no legitimate criteria existed to measure workers' merit or to calibrate living standards to productivity. Housing and other prizes for Soviet heroes such as astronauts, Olympians, war veterans, pathbreaking scientists, and shock workers provoked little controversy (Matthews 1978, 43). The grounds for other forms of privilege were shakier. According to Marxist-Leninist ideology, skilled workers constituted the core of a revolutionary socialist society and should have received the bulk of consumer resources. But professionals and party functionaries also expected rewards for their expertise, education, and party participation. The latter group, who controlled the distributive apparatus, resolved the matter in their own favor.

The internal passport system further tied housing chances to work. As in Stalin's time, people could not move legally without a local propiska stamp in their passports. Although peasants gained the right to internal passports in 1974, the propiska system continued to restrict population flows into large cities, which had better supplies of goods and services (Zaslavsky 1980). A propiska was required not only to apply for a job or housing, but also to access medical care, education, pension payments, and ration cards for deficit goods (Höjdestrand 2009, 24). Although this system helped enterprises recruit workers, it also impeded labor mobility because people were reluctant to move if it meant giving up their propiskas, and therefore their right to return home (Matthews 1993, 51; Buckley 1995, 900).

Bending the Rules of Housing Allocation

Formal principles of state allocation, although important, do not tell the entire story of who got what and how. The discretion left to managers for issuing propiskas and administering queues enabled informal exchange of favors. Housing catalyzed complaints over corruption and unfairness in Soviet society. One woman I interviewed in 2002 recalled the manifest unfairness of queue jumping: "I hated the communists. My husband and I lived in a dormitory for ten years. We were young and thought if we worked our turn would come. And we watched while others got apartments before us, not because they worked harder, but because they worked at a rich enterprise, or because they knew somebody. It was unpleasant to realize that the party and union committees were giving each other gifts."

According to official communist morality, housing was a right but not a proper end in itself. In reality, many people adjusted their work and family strategies to pursue housing. People changed jobs and even careers to improve their housing chances (Zavisca 2004, chapter 3). Getting married and having children were not just stages in the life course; they were means of getting onto waiting lists (Gerasimova 1999, 109). Some people contracted fictitious marriages to gain propiskas, which may explain why divorce rates in Moscow and Leningrad were twice the national average (Matthews 1993, 51–52).

A quasi-market sector also created opportunities to circumvent housing queues. In 1962 the party-state banned private home building in major cities (Herman 1971, 213–14). However, a residual market remained in privately owned dwellings, mostly dilapidated prewar houses, which could be bought and sold. Cooperatives were also legalized, although they constituted a tiny portion of the housing sector. Members had to pay to join coops at rates that were expensive compared to incomes. Most Russians could not afford a deposit, and planning targets gave the construction industry little incentive to build cooperatives (Andrusz 1992).

More significant was a lively market in state-owned housing. People were allowed to swap government apartments, complete with propiskas. Although payments were not allowed, two marketlike mechanisms governed swaps. First, the attributes of swapped apartments suggested an implicit market. Small apartments in Moscow were exchanged for much larger apartments in the provinces (Sidorov 1992). Would-be swappers whose apartments had undesirable attributes, such as ground-floor locations or little natural light, had to compromise on size or location to find a taker. Second, illegal side-payments often accompanied swaps. People with second-economy incomes tended to occupy better state apartments, indicating that illegal income could be laundered into housing (Alexeev 1988) and confirming Katherine Verdery's observation that the Soviet second economy was both "parasitic upon the state economy and inseparable from it" (1996, 27).

The right to exchange propiskas as well as property, and to register others at one's address, made housing a source of social capital. People who had extra living space could help relatives acquire propiskas and join housing queues. For example, extended families might decide with which set of in-laws a couple would register (although not necessarily live) based on which arrangement would create sufficient crowding to give the young couple priority status in queues for separate apartments. Family networks could also yield a propiska in a desirable location. A person with extended family in Moscow had a better chance of moving there than someone who did not. People without social support, such as ex-prisoners or elderly residents of hostels, might find themselves with no propiska at all, members of a stigmatized class of *bomzhi,* an acronym meaning people without a defined place of residence (Höjdestrand 2009).

Housing Inequality in the Soviet Union

Despite some quasi-market mechanisms, state distribution predominated in the housing sector. By 1990, 80 percent of housing was owned and allocated by the state (Goskomstat 1991). What was the end result of this distributive apparatus, with its dual principles of work and need? Scholars have not reached consensus about the consequences of state distribution for inequality. Some maintain that the Soviet housing system exacerbated inequality. Because everyone got housing for free, the better off were more heavily subsidized in a system governed by the principle "equal payments for unequal housing conditions" (Andrusz 1990c, 313). Others contend that housing subsidies mitigated inequality, because they constituted a greater share of the permanent income of poor households (Alexeev 1990; Buckley and Gurenko 1997).

To theorize the significance of housing for socialist inequality, Iván Szelényi (1983) adopted the concept of "housing class," which was introduced by John Rex (1968) in a study of the United Kingdom. Rex drew on Max Weber's conception of class as shared market position to argue that housing can create classes with shared interests under capitalism. The Marxist position that relations of production account for unequal living standards was wrong, he argued, for two reasons. First, the state differentiates access to housing through subsidies and tax policy. Second, inheritance transfers housing wealth to children, independently of their occupations or wages.

Both of these mechanisms operated in the Soviet bloc: the state distributed most housing, and tenancy rights could be passed to descendants. Furthermore, a new class had emerged under state socialism, whose power and resources derived not from relations of production but from control over distribution (Konrád and Szelényi 1979). These redistributors tended to reserve the scarcest resources for themselves, their relatives, and friends. As a result, employees at the same enterprise earning the same income could have different housing conditions. Thus, Szelényi argued, socialist housing generated a particular form of inequality: "Privileged housing carried with it an almost feudal distinction. To receive it was to stride eight or ten years ahead along the road to consumer security. . . . That traditional vertical inequality was soon accompanied by specific horizontal inequalities. Among people within similar social categories there were the elderly who had homes, and the young who did not have them yet; there were the original urban residents with homes and the newer immigrants" (1983, 34).

Numerous studies found support for Szelényi's argument across the Soviet bloc.[11] However, most of this research was conducted in Eastern European countries, which, unlike the USSR, had substantial private housing sectors. The first relevant survey of the USSR, the General Social Survey of the European USSR, was conducted in spring 1991 (Swafford et al. 1995). Using this data, Zhou and Suhomlinova found that upper-level administrators and managers with authority in the workplace had more living space (2001, 185–93).[12] Communist party membership, after controlling for occupation, did not appear to bring housing rewards. This is consistent with Szelényi's argument: high-level administrators, not rank-and-file party members, constituted the redistributive class. The most important predictor of living space, however, was household size, reflecting some correspondence between need and housing conditions.

The literature on socialist housing inequality typically measures inequality in terms of space (square meters or rooms, in total or per capita), a conventional approach in the cross-national literature. However, in the USSR the number of generations per room, and of families per apartment, were important measures of housing status that have so far been overlooked. Previous studies have also not accounted for key demographic variables—being married and having children—that underlay the logic of distribution. I reanalyzed the GSS-USSR data to consider the determinants of housing status using new measures more appropriate to the Soviet context: having a separate apartment for the nuclear family, and having at least one room for each generation in the household. Table 1.1 gives descriptive statistics on the correlates of housing inequality for these two new measures, as well as for the traditional measure of housing space per capita.

As table 1.1 indicates, young adults age twenty-one to thirty were less than half as likely as older adults to have separate apartments. Only half even had their own rooms (to themselves or shared with a partner), compared with four out of five adults over age fifty. The family structure variable makes clear why this is the case. Young people are far more likely to be unmarried and/or childless. Unmarried Soviet citizens had very little chance of getting a separate apartment (regardless of whether they had children). About two-thirds

Table 1.1   Correlates of housing status in the urban USSR in 1991

	Separate Apartment[a]	Separate Room[b]	Space per Capita[c]
All (N = 1,583)	56	67	10
Age			
21–30	29	55	9
31–40	62	61	9
41–50	68	69	10
≥51	66	79	13
Marital status			
Single	12	67	13
Married	63	69	10
Divorced/widowed	49	59	13
Has children			
No	23	71	12
Yes	62	67	10
Education			
< secondary	57	70	11
Secondary (with degree)	54	64	10
Higher (including incomplete)	59	70	10
Occupation (current or last)			
Manager/ upper prof.	67	80	10
Lower professional	65	72	10
Routine nonmanual	52	64	10
Upper manual	54	64	10
Lower manual	54	70	10
Party member			
No	54	66	10
Yes	71	78	11

Source: General Social Survey of the European USSR.

[a] Percent living only with spouse & minor children; not dorm, communal, or rental.

[b] Percent having at least one room per generation as well as for each child age ≥15; not dorm or communal apartment.

[c] Median square meters per capita.

of married people, by contrast, had their own apartments, as did half of those who were divorced or widowed. The combination of being married and having at least one child (not shown in the table) greatly increased the likelihood of a separate apartment: among married people, having children improved one's odds of having a separate apartment by 62 percent, compared to childless couples.

These differences in housing quality by age and family structure are far less evident when we use the standard measure of living space per capita (see the last column of table 1.1). Likewise, living space does not vary by indicators of socioeconomic status—education, occupation, and party membership. Education is also not correlated with either of the other indicators of housing status—having a separate apartment or a separate room. However, occupational status and party membership are associated with having a separate apartment or separate room. Two-thirds of managers and professionals in the GSS-USSR had a separate apartment, versus about half of others; the differences are similar for party members.

In sum, the two new measures of housing status appear to detect inequalities that the living space measure fails to capture. However, these descriptive statistics must be interpreted with caution. First, the data do not reveal the attributes of the household member (current or previous) who originally acquired the housing unit in which the respondent lived at the time of the survey. Second, the bivariate relationships may be spurious. For example, communist party members are typically older than nonmembers, so the apparent benefits of party membership may really be a function of age. Multivariate regression models take into account such covariance between multiple predictors of housing status.

Table 1.2 shows the results for a logistic regression of various factors on the odds of having a separate apartment. Demographic variables—age, marital status, and having had children—strongly increased these odds. For example, the odds are nearly triple for a married individual compared to a single person, controlling for other variables. Likewise, having at least one child nearly doubles the odds (controlling for other variables in the model). Indicators of socioeconomic status—occupation, education, and party membership—had weak and statistically insignificant associations with having a separate apartment. Results were similar for multivariate analysis of the odds of having a separate room for each generation.[13]

How should we interpret the preponderance of demographic as opposed to socioeconomic variables in the structure of housing inequality? Zhou and Suhomlinova conclude that the association between household structure (which they measure as household size) and housing quality (which

Table 1.2   Logistic regression for odds of having a separate apartment, urban adults, 1991

	Odds Ratio	Confidence Interval
Age	1.15*	(1.08, 1.22)
Age squared	0.999*	(.9982, 1.0005)
Male	0.77	(.58, 1.12)
Married	2.64*	(1.97, 3.54)
Number of children (0 = reference)		
One	1.71*	(1.13, 2.59)
Two or more	1.86*	(1.22, 2.83)
Occupation (Lower manual = reference)		
Manager/upper prof.	1.25	(.67, 2.3)
Lower professional	1.25	(.73, 2.14)
Routine non-manual	0.79	(.50, 1.25)
Upper manual	1.08	(.69, 1.71)
Higher education	1.05	(.74, 1.48)
Communist party member	1.18	(.78, 1.79)

Notes: Other variables in the model not shown here include sector of employment and region.
* = significant at p =.05 level; N = 1476; pseudo R2 = 0.13.

they measure as living space) reflected a "'need-based' housing policy—an egalitarian principle of state socialist redistribution" (2001, 187). The concept of housing class, combined with the new measures I propose, suggests an alternative interpretation. When housing is not strongly related to either occupation or income, it becomes a principle of stratification in its own right, autonomous from relations of production. The familial basis for distributing housing created a new basis for inequality. The strong relationship between housing conditions and completed life course transitions—to marriage and parenthood—indicates that housing was a reward for reproduction, and not just need. Furthermore, the right to transfer usage rights to one's descendants and to swap housing at will turned housing into a household asset, unequally distributed across families.

In comparative perspective, despite these inequities, housing inequality in the USSR was quite low. Variation in housing space in the United States, for example, was twice as high as in the USSR.[14] Standardized construction limited the range of housing possibilities. Only 5 percent of government housing units had more than three rooms in 1988. Housing quality also depended much more on the time period of construction than on unequal construction at any given time. By late Soviet standards, a high-quality apartment was one with at least two isolated rooms, a kitchen no less than eight square meters in size, and all key utilities, including running water, hot water, sanitation, and central heat. According to GSS-USSR data, 29 percent of Soviet adults occupied such apartments. In the 1980s, 60 percent of new apartments met these standards, compared to 23 percent in the 1970s, and just 10 percent for earlier construction. Given that two-thirds of all high-quality apartments were built after 1980, timing mattered most for one's odds of inhabiting one.

We should not underestimate the social significance of apparently small differences. A few extra square meters provided play or study areas for children, space for durable goods, and opportunities to entertain. A separate apartment for the nuclear family provided a sense of normalcy, yet only half of urban adults lived in separate apartments by 1991. An extra room made it possible to separate sleeping quarters across generations, but one-third of adults lived in apartments with fewer rooms than there were generations in the household. During the long wait for a separate apartment, housing remained a source of stress and suffering.

How the Separate Apartment Became Normal

In reminiscences of the Soviet era, having had a separate apartment—along with a car and a dacha—is a sign of having lived well.[15] Shortage and inequality only made people covet apartments more. Soviet moralists worried that the privacy, prosperity, and de facto sense of ownership afforded by separate apartments would degrade socialist consciousness. The party-state used design and discourse to maintain its presence in the home. Apartment layouts and furniture styles physically limited the potential for individualism (Humphrey 2005; Reid 2009, 479). Convertible sofas and hideaway tables, for example, normalized living and sleeping in the same room. Tiny kitchens discouraged elaborate meal preparation and suggested that socialist citizens would prefer to dine in public settings (Reid 2005). Nevertheless, these cramped kitchens became the heart of Soviet homes, a locus for hospitality and private conversation (Ries 1997). Large windows promoted openness to the collective gaze, although people sewed curtains as soon as they moved in (Reid 2009, 489).

Cultural authorities also used discourse to influence how people understood and used their apartments. Media ranging from explicit propaganda in newspapers to depictions of everyday life in film framed housing as a right of Soviet citizens, a reward for socialist workers, and a responsibility for rational consumers. The volume of advice on how to live belied concerns that citizens were developing unhealthy relationships to their apartments (Kelly 2001, chapter 5; Varga-Harris 2008, 574). As Susan Reid put it, "In making housing into a home, it was the occupant who had the last word" (2009, 470). Nevertheless, the state's attempts to shape meaning had significant, if unintended, effects. The separate apartment was defined through a series of contrasts: familial versus communal; modern versus old-fashioned; rational versus consumerist; married with children versus childless and single. This set of meanings encouraged people to interpret the separate apartment as "normal."

The romantic comedy *The Irony of Fate,* produced in 1975, encapsulates these contrasts. This popular Soviet film is still shown on Russian television on New Year's Eve. The film's protagonists Zhenya and Nadya, two singles in their thirties, fall in love after they meet by chance when Zhenya mistakes her apartment for his own, a mishap made possible by standardized housing. The film opens with a cartoon: an architect is shown drawing blueprints for an attractive residential building. His superiors reject his design as too ornate. A series of revisions, successively simpler, is also rejected, until nothing remains but a bland box. Replicates of this final model march and settle all over the world.

After the cartoon ends, the camera pans across a new neighborhood in Moscow. The narrator asks, "Isn't it wonderful that in every Soviet city, you can find streets with the same names, apartments with the same addresses, and standard locks that can be opened with standard keys?" The narrator's tone is sarcastic but warm, and passersby appear content as they shop for gifts for New Year's Eve. The message is clear: prosperity in the USSR is founded on modernist simplicity.

Zhenya has just moved with his mother into a new, two-room apartment in Moscow. Having reluctantly agreed to propose to his girlfriend Galya at midnight, Zhenya gets very drunk and winds up on a plane to Leningrad. When he sobers up at the airport, he thinks he is still in Moscow and takes a taxi to his address. His key turns the lock, the furniture is familiar, and he goes to bed. When the rightful resident, Nadya, returns home, the two argue about whose apartment it is. The moment of truth comes when they compare propiskas. Zhenya cries, "This is my apartment, I'm registered here!" He recites his address and living space. Nadya's data are identical—except for the city! Nadya, it turns out, also lives with her mother (fathers are never mentioned). Both mothers disappear at the right times, only showing up to supply food or nuggets of maternal wisdom. The pathology of Zhenya's and Nadya's situations, the film suggests, is not that they still live with their parents; it is that they are unmarried and childless.

The film also offers a lesson in socialist taste. The apartment's design is socialist realist, with stylish furniture and lots of open space. The set occupied more than 100 square meters, triple the size of the apartment it was supposed to represent. The furniture and decor depicted things as they were supposed to be, rather than as they typically were. The contrast between Nadya and Galya is also typical of Soviet romantic comedies. Galya is pretty but silly and vain; Nadya is beautiful but restrained. Although Zhenya and Nadya meet due to an "irony of fate," their parallel apartments lead them to each other, and to a normal life at last.

An Escape from Communal Abnormalcy

The official rationale for Khrushchev's housing campaign was to "isolate" and "separate" people from the "social strain" of communal living (Gerasimova 2003, 168; Semenova 2004, 58). People were encouraged to regard state-provided apartments as "their own." For example, a worker quoted in the newspaper *Pravda* said, "I have my own apartment in a new eight-story build-ing, with all conveniences. It has two rooms. I received this apartment not as a loan, but for my entire life."[16] The transition to a separate apartment was con-secrated in the ritual of "Happy Housewarming." Soviet media depicted this experience as a "joyous rite of passage, associated with brightness, coziness, stability, and happiness, through which the new Soviet person would emerge, remade, in readiness for the new life under communism" (Reid 2009, 475).

These transitions were significant events in people's life histories. My older interviewees in Kaluga in 2002 recalled moves into separate apartments viv-idly and happily. In an analysis of citizens' letters, Steven Harris demonstrates how people "defined the 'normality' of the separate apartment" in contrast to communal living. Normalcy meant having no neighbors inside one's apart-ment and living with only two to three generations of one's family (2003, 9). As Lynn Atwood concluded from retrospective interviews: "Not having to share cooking and washing facilities with strangers was a huge relief. Despite the party's attempts to present the move to single-family housing as a new form of socialist living, in reality it resulted in a more privatized form of family life" (2004, 193–94).

The privacy afforded by the separate apartment created an ideological problem. Soviet citizens might succumb to consumerism as they made their apartments their own. If they spent too much time at home, they would withdraw from the life of the collective. This dangerous disposition was labeled *meshchanstvo*, which meant "materialism, small-mindedness, an exclusive concern with family and personal life, and a corresponding lack of social involvement" (Field 2007, 16). Soviet moralists called for "strict social and political control" over this new private sphere the state had cre-ated (18). The title of a brochure for party activists warned: "Everyday life is not a private matter" (Reid 2002, 249).

A Right and Responsibility of the Rational Consumer

A Soviet slogan chided, "There are not rights without responsibilities."[17] Promising every family an apartment constructed the family as a discrete social entity and the apartment as an entitlement. Yet the collective retained the right to define needs, and citizens were expected to eschew "thingism" (*veshchism*). To cultivate a "communist culture of needs," Soviet planners developed "rational consumption norms" (Bigulov et al. 1984). For example, citizens could expect to consume eighty-two kilograms of meat per year and eight pairs of socks or hosiery (Maier 1988). Although planning norms were rarely fulfilled, they helped the regime "simultaneously to meet and depress consumer expectations" (Breslauer 1982, 139–40). The sanitary norm for living space fit neatly into this paradigm.

Rational consumption began with the pursuit of an apartment. Legal and moral ways existed for obtaining whatever one rationally needed; to desire more was irrational and immoral. The novella *Just Another Week* provides a portrait of a good socialist consumer in the figure of Olga, a working mother struggling to juggle her responsibilities (Baranskaya 1989). Although Olga is strapped for time, she describes her housing conditions as "superb" (5). She occupies a new, three-room apartment of thirty-four square meters, nearly the sanitary norm for her family of four. Cautionary tales on the dangers of "malicious consumption," on the other hand, told of the consequences of greed. One story, published in a national magazine, described a young engineer who lost his job, his wife, and his party membership after he was caught maintaining a mistress in an illegal second apartment. He is "a portrait of a 'terminal consumer.'. . . His hands only took from people and society, and gave nothing in return."[18]

Rational norms also extended into the interior of the apartment. Soviet authorities perpetually waged campaigns against "domestic trash," which depending on the time period, ranged from porcelain knickknacks to pets (Dunham 1976; Boym 1994). Such petit-bourgeois clutter was not just bad taste—it led to commodity fetishism and impeded the development of social-ist consciousness. People were admonished to throw away superfluous things; to redecorate walls, windows, and floors with light, uniform materials; and to rearrange rooms to decenter or eliminate the family table and create multiple zones for socializing, sleeping, and studying (Buchli 1997).

Insistence that consumption should be collectively oriented was at odds with expanding opportunities for personal consumption. Authorities were dismayed when sociological time-budget surveys found that attendance at cultural events was poor (Moskoff 1984; White 1990). People preferred to stay home and watch television or visit with friends. The party-state propagated a discourse on "active leisure" to encourage people to spend less time at home and to transform personal time into socially useful time. Dachas—garden plots with small cottages—were distributed to people in hopes that they would grow their own fruits and vegetables and enjoy the fresh air. Cultural authorities worried, however, that the dacha could become a locus of private consumption instead of informal production. Preventative measures included requirements that plots be cultivated; strict limits on the dimensions of cottages; and a prohibition on heating systems. Nevertheless, just as with apartments, people came to think of the dachas assigned to them as their own (Lovell 2003; Zavisca 2003).

Based on the sheer volume of propaganda on lifestyle, the fight against consumerism—whether framed as "domestic trash" or "inactive leisure"—was a battle the party-state did not believe it was winning. In fact, the state had built the infrastructure for privatized leisure by housing people in separate apartments, distributing dacha plots, and producing entertainment that could be consumed at home. Television symbolized the right to retreat into a private sphere, "as in the aphorism 'the Soviet person has the right to relax in front of the television after a day's work,' attributed to none other than Leonid Brezhnev" (Roth-Ey 2007, 295–96).

The Normalcy of the Nuclear Family

Soviet demographers defined the nuclear family as the natural household unit; deviation from this arrangement, they argued, contributed to a declining birthrate and increasing divorce rate (Field 2007, 70). A prominent demographer in 1977 framed housing conditions as the key to proper demographic development: "The earlier departure of grown children from the family is also facilitated by the general rise in material well-being, notably the steady improvement in housing conditions.... This confirms...that the family is moving toward a common structure: a group based on monogamous marriage and reduced to its 'natural size'—parents and their children" (Volkov 1982, 228). The presumed effect of housing on fertility was a foundational premise of Soviet social policy (Andrusz 1984, 141–42).

Some demographers questioned whether improving housing conditions would increase the birthrate. Housing alone could not alleviate women's double burden as workers and mothers, and Soviet family policy did not seriously address unequal division of labor within the household. An alternative explanation attributed fertility decline to a cultural shift in preferences for smaller families. Fertility had declined just as living standards improved, leading some to accuse women of a "selfish interest in consumerism" (Rivkin-Fish

2010, 707). The spoiled only child was the pathological result: "The child constantly feels itself the focus of attention of the older members of the family, the object of their love and admiration, which often leads to egocentrism, inflated self-image, and the mentality of a parasite" (Sheptulina 1982, 160).

Campaigns to encourage childbearing in the interest of society targeted women for two reasons. First childbearing and childrearing were presumed to be women's responsibility. Second, Soviet moralists perceived women as prone to acquisitiveness and irrational consumer behavior (Varga-Harris 2008, 573–74). Since Khrushchev had relegalized abortion, the birthrate could only be lifted through moral education and persuasion. Advice literature on parenting presumed that families' housing needs had been met. For example, injunctions to construct "children's corners" at home assumed that parents had "enough room to set up a desk or workspace for their children" (Field 2007, 87–89). The problem, according to this discourse, was not insufficient living space, but more space than women were capable of handling.

The underlying causes of fertility decline were complex and the birthrate was already declining before Khrushchev took power. However, the separate apartment campaign, and the moral campaigns that accompanied it, may have contributed to Russians' reluctance to have multiple children. By promising each family a separate apartment and defining the family as nuclear, the party-state created new expectations for a normal life, but then failed to meet these expectations. As the first generation of children grew into adults, khrushchevkas became overcrowded with multiple generations. Although most couples had one child regardless of housing circumstances, many calibrated their decisions about a second child to their housing prospects. When the government began to allocate roomier apartments for multiple children, this in turn generated expectations that a separate room for each child, not just a separate apartment for each family, was needed to live normally.

Housing as a Gift of the Party-State

By promising every family a separate apartment, the party-state signaled that it cared for all its citizens. Mass housing opened the door for the mass consumption of other goods such as furniture suites and televisions, which symbolized modernity, progress, and ever-improving living standards. In turn, the party-state expected gratitude for its "gifts to the people." In Kaluga's local newspaper, one lucky recipient exclaimed, "We are grateful to the factory for this gift. The apartment is convenient: three isolated rooms, fifty square meters of floor space, a large, well-lit kitchen, and a wide corridor. My wife and I are also glad that our children can walk to the school right in our courtyard. Our neighbors, most of whom are workers, share this opinion." The article concluded by reminding readers that apartment rents had not been raised since 1928.[19]

This discourse resonated with Soviet people, who tended to describe housing trajectories "in the passive tense: 'I've been given an apartment/room,' 'I was allocated an apartment/room'" (Semenova 2004, 54). My interviewees in Kaluga, including older respondents in 2002 and younger respondents in 2009, used similar language to describe housing distribution in the Soviet era, and to ask of the post-Soviet epoch: "Who will give us housing now?" Despite inequalities, people typically recall housing as a universal entitlement and evidence that "we all lived more or less the same."

Propiskas also contributed to Soviet sensibilities on entitlement and normalcy. Tova Höjdestrand (2009), in her work on homelessness, argues that the propiska system was a form of Foucaultian governmentality. Not having a propiska signified worthlessness and led to social as well as civic exclusion. Conversely, having a propiska symbolized one's status as a normal person, with social as well as civic entitlements. Among these entitlements was the practical sense of ownership of housing that secure tenancy rights provided (Matthews 1993, 47–48; Buckley 1995, 911–12).

Perestroika: Renewing the Promise of a Separate Apartment

By the close of the Soviet epoch, most people took for granted the housing regime and the tactics they had devised to work within and around it. However, the separate apartment's normalcy produced a sense of abnormalcy among those who lacked one. Recognizing frustration with long waiting lists, the Twenty-Seventh Party Congress in 1986 resolved to provide every family with a separate apartment by the year 2000 (Andrusz 1990b, 228–30). Housing construction reached its maximum volume in 1987, when the state produced more than 70 million square meters of living space in one year (Goskomstat 1991).

Glasnost opened a public dialogue about the housing question. Letters to the editor reflected anger over unjustified inequality, with the best flats going to people with the best connections, not the best work ethics (Andrusz 1990a, 557). Gorbachev railed against the Brezhnev regime's "violation of the most important principle of socialism—distribution according to work."[20] Social justice required "justified inequality." Inequality had become an end in itself, as long as the right people were rewarded.

In 1988, several decrees encouraged individual housing construction in urban areas to "activate the human factor," reversing thirty years of policy that discouraged an urban private sector. New programs provided generous terms of credit and improved access to roads and utilities to facilitate individual housing development. Another provision enabled converting some of the state-owned housing stock to cooperative ownership and adjusting prices to reflect a location's desirability. Enterprises were also allowed to build housing and sell it to cooperatives (Andrusz 1990a, 562–64; 2002, 136–37).

Nevertheless, an acute housing shortage persisted as the Soviet period drew to a close. In 1985 the government estimated that 40 million new housing units, or a doubling of the housing stock, would be needed to provide separate dwellings for all families (Andrusz 1990b, 228). In 1990 20 percent of families were standing in queues for housing, and an additional 25 percent hoped to join waiting lists (Kosareva and Struyk 1993; Goskomstat 2000). The average queue was about ten years, although the right job and connections could shorten the wait (Andrusz 1990b, 239). Differential waits became extremely consequential when communist rule collapsed. People without separate apartments, who were disproportionately young, lost their chance for a free apartment when market transition began.

 **CHAPTER 2**

Transplant Failure

The American Housing Model in Russia

After Soviet rule collapsed, the new government tried to construct a housing market. This chapter traces the process of transplanting American housing institutions to Russia through three stages: from an initial focus on privatization, to the establishment of mortgage finance, to the government's attempts to rescue the market from failure. To jump-start a housing market, the Russian Federation signed an agreement with the US Agency for International Development (USAID) to implement the Housing Sector Reform Project (HSRP). The project, one of USAID's largest in the region, was funded by the US Freedom for Russian and Emerging Eurasian Democracies and Open Markets (FREEDOM) Support Act. Project management was subcontracted to the Urban Institute, an American nongovernmental organization. The Yeltsin administration and its American advisers had three goals: to reduce the state's role in the housing sector, to enable markets to allocate housing according to resources and preferences, and to convince the public that housing markets are efficient and fair.

The HSRP shared many tenets of the "Washington Consensus," a set of policies for building markets embraced by political and financial institutions based in Washington, DC (Williamson 1990). The consensus held that governments in developing countries needed to privatize state assets, deregulate business, liberalize finance, and limit public expenditures. A World Bank report, entitled *Housing: Enabling Markets to Work* (1993), applied the

Washington Consensus to housing. Policy analysts frequently reference—and criticize—this report's international influence (Jones and Datta 2000; Rojas 2001; Mukhija 2004).

World Bank prescriptions and HSRP goals parallel one another. Both conceptualize the housing sector as a market, founded on private property and regulated by supply and demand. Both urge governments to privatize dwellings, land, construction, and maintenance; to free housing prices; to rationalize registries of property rights; to deregulate barriers to private construction; to develop mortgage finance; to recover infrastructure costs; and to subsidize needy people, not housing units or interest rates (World Bank 1993, chapter 3; Struyk 1997, 1–8).

The HSRP departed from the World Bank's approach in two respects. First, USAID sought to maximize homeownership, which symbolized American capitalism and was expected to give Russians a stake in market reform (Mandić and Clapham 1996). A housing market, however, does not require that everyone own a home. The World Bank cautioned that enabling markets requires opportunities to rent as well as to own and attributed underdeveloped rental markets in the former Soviet region to USAID's influence (Dübel et al. 2006, 54–55). Second, USAID attempted to create "a Russian copy of the American secondary mortgage market system" (Mints 2000, 50). In the United States, government-sponsored enterprises (GSEs) and private financial institutions purchase mortgages from banks and resell loan payments as mortgage-backed securities (MBS). This system removes mortgages from originators' balance sheets and creates liquidity, enabling "individual mortgages... to be turned into homogenous goods by a government agency set up to make a market out of mortgage payments" (Carruthers and Stinchcombe 1999, 354).

United States reliance on securities to capitalize housing markets is exceptional; most other market economies employ alternative means (Green and Wachter 2010). Some postsocialist nations, such as the Czech Republic and Hungary, modeled their mortgage systems after Germany's *Bausparkassen*, a form of savings and loan association (Roy 2008, 140). Another potential model was European mortgage banks, which raise capital with covered bonds, whose underlying assets remain on a bank's balance sheet (UNECE 2005). HSRP leadership ruled out these alternatives, however, as "costly populism" unsuitable for postsocialist contexts. HSRP leaders warned against a "follow-the-leader mentality.... Governments have seemed to follow 'housing finance trends,' the most recent being the introduction of European-style mortgage banks" (Struyk 2000, x). Securitization made more sense for Russia, they argued, because its fragile banks, which were already undercapitalized, needed to mobilize and reinvest capital rather than tie it up in long-term loans (Kosareva 2007, 296–97).[1] This early influence of the American model has had lasting effects; as of 2010, despite the crisis that had overtaken the American system, securitized mortgages remained the ideological core of Russian housing policy.

Transplanting the Housing Market: 1992–1998

Privatizing Housing and Scaling Back the State

Privatization, the core principle of the Washington Consensus, "became the Government's key instrument in establishing market relations throughout the [housing] sector" (UNECE 2004, 1). Construction firms, like most state-controlled businesses, were privatized using voucher schemes that enabled managers to consolidate controlling shares (Sutela 1994). The question remained what to do with the state–owned housing stock. Nadezhda Kosareva and Raymond Struyk, the Russian and American directors of the HSRP, advised the Russian government to privatize housing and raise maintenance fees to "shock the housing sector into operating more on market principles" (1993, 99).

The 1992 Law on the Fundamentals of Housing Policy gave occupants the right to privatize the dwellings they inhabited for free. The policy was simple to implement and popular among privileged groups, but it had flaws (Pickvance 1994). For one, it did not try to mitigate inequality. As Kosareva and Struyk put it, "There is little hope of equal treatment.... Those occupying the better units at the beginning of the privatization process will receive larger transfers of wealth" (1993, 98). Residents of quality apartments in prestigious neighborhoods rushed to claim their shares, privatizing one-third of eligible dwellings within two years. The pace of privatization then slowed: only about half of eligible units had been privatized by 2000 (Rosstat). People in subpar apartments had little to gain by privatizing, and perhaps a lot to lose. The government charged identical maintenance rates for privatized and unprivatized dwellings. Citizens could privatize only once in their lifetimes, and some held out hope of first receiving a better municipal apartment. Persistent property rights conferred by propiskas—Soviet-era residency permits—also complicated the process (see chapter 6). Many tenants, uncertain about long-term costs and benefits, decided to wait (Daniell and Struyk 1994; Guzanova 1998).[2]

Maintenance subsidies conflicted with a second principle of the Washington Consensus: the state should recover infrastructure costs. The average tenant in 1992 spent just 2 percent of household income on rent and utilities, which covered less than 1 percent of the cost.[3] The HSRP proposed to align fees with costs by 1998, while targeting subsidies to the poor. Nevertheless, the government extended the timeline for full cost recovery until 2003, and then again until 2008 (Struyk et al. 1997, 1794; Lykova et al. 2004, 620).

Housing subsidies were a popular safety net that ensured the survival of the government as well as of the population. The 1993 constitution declared that "everyone shall have the right to a home," enjoined the state to "encourage housing construction and create conditions for exercising the right to a home," and guaranteed free or subsidized housing for "low-income people and other persons mentioned in law and in need of a home."[4] Citizens who had been queuing for housing in 1991 retained the right to stand on municipal waiting lists. Other categories of entitled citizens included people living in communal or extremely crowded apartments, residents of condemned buildings, as well as military officers, war veterans, Chernobyl victims, and refugees from former Soviet republics.

This constitutional right, however, was an empty promise. The federal government slashed the housing budget and devolved responsibility for most social housing to municipalities (Kosareva et al. 2000). Local governments lacked the resources to fulfill this unfunded mandate, and government distribution of housing plummeted. Some numbers from Kaluga give a sense of how hopeless it was to queue: just 159 households were resettled from a queue of 8,500 in the year 2001. The city's waiting list had shrunk 60 percent in ten years, in part due to tightened criteria, but also because many eligible families did not bother to wait in a line that had stopped moving. Nationally, 0.5 percent of households received an apartment in 2000; 10 percent were still waiting in line (Rosstat).

This retreat from redistribution fulfilled a third tenet of the Washington Consensus: the state should get out of the business of housing supply. Government investment in construction dropped as well. By 2000 just 20 percent of new housing construction was commissioned by federal or municipal governments, down from 80 percent in 1990. Most new construction was for retired military officers; but even that program was so underfunded that the average waiting period exceeded three years. As for the existing housing stock, public expenditures on maintenance and capital repairs fell by 80 percent within a decade (Rosstat).

For proponents of the Washington Consensus, the state's decline was a good sign. Shock therapy, a variant of the Washington Consensus for post-socialist transitions, held that markets could be created by destroying their impediments—government ownership and price controls. Speed would shorten the pain of transition and deprive political opponents of time to organize and resist reform. Supporting institutions, such as a central bank and taxation system, were mere technicalities that could be copied from Western models (Murrell 1993). In the housing sector, rapid privatization was supposed to catalyze the market. Newly minted owners dissatisfied with their apartments could sell and buy a more suitable home. Private builders and lenders would meet demand from those passed over by privatization (Kosareva and Struyk 1993).

Importing Mortgage Institutions

Because housing is so expensive compared to household income, markets based on homeownership require a system of credit. HSRP leadership shifted the project's focus to institutionalizing mortgage lending in 1995. To that end, the Russian staff of the Urban Institute founded the Moscow-based Institute for Urban Economics (IUE). Its board of trustees included the chairman of the central bank and a deputy prime minister. The institute helped to draft laws on mortgages, securitization, bankruptcy, and foreclosure. It also introduced a Certified Mortgage Lender program in 1996, developed in consultation with Fannie Mae. The program trained bankers in "classical housing purchase mortgage loans" and discouraged "pseudo-mortgage lease loans," installment loan programs (*rassrochka*) that offered few legal protections for either buyers or sellers (Struyk 1998; Kosareva et al. 2000, 182–87).[5]

In 1997 the Russian government created the Agency for Home Mortgage Lending (AHML) to establish lending standards and provide liquidity. The agency was modeled on the US's Fannie Mae, whose experts helped set up AHML's operating procedures. Like Fannie Mae, AHML is a GSE. Although AHML is formally a joint stock company, the government is required to hold the majority of shares, giving an implicit state guarantee to AHML debt. The AHML initially planned to purchase loans from banks with personnel trained by the IUE's Certified Mortgage Lender program. Loan standards included a minimum down payment of 30 percent, a maximum loan amount of seventy thousand dollars, and a loan term of five to ten years. Interest rates were set via a deferred adjustable instrument (DAIR) that placed most inflationary risk on the borrower (Struyk 1998).

Russia thus became the first post-Soviet nation to have a formal institution to create a secondary mortgage market. Struyk (1998), in the HSRP's final report to USAID, attributed this accomplishment to a minimally adequate legal base; demand for liquidity from private banks that did not want to hold long-term loans; and lack of competition in home lending from government banks. Legal reforms had created a registry of real estate rights and transactions, enabled the use of real estate as a pledge to secure a loan, and established grounds for foreclosure. "USAID... has built the sturdy foundation and partially completed the superstructure for housing sector reform in the Russian Federation," he claimed, citing privatization, increasing market transactions, and declining state expenditures as signs of success (4). With the state out of the way, the private sector could organically begin to meet demand. Institutions for mortgage finance, although more complex to organize, were ready to take off as soon as the economy stabilized. This success story emphasized formal institutionalization rather than market performance.

The Market Fails: 1999–2004

AHML remained a hollow transplant, a formal copy with little practical effect. Its first loan purchases, scheduled for September 1998, had to be postponed when Russia defaulted on its debt in August. The AHML had been planning to raise capital on the international market, but the default made investors wary of long-term assets backed by the Russian government (Struyk 1998, 88–89). Legal barriers further diminished development of a secondary mortgage market (Skyner 2005). Two similar projects to jump-start mortgages in Russia—one led by Harvard consultants for the city of Moscow, the other a joint project of the US Congress and the Russian Duma—also tried but failed to create functioning facilities to securitize mortgages (Mints 2000).

The tiny mortgage sector survived on American subsidies. Although the HSRP ended in 1998, USAID sponsored the US-Russian Investment Fund, which provided starting capital for the firm Delta Capital and began marketing mortgages in Russia under the brand "Delta Credit."[6] A USAID report boasted in 2002: "Building on USAID's support for landmark reform of mortgage lending, Delta Capital is now the leading mortgage financier in Russia."[7] It wasn't difficult to lead in the minuscule sector, which was more a demonstration project than a market. In 2001–2, only about ten thousand mortgage loans were originated in Russia (Kosareva 2007, 42). Investors in Russian mortgages—i.e., the American government—entered the field not to turn a profit, but to promote markets as a political project. The result was "cheap mortgages for approximately 5,000 highly paid Russian qualified professionals... provided... by American taxpayers" (Mints 2000, 53).

A housing market did not flourish while mortgages sputtered and the state withered away. The relative growth of the private sector was a function of state collapse more than of market emergence. Construction of new housing units fell by two-thirds from 1990 to 2000. During the same period, the average size of new apartments rose by nearly 50 percent (Rosstat). Builders developed fewer, more luxurious homes for wealthy people who could pay cash. Figure 2.1 depicts a luxury apartment building constructed in the mid-2000s in Kaluga. Such buildings are located close to dilapidated Soviet-era residences in the city center, where space for new construction is limited. Suburban construction is also developing, but is less popular because of poorly developed infrastructure for utilities and transportation, as well as difficulty securing loans or contracts for new construction. The director of a privatized construction firm in Kaluga told me in 2002 that he felt guilty he could no longer build housing for the masses. He had to operate on a cash-only basis because the state would neither give him credit nor enforce contracts with consumers. Some builders offered installment loans: buyers could make a down payment to help finance construction, and then pay the remainder when the project was complete. However, consumers risked losing everything if the builder went bankrupt or disappeared (Kosareva 2007, 52–54). Both builders and buyers preferred to deal with counterparts who did not need credit.

Most families could not afford to pay cash for a home. Figure 2.2 calculates how long a family of three with average wages would have to save to afford an apartment, assuming they lived only on the paltry official subsistence minimum. Affordability declines as the index rises. This index conservatively measures housing prices and living expenses and surely underestimates the

FIGURE 2.1   Luxury apartment building in Kaluga. Photo by Anastasia Smirnova.

time to save.[8] Three is the maximum value typically found in stable housing markets, and the Russian government predicted the index would decline to that level by 2010.[9] Yet the index was at least twice as large as that target through 2010. Although the index did fall dramatically as the economy recovered after the 1998 default, housing prices remained so high compared to incomes that most households could not realistically purchase homes with savings alone.

Most Russians were compelled to live in the sediment of Soviet housing, much of which had outlasted its intended lifespan and was falling into disrepair. Khrushchevki of the 1960s, which were not built to last, were in critical condition. As of 2006, 41 percent of Russian housing space had been built before 1970 (the figure was 51 percent for the Kaluga region) (Rosstat 2007). Gosstroi, the federal housing agency, estimated in 2001 that 9 percent of housing was beyond repair. But less than 5 percent of condemned housing was being demolished annually. Another 11 percent of housing needed urgent repair, and Gosstroi projected that each year an additional 5 percent would require capital repairs. However, just 0.3 percent of the housing stock was actually renovated per year (UNECE 2004).

Of course, people could still move within the existing housing stock. Privatization provided starting capital for a secondary housing market: people

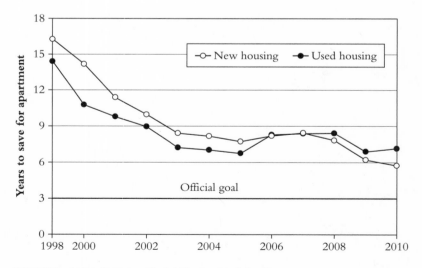

FIGURE 2.2   Index of housing affordability, Russian Federation
Source: Data from Rosstat.
Note: The index is calculated as the average price of fifty-four square meters of housing, divided by average annual income (less the official subsistence minimum) for a family comprised of two working-age adults and one child.

could sell their privatized apartments and trade up for additional cash. One study estimated that the percentage of Russian movers using market methods rose from 43 percent in 1992 to 70 percent in 2002. Yet the same report estimates that only 10 percent of households could afford to buy an apartment (UNECE 2004). As with housing construction, the rising share of market transactions reflected less a flourishing market than a shrinking state, since fewer people received housing from waiting lists. Many housing transactions, unmeasured by these studies, were neither state nor market—they were transfers among family. Relatively little privatized housing reached the open market. As of 1996, 40 percent of privatized housing units were occupied by pensioners, most of whom planned to bequeath their apartments to their children (Guzanova 1998).

Furthermore, rates of mobility within the existing housing stock remained low compared to developed housing markets. As of 2007, the estimated coefficient of multiplication of the secondary market (the ratio of transactions on the secondary versus primary market) was quite small—less than 2. In Europe, the analogous coefficient is around 3 to 4, and in the US, 4 to 5 (Berezin 2007).

The result is a housing regime I call property without markets, in which housing is privately owned but not fully commodified, and housing opportunities depend on privatized wealth rather than wages. Russians did move, but as chapter 4 will show, mobility was weakly correlated with standard measures of market position such as income, occupation, or education. This pattern also emerged in other former Soviet territories that prioritized privatization in housing reform (Buckley and Tsenkova 2001; Lux 2003).

Low living standards and hopeless housing conditions were frequent themes in Vladimir Putin's speeches after he became president in 2000. Yet housing policy during his first term in office departed little from that of his predecessor. His main achievement was completing an HSRP task that Yeltsin had begun: reducing and recovering the cost of state expenditures (Cook 2007). Maintenance and utilities rates skyrocketed, quadrupling between 1999 and 2002. A social marketing campaign portrayed paying for housing as patriotic. The city of Moscow in January 2002 mailed two versions of bills, a regular bill asking for a 60 percent payment, and a voluntary bill for the full price. Just 44 families paid the full price (UNECE 2004, 95). Kaluga also redesigned housing bills in 2002. I witnessed confusion turn into outrage as an acquaintance puzzled over her new bill, which itemized both the full cost of services and the percentage she was required to pay. In Moscow, a friend and I inspected a billboard urging residents to "Love Your City 100 percent!" My friend asked, "100 percent of what? Who decides what heat or electricity should cost? Those very bureaucrats who are in the pocket of the energy monopoly."

The Soviet concept of living space guided how prices were set. Fees were charged per square meter, and space beyond the sanitary norm (eighteen square meters per capita, increased from nine square meters in the Soviet period) did not qualify for subsidies. The intent was to encourage "over-housed" low-income families, mainly widowed pensioners, to move to smaller homes (Struyk, Puzanov, and Lee 1997). Many consumers instead stopped paying for utilities—one in five households was in arrears in 2002 (Mroz et al. 2004). To discourage nonpayment, the federal government in 2003 passed a law that approved evicting people whose delinquencies exceeded six months and resettling them in dormitories. Privately, however, authorities said that evictions were unlikely. Instead utilities were turned off for nonpayment, infrastructure and weather permitting.[10]

While rates soared, over 40 percent of the population remained entitled to a subsidy. Shortly after winning reelection in 2004, Putin introduced legislation to replace most in-kind subsidies with cash transfers to the elderly, disabled, and poor. Over half of surveyed Russians opposed the initiative.[11] Monetarization was "an obvious ruse," said a pensioner I interviewed in 2005. "They promise to raise pensions 100 rubles, and simpleminded people say, 'Thank you Mr. Putin!' But the next month, they will raise the electric bill 300 rubles." In early 2005 mass demonstrations around Russia protested the law.

Benefits were monetized despite opposition, and Putin's popularity did not suffer. How did he reconcile rolling back entitlements with expressing sympathy for the plight of average Russians? He echoed populist indignation by blaming high prices on resource monopolies and business oligarchs. Subsidies should go "not to the housing and utility complex, but to the people directly." Giving subsidies in cash instead of in kind would bring freedom and fairness, giving needy citizens "the right to allocate budget subsidies themselves, rather than having to share universal entitlements with the rich who could afford to pay."[12]

In his state of the union speech of 2004, Putin foregrounded affordable housing as a top priority: "People need decent housing for rest, for work and for starting a normal family. . . . It must be admitted that many people still live in dilapidated and unsafe apartments. . . . Only people with high incomes can afford to buy new housing. The fact that young families are unable to afford housing of their own affects their plans to have children, and it is still quite common to find several generations all having to share the same apartment." The solution to the housing question, he maintained, was mortgages.

We should stop deceiving people, forcing them to wait for years and even decades in line for housing. We need to create possibilities for the bulk of the working population to buy housing on the market, while ensuring that low-income groups have access to social housing. The government, regional and local authorities should work toward having at least a third of the population (and not a tenth, as is currently the case) able to buy housing that meets modern standards by 2010. They will buy housing through their own savings and with the help of mortgage schemes, ... [which] must become long term and affordable.... We must have a functioning state system for registering real estate rights, a credit history bureau, and a developed market for mortgage securities.[13]

The State Sponsors the Market: 2005–2009

The Mortgage Market Emerges

In 2005, the mortgage sector suddenly began to grow. As figure 2.3 demonstrates, the volume of mortgage lending grew from nil to about 25 million rubles within one year. Lending tripled by 2007, and doubled again by 2008. This growth did not last: the market was decimated in 2009 when the international financial crisis hit Russia, a topic to which I return at the end of this chapter.

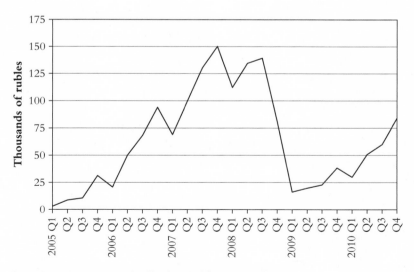

FIGURE 2.3 New mortgage lending (quarterly), Russian Federation
Source: Data from Central Bank of Russia.
Note: Adjusted for inflation using 2005 (first quarter) constant rubles.

Mortgage terms improved during the short-lived boom. A typical mortgage loan in 2001 had a 20 percent adjustable interest rate on a ten-year loan. By 2007, the average loan offered a 12 percent fixed rate over sixteen years, with a down payment of 30 percent. These rates are conventional in historical and comparative perspective. Internationally, a minimum down payment of 30 percent was typical before the subprime bubble, and few countries offered fixed-rate loans over long terms. Average interest rates were typically above 10 percent until the early 1990s (Green and Wachter 2005, 100–102; 2010, 419).

Nevertheless, housing did not become more affordable. Housing prices doubled from 2005 to 2007 and the index of housing affordability increased by 50 percent (figure 2.2; higher numbers indicate worsening conditions for consumers). To qualify for a typical loan, an applicant needed a family income of about forty-five thousand rubles a month, twice the average earnings of two full-time workers in 2007. Estimates of how many families could afford a mortgage during this period ranged from 10 to 20 percent (Kosareva and Tumanov 2008).

Even at its peak, Russia's mortgage market remained tiny. Mortgage debt in 2007 was worth less than 3 percent of GDP, dead last among thirty-two countries ranked by the European Mortgage Federation.[14] Most other former Soviet states had mortgage sectors worth from 10 to 20 percent of GDP in 2007. The ratio stood at about 50 percent in the European Union and 80 percent in the United States. Registries of housing transactions also reveal the small weight of mortgages in the housing market. In the second half of 2007, 17 percent of registered sales involved a mortgage. That figure had declined to 12 percent by the second half of 2009.[15] Most market transactions were still paid in full at the time of sale, suggesting that the construction boom that occurred from 2004 to 2008 mostly went to wealthy buyers with cash in hand. Furthermore, nearly half of all housing transactions were inheritances or gifts, not sales. After accounting for these nonmarket transactions, mortgages constituted just 7 percent of all transfers of property rights.

Still, a market had begun to emerge, a trend that HSRP's former leadership attributed to the maturing of the institutions it had created (IUE 2007, 22). This growth began, however, only after the government stepped in to sponsor the market: it began to subsidize mortgage loans and dominate mortgage lending.

From Plan to Project

"Throughout the world, mortgage lending is the most effective and civilized mechanism for dealing with housing problems," President Putin declared in

2003. "The system of mortgage crediting must be market-based and not subsidy-based," he added. "Only then shall we be able to attract private investment funds to match the scale of the nation's housing problem."[16] However, during his second term in office, his administration began to subsidize and manage the market. In 2006 Putin reformulated the state's role in the market under the auspices of the Priority National Projects (PNP), a federal initiative in four sectors—housing, health, education, and agriculture—to overcome a demographic crisis. The housing subproject, entitled "Affordable and Comfortable Housing for the Citizens of Russia," aimed to reduce the coefficient of housing affordability to 3 (see figure 2.2) and to increase the percentage of families who could afford a mortgage to 30 percent by 2010. The program sought to stimulate both supply and demand for housing and credit.

Supply-side efforts included subsidized credit and tax incentives for builders and for manufacturers of construction materials. A strong dose of cajoling supplemented these financial transfers. Government directives echoed Soviet-era production drives. If the Soviet government had spoken of fulfilling the "plan," the new government spoke of completing the "project." Vladimir Yakovlev, Russia's minister of regional development, claimed in 2007 that by 2010 the volume of housing construction would exceed the best years of the Soviet Union. Putin set a goal to construct one square meter of housing per capita per year, a standard that would place Russia on par with the European Union. PNP press releases trumpeted progress via litanies of statistics. "In the first eight months of 2007 housing construction grew by one-third.... The construction of cement and plaster grew by 20 percent, of glass by 17 percent, and of brick by 14 percent," said Medvedev, then director of the PNP. Nevertheless, domestic production was insufficient. Builders had to import cement from China, which was "not only offensive, but impermissible," evidence of "an extreme lack of new ideas." Likewise, the proportion of families who could afford mortgages, claimed Medvedev, had increased from 3 percent to 10 percent within five years. But "this figure cannot satisfy us. This indicator must be raised to at least 17 percent." The solution? "AHML must become bolder in introducing new mortgage products." Anyone familiar with Soviet policy discourse will recognize this style of making grandiose promises, celebrating progress, and attributing shortcomings to insufficient effort by producers.[17]

Under federal pressure, regional governments tried to stimulate local construction. Moscow was the most active: a city-owned company constructed low-cost apartments. Other regional governments subsidized private builders. For example, Kaluga invested in several suburban developments of small single-family houses. They were advertised as a PNP initiative for young families; a local reality television show even awarded a free model home to the winner. The pilot project was unpopular, however, because the homes were poorly designed, shoddily constructed, and expensive. Kalugans interviewed in 2009 scorned the homes as overpriced "cardboard shacks."

The government expanded the supply of mortgages by stepping up lending through banks that it controlled. Public-sector banks had easier access to credit and to the state's social marketing apparatus than did private banks. Sberbank, the largest government bank, controlled 36 percent of mortgage market volume by 2007; AHML and VTB-24 each held about 10 percent (Fitch Ratings 2007; Grishin and Raskosnov 2007). This reflected a broader trend in the banking sector. Before the 1998 financial crisis, private banks had profited from political patronage and skimming off privatization (Johnson 2000). Under Putin, government support was redirected toward government banks.

The government also began to subsidize mortgage demand. The PNP introduced two new mortgage subsidies: the Young Families Program (YFP) and maternity capital. The YFP provided a 30-percent down payment, which did not have to be repaid, and a low-interest loan to pay for a portion of the remainder. The maximum loan amount was set at the average regional cost of the normative number of square meters of living space. The definition of young families belied the program's pronatalist intent: only married couples or single parents under age thirty were eligible (the age limit was raised to thirty-five in 2009). Single adults without children could not apply. Financing was left to regional governments and few families qualified for assistance. People were disqualified if they owned any housing space, even if only a share of a parent's privatized apartment, or if they wished to purchase a home in another city. They had to be classified as needy according to miserly regional housing norms, but also to earn enough to qualify for a mortgage. Most interviewees in Kaluga who looked into the YFP were either rebuffed by eligibility restrictions or put off by the requirement to take out a mortgage.

More significant was so-called maternity capital, the material and symbolic centerpiece of the PNP. Flush with petrodollars, the Russian government offered one-time baby bonuses for all mothers who had a second child after January 1, 2007 (or for a further child if they already had two children). Maternity capital is not cash in hand; it is a certificate worth about ten thousand dollars (indexed to inflation) that can be used for one of three purposes: to purchase or build housing, to educate a child under twenty-five, or to invest in the mother's pension fund. Certificates could not be used until qualifying children turned three, so payouts were not scheduled to begin until 2010. However, in light of the economic crisis, the government changed the rules in January 2009 to allow people to cash in maternity capital immediately to pay down home loans. The three-year waiting period still applied to expenditures on housing not financed by credit.[18]

A social marketing campaign advertised the potential to use maternity capital as a down payment on a mortgage. Seventy percent of eligible women surveyed in 2008 said they hoped to apply maternity capital toward housing. By April 2010, Russia had distributed more than 2 million maternity capital certificates. Of these, 6 percent had used their certificates to pay off housing debt. The government projected that, out of the 300,000 families who were likely to spend maternity capital in 2010, one-third would pay down housing debt, whereas half would pay for housing without using credit (the remainder would apply it toward education or pension savings). As more families pass the three-year waiting period, the relative proportion using maternity capital to buy or build housing without a mortgage will likely grow.[19]

A maximum of 5 percent of young Russian adults will have received housing subsidies through the YFP or maternity capital through 2010. I assume that about half a million households will have received a housing subsidy: 150,000 participants in YFP, 200,000 using maternity capital to pay down housing debt, and 150,000 using maternity capital to purchase housing without a loan. If we assume that each recipient household has two adults age twenty-five to thirty-five, 1 million of the 25 million Russians of that age group would have received a subsidy. This is surely an overestimate, because not all households qualifying for help have two adults in this age range. Although these subsidies did not reach the average Russian, government hype about them did. Most Russians were aware of the policies, even if they had not benefited from them. According to a national survey in 2007, 75 percent of Russians age nineteen to thirty-five knew about the program, and another 20 percent had heard of it (FOM 2007a). Interviewees in Kaluga in 2009 remarked on the constant coverage of maternity capital and YFP on television news.

These programs are a legitimation project as well as an economic policy. While rolling out the PNP, Putin described affordable housing as a moral and demographic imperative. Mortgages were a potential but unrealized remedy for suffering and injustice: "One of the sharpest socioeconomic problems in today's Russia is the large difference in incomes between various groups of the population.... Providing the low-income population with housing is very important in relation to that problem.... But let us be frank: mortgages remain inaccessible to many. Many people have no prospects for solving their housing problems." In the same year, however, Putin declared that the PNP had already achieved its chief goal—legitimacy. "The most important result is that people believe the state cares about them.... There's something else: people have begun to change how they relate to the demands that life presents. Their eyes are sparkling! People want to work efficiently in the jobs they have now."[20]

These speeches reveal a tension between state and market in Russian housing policy. The Washington Consensus advised states to transplant market institutions and then withdraw from the housing sector. But this had not worked in Russia. New mortgage subsidies signaled that the state was responsible for making housing affordable. Yet the leadership insisted that markets should govern the housing sector. Putin's pledge to "civilize the market" encapsulates this tension. "The government can't allow itself to exit the housing sector, despite its market priorities. The government must actively form a civilized market arena.... We can only untangle this tight housing knot," he said, "on the basis of market mechanisms. All levels of government must work toward its more effective operation."[21]

A Transplant, Not a Copy

Russia did not copy the American housing system. The US template was overlaid onto preexisting conditions. In turn, the Russian government grafted other policy concerns—demographic and political—onto transplanted institutions. Russia departed from the American example when it introduced pronatalist mortgage subsidies, a topic the next chapter examines in depth. Russian mortgage law also differs from its American prototype.[22] The law evolved in response to risks inherent in postsocialism: economic instability, uncertain property rights, and difficulty evaluating creditworthiness.

In the United States, GSEs (Fannie and Freddie) managed risk in three ways prior to the subprime crisis. First, the GSEs established standards for "conforming loans," eligible for purchase and resale on the secondary market. Second, many of the loans the GSEs purchased were insured by the Federal Housing Authority (FHA) or the Veteran's Administration (VA). Third, after the GSEs began loosening standards for conforming loans, it pooled loan payments into MBS to disperse risk. Institutional investors—pension funds, insurance companies, and foreign governments (including Russia)—viewed American MBS as low-risk and implicitly guaranteed by the government.[23] Private banks piggybacked on the global confidence in American MBS by issuing their own securities, to which ratings agencies gave their stamp of approval.

In Russia there was no equivalent to FHA to insure the mortgages that AHML purchased, and there was little demand from institutional investors for Russian MBS. Therefore AHML developed standards for conforming loans that transferred risk to consumers. Borrowers had to purchase insurance against loss of life or ability to work, as well as property and mortgage insurance.[24] AHML template contracts penalized prepayment of loans, making it more costly for borrowers to refinance loans. Primary lenders were required to buy back loans if underwriting standards had been violated; in the West such repurchase agreements are normally only seen in subprime markets. Banks in turn transferred the risk of repurchase agreements to borrowers, who could lose their properties even if they had not perpetrated the fraud (Guseva 2009).

Foreclosure provisions also grew more severe. An early impediment to mortgage lending had been the strong property rights conferred by residency permits (propiskas). Until 2004, banks could neither evict families in default if they had no other living space, nor displace minor children (Skyner 2005). Legal reform made foreclosure a real possibility; municipalities were directed to offer evicted families public housing. Unlike US law, Russian law does not require banks to offer a grace period before foreclosure. Minor delays in payment, for example, three late payments within a year, even if late only by a day, could trigger foreclosure proceedings. Personal liability was also unlimited—if the sale of a foreclosed property did not satisfy a debt, a bank could go after other assets of the borrower indefinitely (Guseva 2009).

Despite these distinctions, Russian housing policy continued to pursue the American model of a securitized, mortgage-based market. Harsh treatment of borrowers, which likely dampened demand, was intended to generate confidence among potential lenders and investors. New securities legislation, coupled with an oil-based economic boom, enabled AHML to finally issue its first three series of MBS in 2007–8. Other banks also issued small volumes of MBS. AHML celebrated the issuance of these securities as a milestone in a press release to potential investors: "Developing a securities market in Russia is a major component of the priority national project 'Affordable and Comfortable Housing for the Citizens of Russia.' The Agency, in its capacity as a government institution for development, is enabling the formation of this segment of the financial market."[25] This statement (minus the reference to the PNP) could have been lifted from HSRP guidelines written a decade earlier.

Government intervention in the housing sector does not in itself make Russia exceptional among market economies. Both the American and European housing systems were jump-started with public financing, a history that the Washington Consensus forgot (Gilbert 2002; Arku and Harris 2005). American mortgage institutions are a product of government responses to crises. Traditional mortgage loans had high down payments, variable interest rates, and short terms. When millions of borrowers faced default during the

Great Depression, the US government purchased and restructured loans with what are now conventional terms: fixed interest rates, high loan-to-value ratios, and long terms. The FHA insured the loans, and Fannie Mae bought FHA loans (and later VA loans) and resold them to investors, creating the secondary mortgage market (Green and Wachter 2010).

Securitization, the next American innovation in housing finance, was also born of crisis, this time the stagflation of the 1970s. The government established Freddie Mac to help the troubled savings and loan sector, whose dwindling deposits prevented them from meeting their debt obligations. Freddie Mac was authorized to purchase private loans that were not insured or guaranteed by the government. Fannie Mae was given similar authority (Ginnie Mae, Fannie Mae's legacy institution, still guaranteed loans that met traditional criteria). MBS were invented to capitalize this expansion of the secondary mortgage market (Carrozzo 2004). The subprime crisis emerged when Fannie and Freddie, as well as private issuers of MBS, were deregulated and began pooling riskier loans (McCoy and Renuart 2008). Once again, the government stepped in: it nationalized Fannie and Freddie, bailed out banks, and promised a new regulatory regime.

When the international financial crisis began in late 2007, Russian authorities tried to calm markets, and the population, by asserting: "Russia is not America." Banks claimed that strict underwriting standards had immunized the fledgling mortgage sector from a subprime crisis. The government pointed to Russia's sizable stabilization fund, accumulated when oil prices were high.[26] Nevertheless, loan defaults grew as Russia descended into a recession, fueled by falling oil prices and losses in financial markets. By the end of 2009, 3 percent of outstanding mortgage debt was in arrears, compared with 1 percent a year earlier. Mortgage lending contracted by 80 percent in 2009, and interest rates increased from 11 percent to 13 percent on ruble-denominated loans.[27]

Ensuing anticrisis measures resemble those of the United States: massive bailouts for banks and toothless programs for borrowers. If after the 1998 ruble crisis, the American government kept the tiny mortgage sector afloat, this time the Russian government came to the rescue. In October 2008 the government allocated $36 billion from its stabilization fund to bail out banks and gave the central bank "broad executive privilege in disbursing the money." The share of new mortgage loans issued by government-controlled banks grew from 47 percent to 68 percent in 2009 (another estimate that includes banks indirectly under government control puts the share at 80 percent). These banks received the bulk of bailout money and were able to borrow at below-market rates. Prime Minister Putin also put forth proposals (unimplemented as of this writing) to purchase Russian MBS and capitalize the mortgage sector using three sources—the sovereign wealth fund, the pension fund, and the capital of AHML and VTB. In other words, the Russian government would be its own institutional investor—investing state funds in MBS issued by state-controlled banks.[28]

For troubled borrowers, the state decided to "extend and pretend," a phrase critics have applied to American loan modifications that delay but do not stop foreclosure.[29] For example, the Russian government offered to make mortgage payments for up to a year for qualified unemployed borrowers. However, this aid was a loan, not a gift, and drove borrowers deeper into debt. In 2009, thirty thousand borrowers (with 4 percent of all outstanding loans) used the program. But only one-third were able to resume payments within a year; the remainder entered foreclosure proceedings. Similarly, Sberbank offered to reduce loan payments for three years after the birth of a child, but interest would continue to accumulate. The government's "second chance" program permanently restructured loans over longer terms or at lower interest rates. Alternatively, borrowers could sell their apartments to the government and move into public housing. Eligibility restrictions on maximum income and property value excluded many borrowers. Furthermore, as in the United States, borrowers had to apply for these loan modifications through their banks, which were not obliged to participate in the program.[30]

Meanwhile, interest rates increased, ranging from 12 to 15 percent in the first half of 2010; they had fallen back to 12 percent by early 2011. AHML loosened its standards for conforming loans to try to make mortgages more affordable. The minimum down payment declined from 30 percent to 10 percent, although loans for more than 70 percent of the home value required additional mortgage insurance. The maximum mortgage payment as a proportion of household income increased from 35 percent to 45 percent.[31] These changes increased the pool of people who could potentially qualify for mortgages, but only on condition that they take on large amounts of debt relative to their incomes.

The financial crisis that began in 2008 led not to questioning the American model of housing finance, but to digging in. Private ownership and mortgage financing remained the orienting goal of policy. In July 2010, the government issued a new planning document, "Strategy for Development of Mortgage Credit in the Russian Federation through 2030." It reads like a Soviet plan and predicts rapid growth within just two years. The planning targets, however, are a product of transplant: to triple the volume of mortgage lending and double the percentage of mortgages that are securitized by 2012.[32]

Despite the crisis, Putin and Medvedev promised to fulfill the state's existing social obligations: maternity capital would still be paid. To prove the point, the three-year waiting period was waived for those who wanted to spend maternity capital on mortgage debt. The government also authorized one-time cash payments from maternity capital of about four hundred dollars for eligible children. By the year's end, nearly 80 percent of families with maternity capital certificates had applied for the disbursement. Both policies were labeled "anticrisis measures," set to expire in 2010.[33] These emergency measures did little to help families with their financial troubles or housing woes. But the purpose was as much symbolic as material. "Owners of maternity capital can count on receiving 12,000 rubles this year," said Liliya Chizhik, deputy minister of the Pension Fund, which disburses maternity capital. "This is very good news, because, like those who have had the opportunity to pay down housing debt, citizens can sense that the program is really working."[34] In the same interview, she attributed the bump in the birthrate to the program: "The number of families who decided to have a second or third child went up in recent years. Is this a result of the government decision to support such families? The proof is in the statistics." In later chapters, I analyze both statistics and qualitative evidence to evaluate the political as well as demographic effects of maternity capital. But first, I explain how and why the government grafted demographic policy onto housing policy.

 CHAPTER 3

Maternity Capitalism

Grafting Pronatalism onto Housing Policy

All Russian women who give birth to a second child receive maternity capital, a ten-thousand-dollar voucher that they can apply toward housing.[1] Maternity capital is now one of Russia's largest social commitments besides the pension system and is its most significant housing subsidy. Worth over a year's average wages, maternity capital is the largest baby bonus in the world relative to income. To give a sense of scale, the equivalent bonus in the United States would be worth more than forty thousand dollars. Existing baby bonuses for second children in other countries, including Australia, Italy, Poland, Singapore, and Spain, are typically worth less than 10 percent of average annual wages.[2] Maternity capital also stands out for its overt pronatalist intent. Most European governments are more discreet about their reproductive aspirations for their citizens so as to avoid the label "pronatalist," which evokes fascist cults of motherhood.

Demographers and gender scholars understand maternity capital mainly as a pronatalist population policy. In anthropologist Michele Rivkin-Fish's estimation, maternity capital had two goals: "raising fertility and establishing political legitimacy" (2010, 724). There was also a third goal: to build and legitimate mortgage markets. To my knowledge, no other nation channels baby bonuses into the housing sector. Russia's housing regime therefore can only be understood in the context of demographic politics. Conversely, attending to the housing dimension of maternity capital sheds new light on Russia's variety of pronatalism, which I call "maternity capitalism."

A new and expensive subsidy from a government that had been retreating from the housing sector, maternity capital appears to depart from the path of market reform. Given the Soviet Union's long history of pronatalism, maternity capital also calls to mind the Soviet legacy.[3] However, maternity capital is not a retreat from capitalism back to socialism. Rather, the policy attempts to save both the market and the nation by grafting pronatalist incentives onto the failing transplant of American-style mortgage markets. Housing policy and demographic policy were fused: baby bonuses injected capital into the housing market, and the state invested in housing to encourage demographic growth.

Its pronatalist objectives notwithstanding, maternity capital conformed to the Washington Consensus on how to subsidize housing. According to the World Bank's *Enabling Markets* report, lump-sum grants to households to purchase houses are the best kind of subsidy because they minimize price distortions and maximize transparency. Supply-side subsidies of construction or interest rates, by contrast, derail markets (World Bank 1993, 48–49, 65, 117–18). IUE analysts came to a similar conclusion when they evaluated regional pilot programs (Kosareva 2007, 54–65). Targeting subsidies to families with multiple children could also reduce inequality, because per capita income decreases with family size (United Nations in Russia 2008, 22).

Maternity capital is a Russian variant of the "Washington Consensus Plus," which Joseph Stiglitz defines as correctives proposed by adherents of the consensus when it faltered: "When growth failed to materialize, 'second generation reforms'... were added. When problems of equity were noted, the 'Plus' included female education or improved safety nets" (2008, 49). In Russia, the "Plus" is baby bonuses designed to stimulate markets as well as births.

Maternity capital's dual purpose is captured by its name, which Putin claims to have coined: "The very term—maternity capital—is one I thought of myself. I started from the premise that women bear the main burden of bearing a child and bringing it up. And I thought that the state should provide help in particular for women, both moral and material help....These funds can become part of the family's capital, to be saved up or spent on a mortgage."[4]

Feminist scholars have analyzed the paternalism of the policy, whose focus on women had origins in the Soviet "gender contract": the state, rather than men, helped women bear the burden of the second shift by compensating for their losses in the labor market (Rotkirch et al. 2007). Men became irrelevant, bereft of breadwinner status yet absolved of domestic duties. Rivkin-Fish, in her analysis of public discourse on the matter, concludes that the policy obscured the "instrumentalization of women's bodies and lives" by resonating with local understandings of the state's responsibility to support families (2010, 724).

Russia's pronatalist turn acquired specific meanings in the context of market transition: I label this cultural logic "maternity capitalism." The metaphor of capital has several meanings corresponding to the policy's multiple objectives. Maternity capital provided *starting capital* for women and their families; *investment capital* for the housing market; and *human capital* for the nation. The state, by determining who deserved this capital and how it could be invested, claimed for itself the right to manage the macroeconomy of reproduction. If citizens endorsed the policy, the state could accrue *symbolic capital,* that is, legitimacy.

This dual set of meanings—gendered and capitalist—makes Russia difficult to classify in the literature on varieties of pronatalism. In the next section, I place Russian pronatalism in comparative perspective and argue that maternity capital is best understood as an economistic variant of civic nationalism. Next, I explicate the cultural logic of Russian pronatalism through two lenses: official discourse that explained and justified the policy to the public, and the distributive apparatus that determined who would receive maternity capital and how they could use it. Later chapters examine maternity capital's effects in its three target domains: supporting housing and mortgage markets; increasing the birthrate; and legitimizing the state.

To elucidate the state's objectives in disbursing maternity capital, I analyze how official policy discourse framed the nature of the problem at hand, the problem's causes, and its solutions. This is a standard approach to analyzing policy discourse in the sociological literature on social problems (Benford and Snow 2000; Ferree et al. 2002; Stark and Kohler 2002). Discursive claims, however, are not identical to actual objectives (Rivkin-Fish 2010, 714–15). Intent is also implicit in the logic of distribution. I explicate this logic by examining who was entitled to maternity capital and who could put it to use.

Evidence includes more than three hundred texts and images disseminated by the federal government to the public between 2006 and 2010. Data sources include transcripts of speeches, press releases, and interviews in news sources controlled by the government. I also examined visual images from social marketing campaigns on billboards, websites, and brochures.[5] Other work on pronatalist discourse typically analyzes media and academic texts (Stark and Kohler 2002, 2004; Rivkin-Fish 2003; Brown and Ferree 2005).[6] The focus here is on how the state frames policy in authoritative discourse, which circulates extensively in the media. The federal government under Putin consolidated control over the media, especially television and radio, from which most Russians get their information.[7]

Russian Pronatalism in Comparative Perspective

Russia has one of the lowest birthrates in the world. The total fertility rate (TFR), a common measure of fertility, declined sharply during the period of market transition. In 1985 the TFR was just above 2, the level required to replace the population across generations. By 1995 the TFR had plummeted to 1.3, placing it among the nations with "lowest-low fertility." At this level the population halves every 45 years, rendering demographic equilibrium impossible (Kohler et al. 2002, 642). Russia's TFR bottomed out at 1.16 in 1999, hovered around 1.3 until 2006, and had recovered to 1.5 by 2008.[8] Demographers debate over how to interpret and explain this trend.[9] Although the fertility rate has changed with the economy, this is not necessarily causal. Fluctuations in fertility are likely driven by a combination of changing gender relations, shifting cultural preferences, economic uncertainty, and downstream effects of wartime demographic losses. Whatever the causes, fertility decline in the post-Soviet period has been significant and sustained.

Russia is not alone—birthrates in many nations have fallen well below replacement rates. According to the United Nations' *World Population Policies* report, forty-seven countries considered their fertility rates to be too low in 2007. Among these, 80 percent had instituted measures to raise fertility, such as tax incentives or parental leave (United Nations 2008, 13–14). Russia numbered among these nations. A decade earlier this was not the case. The equivalent report in 1996 classified Russian fertility policy as "non-interventionist," although it characterized the government as "concerned" about the issue. The introduction of the Priority National Projects (PNP) in 2006 renewed the government's efforts to try to stop fertility decline.

Post-Soviet pronatalism, despite its unique features, is one case in a broader pronatalist trend across low-fertility nations. The United Nations labels policies that attempt to raise birthrates as "interventionist," not pronatalist. This choice of terminology reflects a shift in the nature of population regimes. Comparative scholars classify pronatalist states as either "ethno-nationalist" or "civic-nationalist." Ethno-nationalist pronatalism is a response to paranoia over ethnic threat and moral panic over the traditional family. Most of the literature on culture and population policy concentrates on cases with explicit ethno-nationalist agendas and repressive gender regimes, such as fascist Italy (De Grazia 1992), socialist Romania (Kligman 1992), and early modern Israel (Birenbaum-Carmeli 2003).

After World War II, governments hoping to boost their birthrates introduced civic-nationalist population policies, which were compatible with liberal democratic ideals of ethnic and gender equality. A comparative study of Israel,

France, Singapore, and Romania in the 1990s found that policies to stimulate reproduction were universally applied across ethnic groups, and offered both women and men more egalitarian opportunities to work as well as to parent (King 2002). By relying on popular family policies such as child allowances and paid parental leave, governments could indirectly try to raise the birthrate while avoiding controversy about whether and how it should do so (McIntosh 1986). Euphemisms such as "family policy" and "demographic renewal" distanced these efforts from their eugenicist predecessors (Demeny 2007).

This is not to say that ethnicity has become irrelevant in liberal pronatalist regimes. A discourse of ethnic threat persists in the conservative politics of most nations, and repressive possibilities lurk in softer efforts to increase the birthrate (Krause 2001; Krause and Marchesi 2007). However, in civic-nationalist regimes, official discourses and policies construct the nation in universalistic terms, not ethnic terms. Even when family policy sparks open debate, the left does not necessarily reject efforts to raise birthrates. Feminists in France, for example, embraced pronatalist ideology as a way to achieve gender equity by redistributing resources and supporting employed women with children (King 1998). In many other countries, conservative ethno-nationalists and liberal feminists both concluded that the state should support mothers, although they disagreed on why (Stark and Kohler 2002; Brown and Ferree 2005).

Given the stigma of pronatalism after fascism, policies intended to increase the birthrate can be difficult to distinguish from policies that happen to affect the birthrate, but are not intended to do so. "Measures adopted under the heading of pronatalist policy or under that of family policy tend to be similar. They often provide similar levels of support, and use similar redistributive instruments. Only their objectives clearly distinguish them" (Gauthier 1996, 4).

Russia stands out because the policy objectives are clear. The government did not disguise its pronatalist intentions—it announced them loudly and proudly. Such overt efforts are more typical of ethno-nationalist than civic-nationalist regimes. Some analysts place Russia in such company. In a discourse analysis of the demographic field in postsocialist (pre-Putin) Russia, Rivkin-Fish (2003) contrasts conservative, nationalist pronatalists with liberal demographers who celebrate fertility decline as a sign of modernity and freedom. In her findings, pronatalism is conservative and ethno-nationalist; there are few signs of a more liberal pronatalism. However, her sources draw from a debate among Russian academics who have had little influence over policy, especially in the Putin era.

Based on the evidence presented below, I view Russian pronatalism as more civic- than ethno-nationalist. This is not to deny either that ethnic

Russians are privileged or that women are repressed—we will see evidence of both. But the state's predominant approach to the birthrate frames the problem as economic, not ethnic. Maternity capitalism is a particular kind of civic nationalism, which aims to build markets while building the nation. The targeting of maternity capital toward mortgages makes Russian pronatalism more of a class project than a race project.

The same was true in the Soviet Union. Historian David Hoffmann (2000) argues that Stalinist population policy was part of an international trend linking population to national power. Western European pronatalism in the interwar period was bifurcated between a Catholic universalism, which "stressed reproduction of all members of society without distinction," versus the eugenics of Germany and Scandinavia (41). Soviet population policy was closer to the former than the latter, even under Stalin, and certainly in the late Soviet period. The Soviet state viewed population as critical to the competition among nations, but "the competition was conceived of as between political systems rather than between races" (38). Other states across the Soviet bloc (except Romania) also tended to view the problem and its solution through a political-material lens (McIntyre 1975; Frejka 1980).

Contemporary capitalist nations also typically frame fertility decline as an economic problem. A comparative study of news coverage of fertility in eleven OECD countries found that more than half of the articles framed low fertility as a threat to the economy (Stark and Kohler 2002). Advocates of pronatalism in the Czech Republic claimed that the new market economy required a balanced age structure (Wolchik 2000, 71–73). There is less consensus in these nations on whether economic factors *cause* fertility decline. In Russian policy discourse, economic decline is not simply an effect of fertility decline; market transition caused the problem of low fertility, and a stimulus package will solve it.

Official Discourses on the Link between Housing and Fertility

The Problem: A Demographic Crisis

Policy discourse in Russia takes for granted that the birthrate is too low. Phrases such as the "demographic problem," the "demographic situation," and the "demographic crisis" presuppose that a problem exists, especially when they appear in a chain of nominal phrases. The linguistic device of nominalization, also common in Soviet political discourse, "converts *claims* into *presuppositions,* presenting ideas as pre-established facts," argues linguistic anthropologist

Alexei Yurchak (2003, 494). Consider for example the following lead sentence from a press release on the PNP: "Dmitry Medvedev proposed a range of effective measures for the resolution of the demographic problem." Each noun in this prepositional chain contains a supposition: there *is* a demographic problem, the problem *can be* resolved, the measures *are* effective, and these effective measures *span* a range. An accompanying photograph portrays the solution: a maternity capital certificate stands on a podium before a beaming young couple holding two children; the baby is spilling out of his mother's arms and grasping the certificate. In the text, Medvedev connects demography to housing, again nominalizing the problem: "There is another key issue, the resolution of which can directly facilitate the resolution of the demographic problem—that is access to housing."[10]

Not everyone agreed that low birthrates were a problem. As mentioned previously in this chapter, liberal Russian demographers celebrated fertility decline as a sign of modernization and women's emancipation (Rivkin-Fish 2003). For example, Anatolii Vishnevskii and his coauthors (2004) interpreted lower birthrates as the arrival in Russia of the "second demographic transition," in which individuals voluntarily restrict family size to pursue a higher quality of life. This was a marginal viewpoint in Putin's Russia, however. The policy documents I reviewed never questioned whether low fertility creates a demographic crisis.

What, then, is the nature of the problem? Medvedev defined it simply: the "demographic crisis" consists of "depopulation, the absolute reduction of the number of Russian people." At stake is "our nation's survival. It's the very question of life for every one of us." When President Putin introduced maternity capital in his 2006 state of the union address, he framed low fertility as a threat to national security: "What is most important for our country? The Defense Ministry knows what is most important. Indeed, what I want to talk about is love, women, children. I want to talk about the family, about the most acute problem facing our country today—the demographic problem." Likewise, the PNP website on maternity capital described the demographic situation as "one of the sharpest socioeconomic problems, with consequences for national security. The population of Russia is shrinking by 700–800 thousand people annually."[11]

This discourse of national security frames reproduction as the legitimate domain of the state. Supporters of Medvedev's presidential candidacy touted his stewardship of demographic policy during his tenure as first deputy prime minister. After Medvedev became president, Putin moved to the position of prime minister and became chief executive in charge of the PNP, affirming its policy significance.

How should we interpret this discourse linking demography with national security? All population policies seek to secure a nation's interests. The question is, how are the nation's interests defined? Modern nation-states have long viewed population as power. The two world wars in Europe heightened a "perceived link between high fertility and military power" (Gauthier 1996, 16). When the nation is defined as ethnos, reproduction preserves a group's power. The state of Israel, for example, tried to stimulate the Jewish birthrate to prevent Palestinians from outnumbering Jews (Fargues 2000).

In postsocialist Russia the chief threat to national security is neither military nor ethnic, but economic. In the discourse of the PNP, demographic decline has depleted the nation's stock of "human capital," needed to develop a competitive national economy. Putin characterized the PNP as "investing in human capital, or, as Alexander Solzhenitsyn put it, 'investing in people.'" Demographic investment defends against the "threats that Russia encounters as part of the world system," and growing the population promotes economic competitiveness.[12] Although military preparedness is also a concern, it is subordinated to economic concerns in discourses on population decline.

Talk of ethnic threat, by contrast, was rare in official documents and press releases about the PNP. Ethno-nationalist discourses did circulate in postsocialist Russia outside of mainstream policy discourse. Some journalists, academics, and provincial authorities maintained that the nation was the victim of a demographic Chernobyl or Holocaust (Rivkin-Fish 2003). They interpreted low birthrates as a form of ethnic suicide or even genocide, perpetrated by capitalists and Jews intent on turning Russia into a debtor's prison (Oushakine 2009). In the PNP, however, there was little place for such talk. Anthropologist Serguei Oushakine explains: "In the spring of 2006, the Russian government, apparently alarmed by the level of nationalist rhetoric associated with the demographic data and by the grave demographic tendency itself, decided to take control of the situation. A new federal council on demographic policies was instituted, and a large-scale system of pronatalist measures was implemented. The intensity of the nationalist rhetoric was significantly toned down" (2009, 103–4).[13]

Nevertheless, subtle messages about ethnicity circulated in visual representations, which can signal what is unspeakable in words (Zubrzycki 2007). Posters for a social marketing campaign for the PNP depicted whom the government wanted to produce. One poster, which appeared at bus stops and metro stations across Russia in 2007, bore the caption: "The country needs you to set records: three people are born every minute in Russia." A woman in the picture effortlessly balances triplets on her arm. She and her children are dressed in fashionable, post-Soviet clothing. They are floating in the sky and appear larger than life, a feature of socialist realist art. The mother in the image represents Russia, and her children the nation. She and the children are light-skinned and presumably ethnically Russian (the father is conspicuously absent), as was true of most images I collected from federal sources.[14] Another advertisement in Moscow in 2007 stated, "Love of the homeland begins with the family." The family in the image was depicted as a series of *matrioshki* nesting dolls, an iconic exemplar of ethnic Russian folk art. The children are nested inside the mother, and once again there is no father in the picture. Prioritizing fertility over migration as the solution to population decline also implicitly privileges ethnic Russians. Nevertheless, federal authorities rarely referred to ethnicity when talking about the birthrate or the PNP, inoculating the state from potential accusations of overt racism.

The Diagnosis: Economic Ills

"What stops young families and women from deciding to have children today, especially when we're speaking of a second or third child?" asked President Putin when he introduced maternity capital in 2006. "The answers are obvious and well-known. They include low incomes, inadequate housing conditions, doubt about their ability to ensure the child a decent level of healthcare and education, and—let's be honest—sometimes doubts about whether they will even be able to feed the child." Putin listed similar constraints in a speech in 2010: "Couples often opt against having a baby for financial reasons, because it is difficult to have a baby and to build a career, and also because they are not sure they can resolve their housing problems or that their children will attend a good kindergarten and subsequently a good school."[15]

Housing conditions are consistently on the list of economic problems that are thought to discourage young Russians from having children: of the documents I coded that discussed the causes of fertility decline, 72 percent mentioned housing. Mortgages could solve the housing problem, but unaffordable mortgages would make the demographic problem worse: "It is no secret that today, in order to receive a mortgage, both spouses need to work just to provide the necessary sum of money. And it is often precisely for this reason that they delay having children," claimed Medvedev. The problem was one of morale more than morality: "People at some point stopped believing in the future, therefore they didn't want to have families. We want to stimulate our citizens to have children." He then enumerated a range of economic incentives to do so.[16]

This singular focus on economic constraint as the cause of low fertility is unusual in historical and comparative perspective. The book *Crisis in the*

Population Question (Myrdal and Myrdal 1934), which inspired the Swedish welfare model, was novel and controversial for framing low fertility as "a natural and rational response of young people to the problems of poverty, unemployment, and sub-standard housing conditions. Contrary to common belief (coming especially from the Church), the main cause of fertility decline was economic and not moral" (Gauthier 1996, 17). However, moral and cultural explanations for low fertility persisted throughout Europe. In Soviet policy discourse, moralists attributed low fertility to women's selfishness and consumerism, for which the separate apartment was partially to blame. In Germany after reunification, East German women who got sterilized were accused of going on a selfish "birth strike" to advance their careers (Dölling et al. 2000). And in the UK in the 1990s, pronatalist commentators were more likely to lecture women on their immoral lifestyle choices than to portray them as victims of structural barriers to motherhood (Brown and Ferree 2005).

Most academic demographers explain the fertility decline in Western Europe as a complex interaction between cultural preference and economic constraint (McDonald 2000). The editors of *Population and Development Review,* a leading demography journal, questioned Putin's "starkly economic interpretation of the problem of low fertility." They speculated that Putin ignored alternative hypotheses because economic factors, "at least in principle, lend themselves to remedial measures that the Russian government, its coffers now swollen with petrodollars, should be able to provide" (PDR 2006, 386). The chief remedy was maternity capital.

The Cure: Injecting Maternity Capital

In the logic of maternity capital, reproduction is akin to a market, in which choices are a function of prices and preferences. If material constraints prevent women from having the number of children they truly want, the state can increase fertility by offering the proper mix of incentives. Among the policy documents I examined that discuss how to solve low fertility, 88 percent advocated some form of material support. In Putin's words:

> If the state is genuinely interested in increasing the birthrate, it must support women who decide to have a second child. The state should provide such women with an initial maternity capital that will raise their social status and help to resolve future problems. Mothers could make use of this capital in different ways: put it toward improving their housing situation, for example, by investing it in buying a house, making use of a mortgage loan or other loan scheme once the child

is three years old; or putting it toward children's education; or, if they wish, putting it into the individual account portion of their own old-age pension.[17]

Maternity capital was the centerpiece of a range of policies designed to change women's calculus of the costs and benefits of having a child. Other incentives included "birth grants" for prenatal care; childcare subsidies; increased income support for an eighteen-month maternity leave (extended for the first time to homemakers as well as to workers); and legal reform to improve job security during maternity leave.[18]

The government also introduced a cultural campaign to "raise the prestige of the family." During 2008, which was declared the "year of the family," numerous festivals celebrated children and motherhood. In a televised interview, President Putin suggested that procreation is patriotic: "What have you personally done to improve the demographic situation?" he asked a female journalist. "I have a wonderful daughter," she replied, "but I promise to work on this problem some more in the future."[19] Social marketing advertisements sent a similar message. One region actually instituted a "conception holiday" on September 12, when workers were encouraged to stay home and procreate. Those who managed to "Give Birth to a Patriot" on June 12—Russian Independence Day—won prizes such as refrigerators and cars.[20]

Yet most resources—both material and discursive—were devoted to economic incentives, not to cultural initiatives. References to family values, although frequent, were typically short and ceremonial, a footnote in the overwhelming economism of pronatalist discourse, which calls to mind an economic stimulus package: the new policy would "stimulate reproduction," "reduce risks and raise confidence," and "provide opportunities to realize maternal ambitions." This is analogous to what Brown and Ferree call the "bribing frame," which "sees the choice [not to have children] as rational, but one that social policy can address by changing the rewards and costs" (2005, 17). Many low fertility countries have policies in place that try to incentivize birth using various forms of payment, often targeted toward the middle class—from tax deductions in the United States (Powell 1999) to cash bonuses in Singapore (Sun 2012). Maternity capital is distinctive among baby bonus schemes, however, for its link to housing investment.

Making a Housing Market with Maternity Capital

The certificates given to mothers are officially called "maternity (family) capital" (*materinskii [semeinyi] kapital*). The term *family,* which is in parentheses on the certificate, is usually dropped in ordinary use. An official at the Pension Fund explained the full name as follows: "The name of the capital—'maternity family'—says a lot, because the right to dispense the means of maternity family capital belongs to the mom, but she can use the funds for the benefit of her entire family, for example to improve housing conditions."[21] Maternity capital was not given out in cash, however, because provincial women could not be trusted with it: "317,000 rubles is a considerable sum for people in the regions. It will simply vanish overnight." Restrictions on expenditures were supposed to ensure that women, who might otherwise squander the money, would invest their capital prudently. "We selected the three options—housing, retirement savings, and the child's education. We tried to protect mothers' interests this way, to prevent wasting this money."[22]

When enumerating the ways a mother can invest her family's capital, officials usually foregrounded housing, which Putin called "the most pressing problem for families today and the most pressing financial issue." Maternity capital provided starting capital to purchase a home with the help of a mortgage. After the PNP was introduced in 2007, Medvedev warned that mortgage instruments needed to be prepared by 2010, so that maternity capital would exist in practice and not just on paper: "We need to be prepared, so that maternity capital does not become inert and will actually enter the housing market." The task for the construction sector, in turn, was to build "modern, low-cost housing—so-called economy-class housing—for those who want to subsequently invest the money they receive as maternity capital."[23]

Maternity capital thus conjoined the fates of families and housing markets. Social marketing advertisements for maternity capital visually make this connection. For example, a press release entitled, "Children Have a Right to Housing Space," depicted children around a playhouse, with a new apartment building in the background. Children not only have a right to housing; they are a path to housing. In other words, children have become a source of capital. In Putin's words: "Our key objective is to provide conditions whereby having children would open up better prospects and opportunities for a family." At the same time, he claimed, maternity capital "has increased demand in the housing market."[24]

In 2009 Russia followed the global economy into a new wave of economic crisis. In response, the government stepped up efforts to stimulate housing markets with maternity capital. The three-year moratorium on spending maternity capital was lifted to allow paying down mortgages "to support people, on the one hand, and to help our construction industry, on the other, so that it does not stop and we can complete all our housing projects," said Medvedev. The director of Kaluga's Pension Fund office highlighted the benefits of maternity capital for builders as well as families: "The government's decision to permit use of maternity capital under conditions of economic crisis came just in time. It allows people to significantly reduce the size of their mortgage and housing debt on purchase or construction of an apartment. At the same time, the money that will be spent during this time will help the construction industry, which needs more support right now."[25]

Maternity capital would inject funds into the faltering mortgage sector while also helping families. In a speech on the PNP, Putin said, "We must create conditions that would allow as many people as possible to purchase new flats and improve their living conditions on their own, primarily through mortgages.... We must support the market and those who want to have their housing conditions improved. We must heat up the market a little bit without overheating it." In a social marketing advertisement produced by the PFRF in 2009, a radiant family of four clutches a maternity capital certificate as they stand in front of a new apartment building. The caption reads, "Maternity capital: pay down your housing debt by 312,000 rubles." The director of mortgage lending at VTB bank included maternity capital among "a number of important steps the Russian government has taken to support mortgage borrowers and boost the market for mortgage lending." According to President Putin, maternity capital helped many young families keep the apartments they had bought on credit, averting the mass foreclosures that happened in some other countries.[26]

Distributing Maternity Capital: Unequal Opportunity to Invest in Housing Markets

On the surface, maternity capital appears to be a universal entitlement for all women willing to bear multiple children, with each qualified woman receiving the same amount. However, there are inherent inequalities in who gets this capital and who can put it to use, which are rarely recognized in official discourse. To better understand policymakers' motivations, this section explores the implicit logic of distribution. Others have already analyzed the gendered implications of the policy, which naturalizes gender inequality within families by singling out women for aid (Rivkin-Fish 2010). Disbursement parameters also create inequality based on family size and class. Despite the moral discourse on helping needy families solve their housing problems, the distributive logic reveals the state's instrumental goals: to raise the birthrate and capitalize housing markets.

Two Children Are Better Than One

Policies to help mothers and children were couched as a universal right to a decent standard of living. But the focus on parity belied a priority on increasing the quantity rather than the quality of life. A journalist asked Yekaterina Lakhova, the head of the Duma committee for women, family, and children, why the government does little to help families with one child. She replied, "The first child just means normal, simple reproduction. This explains why the focus has been put on the second child."[27] Most Russians will have one child regardless of their circumstances. Families who already had two children by 2007 were also ineligible unless they bore additional children. This is further evidence that the policy goal was to stimulate reproduction, not to ease the lives of those who would have been born in any case.

Why, then, were women restricted to receiving just one maternity capital certificate in their lifetimes? Why not provide additional incentives for additional births? Debate about the same issue in the Soviet period provides a possible explanation. Soviet leaders also saw the one-child family as the key problem to be solved: a postcard published in 1981 for International Women's Day read, "One Child is Good; Two are Better." Although all Soviet women were entitled to benefits, targeting resources toward second- and third-order births concentrated resources on European Russia, where birthrates were low, and allocated fewer resources per child to families in Muslim regions, where birthrates were already high (Lapidus 1982, xxxix).

Soviet leadership denied any deliberate regional or ethnic differentiation in its population policy. Post-Soviet leaders have also rebuffed calls for regional differentials. On being asked whether resources should be targeted regions with to the lowest birthrates, Medvedev replied, "All regions of Russia can and should contribute to solving the demographic crisis." Yet, as a critic of Soviet policy pointed out, "Differential effects can be achieved by means of measures that are universal in character and distinguish between citizens by virtue of their demographic circumstances, irrespective of their location or ethnic origin" (McIntyre 1982). Maternity capital directs resources to those who meet the leadership's vision of a normal family: middle-class, ethnically Russian women with two or at most three children.

Starting Capital for a Mythical Middle Class

Maternity capital is the largest baby bonus in the world relative to income. Nevertheless, as a proportion of housing costs, maternity capital is insufficient even to make the minimum down payment of 30 percent for a conventional mortgage. In 2009, maternity capital was worth only about 8 percent of the average cost of seventy-two square meters of living space, the official "sanitary norm" for a family of four. Maternity capital would suffice for a 15 percent down payment in only about 20 percent of Russia's regions.

Figure 3.1 presents another view on how maternity capital could affect mortgage affordability. The chart graphs the ratio of average wages (assuming two full-time workers per family) to the minimum income need to qualify for a typical mortgage, for the various regions of Russia. I assume mortgage terms of a 10 percent down payment, 12.5 percent interest rate, and a maximum payment to income ratio of 45 percent. The light gray bars show the ratio without taking maternity capital into account. At these terms, the average two-income family earned only 54 percent of the amount they would need to qualify for a mortgage. In Moscow, where housing prices are very high, the value is 31 percent; in Kaluga, 46 percent. The dark gray portions of the bars show the difference maternity capital makes if added to the down payment. The effect is smallest in central Russia, where housing is least affordable. For example in Kaluga, maternity capital shifts the ratio from 46 to 51 percent—still well below the amount needed to qualify. In less central regions, where housing is cheaper, maternity capital has a larger proportionate effect on monthly mortgage payments and therefore the income needed to

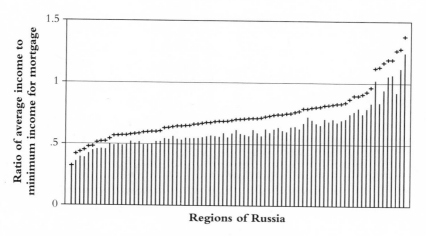

FIGURE 3.1   Mortgage affordability with and without maternity capital, 2010
Source: Data from Rosstat and AHML.
Note: The vertical lines indicate the ratio of average family income to the average minimum income necessary to qualify for a typical mortgage with a 10 percent down payment. Each line represents a region. The plus signs indicate what that ratio would be if maternity capital were to be added to the down payment.
   Calculations assume a family income of twice the average regional wage; a home price based on the average regional cost of seventy-two square meters of housing space (the federal norm for housing space for a family of four, based on the requirement of birth of a second child to qualify for maternity capital); and the minimum income needed to qualify for a mortgage with terms of a 12.5 percent interest rate, thirty-year term, 10 percent down payment, and monthly payment that does not exceed 45 percent of income.

qualify. Nevertheless, in most regions, maternity capital does not bring down monthly payments enough for the average family to qualify for a loan.

Maternity capital would make the difference between qualifying and not qualifying for a mortgage for few families. Most families who could apply maternity capital toward a mortgage would have qualified for a mortgage without the subsidy. Others can use maternity capital to improve their housing conditions only if they possess substantial starting capital—that is, they already have an apartment of their own to trade up.

Restricting maternity capital to housing (and to a lesser extent education) makes the subsidy regressive. A flat cash transfer would have reduced income inequality: for example, a five-thousand-dollar cash subsidy would double the income of a family earning five thousand dollars, but would only increase the income of a family earning fifty thousand dollars by 10 percent. By contrast, constraining maternity capital to be invested in the housing market renders it useless for those without high incomes or preexisting housing wealth. Thus, maternity capital inverts the forms of gender- and class-based inequality that Gal and Kligman (2000) argue characterizes postsocialist state transfers. Means testing, they maintain, contributes to and stigmatizes income inequality (80–82). Maternity capital exemplifies how universalistic, non-means-tested policies can also have unequal effects.

Giving all entitled women a certificate for the same amount of capital symbolically erased this implicit class bias. Policy discourse also increasingly denied or ignored inequality. Prior to the PNP, Putin had stated that only low-income people should receive government subsidies for mortgages. Three years later, maternity capital was framed as a universal entitlement. For example, in a televised interview, a reporter asked Deputy Minister Zhukov: "What if it is a bad family in which the previous children are poorly looked after, yet they give birth to more children and then get this capital? How will the beneficiaries be chosen? How will the needs be tested?" He responded simply: "It should be a universal rule; it should apply to absolutely everyone."[28]

Talk about the poor shifted from questions of how to help the poor to whether maternity capital created moral hazards for the poor. A journalist asked Health Minister Tatyana Golikova in 2007 whether maternity capital might overstimulate reproduction among poor families, who may be less fit to parent. She responded that the three-year waiting period insures against having a child just for the money. Furthermore, "Our families aren't going to give birth in order to exploit their children. The majority of our families, both poor and well-to-do, have children because they want them."[29] Although both officials denied that maternity capital makes a problem out of the poor, they did not discuss how maternity capital could help the poor, especially with their housing problems. By 2009 President Putin openly acknowledged that mortgages were not for poor people: they would continue to rely on subsidized social housing—and implicitly not be encouraged to have more children.

Legitimizing State and Market

Russia's birthrate increased slightly the three years following the introduction of the PNP. In fact, demographers had already predicted such a recovery due to the age structure of the population. Nevertheless, the government is taking credit for this trend. The state-controlled media is filled with pictures of babies and stories about families with two and three children. On reporting a 7 percent rise in the birthrate on national television in December 2008, Prime Minister Putin declared, "The government's efforts are bringing results." The higher birthrate, a policy goal, also indicated achievement of a broader goal: legitimacy. "Perhaps the best indicator of how the nation feels is demographics," said Putin at a convention for the political party United Russia. "Much of the credit for what we have managed to accomplish during this year must be attributed to the mood of the Russian people and their confidence in what we have been doing."[30]

Building legitimacy on the basis of social policy, however, may have unintended consequences. The Soviet promise of a separate apartment raised expectations of what was necessary for a normal life, leading to bitter disappointment when the promise was not fulfilled. Likewise, maternity capital may create problems for the state if experienced as an empty promise. Rivkin-Fish argues, "Putin's demographic agenda has relegitimated citizen claims for state assistance, even as the scope of these claims, and the types of subjects authorized to make them, remain largely circumscribed by pronatalist assumptions about women and the nature of 'family'" (2010, 716–17).

Maternity capital also complicates the political project of transforming housing from an entitlement into a commodity. Creating a housing market, in the logic of the Washington Consensus, required instilling in citizens more modest expectations of the state. Maternity capital, however, reinforced the idea that government should subsidize access to markets. By grafting demographic policy onto housing policy, the state staked its legitimacy on providing normative housing for normative families—that is, a separate apartment for each nuclear family. In the next chapter I examine for whom a separate apartment did and did not become a reality. Part II of the book analyzes how housing market failure has shaped young Russians' experiences and perceptions of inequality, their economic and reproductive strategies, and their dispositions toward state and market.

 CHAPTER 4

Property without Markets
Who Got What as Markets Failed

To fully understand Russia's stratification order, we must understand its housing order. Yet studies of postsocialist stratification rarely consider housing inequality. Most research concentrates on labor market income, the key dependent variable in sociological debates over inequality during market transition (Gerber and Hout 1998; Nee and Cao 2002; Verhoeven et al. 2005). This focus on wages, while important, overlooks an insight from the sociology of wealth: income and occupation are inadequate proxies for living standards in established market economies (Keister 2000; Spilerman 2000; Fischer and Hout 2006, chapter 6) and are even weaker measures of well-being in postsocialist contexts (Burawoy et al. 1999; Bondarenko 2002). Households with similar incomes have varying capacities to consume, depending on their access to property, savings, credit, and government transfers. The disconnection between income and housing consumption is severe in illiquid housing markets, in which it is difficult to convert income into property.

This chapter contrasts empirical trends in housing inequality in Russia with the expectations of the Washington Consensus on housing market transition. The Housing Sector Reform Project was supposed to replace Soviet-style socialism with the American variety of capitalism. Increased inequality is a benchmark of market reform, according to the Washington Consensus, and the necessary tradeoff to improve average living standards. Standardized construction and mass entitlements in the Soviet era had restrained inequality. Correspondingly, shifting control over housing from state to market should have increased inequality. Privatizing the construction industry would enable builders to differentiate their products according to consumers' needs and means. Social policy would provide a safety net for the poor but also encourage "over-housed" people to move to smaller abodes suited to their incomes. In short, a rationalized housing sector would allocate the bulk of housing through the market according to ability to pay.

The Washington Consensus, then, leads to three testable expectations. First, have average housing conditions improved? Second, has housing inequality increased? Third, and most significantly, does "market situation" determine position in the housing hierarchy? Here I adopt Max Weber's definition of market situation as inequality determined by "the possession of goods and opportunities for income...under the conditions of commodity or labor markets," mediated by monetized exchange (1978, 927,83).

To test these hypotheses, I present statistical evidence on the patterns of inequality and mobility that characterize Russia's housing order. The next section describes general trends in housing inequality. Housing status has several dimensions: the amount of space people occupy (housing quantity), the physical features of that space (housing quality), and their rights to that space (housing tenure). In the Russian context, *housing autonomy*—an apartment owned and occupied by the nuclear family—is the most important feature of housing status, a fundamental and necessary condition for decent housing according to local standards. Therefore, although descriptive statistics presented in the chapter include measures of housing quantity and quality, the separate apartment remains my analytical focus.

Stratification researchers examine inequality from two perspectives: "the structure (or degree) of inequality" and "the allocation of individuals to positions within that structure" (Kenworthy 2007, 584). With respect to housing, the structure of inequality is determined by the nature of the housing stock: the number, size, and quality of housing units. The logic of allocation refers to the principles—for example, age or income—that determine who gets what within an unequal housing stock. The next section describes the structure of housing inequality. Then I present hypotheses on the logic of allocation of individuals within that structure and test the hypotheses by analyzing who is most likely to obtain a separate apartment.

I conclude that what has emerged is not a housing market, but a regime of property without markets, in which housing is privately owned but incompletely commodified. In this peculiar stratification order, housing status bears little relationship to wages. Post-Soviet property allocations result mainly from state redistribution and familial reciprocity, not market situation. Coresidence with extended family remains widespread, due to constraint not choice. Privatization carried forward extant Soviet inequality, while introducing a glaring element of chance—prospects for inheritance—into young Russians' housing trajectories.

The Structure of Housing Inequality in the New Russia

What happened to the structure of housing inequality when market transition began? Privatization, which transferred property rights to occupants of Soviet housing, initially reduced total wealth inequality. Housing was more equitably distributed than other privatized assets like factories and oil. Millions of low-income households became homeowners, and privatization initially "had a strongly progressive effect on the distribution of wealth" (Buckley and Gurenko 1997, 29). However, housing privatization barely mitigated skyrocketing inequality in overall household consumption (Yemtsov 2008).

Meanwhile, privatization produced high levels of housing inequality. Occupants of better units benefited from a large and unexpected transfer of wealth; individuals with substandard or no housing by 1992 lost out. Limited new construction was targeted toward the well to do. The Soviet-era housing stock, in which most Russians live, fell into disrepair. Many households still lack basic amenities and tolerate extreme crowding. According to RLMS data from 2009, 17 percent of urban adults lacked a basic utility such as running water, central heat, or a sewage system in the home, and an additional 9 percent lacked hot water (the situation in rural areas is far worse). Just 42 percent owned a separate apartment for the nuclear family. Half were living with extended family,[1] 3 percent were renting with the nuclear family, and 4 percent lived in dormitory or communal settings. Twelve percent had fewer than ten square meters of housing space per capita, while 14 percent lived in dwellings with fewer rooms than generations in the household.

Was the story different for young Russians? Youth, with their capacity to adapt to changing conditions and succeed in new labor markets, should be the vanguard of market transition. Therefore, signs of transition in the housing sector may be more evident among the young. Table 4.1 tracks trends in housing inequality among Russians age twenty-one to forty between 1991 and 2009.

The first two sections of table 4.1 display the distribution of space, in terms of square meters as well as rooms. Trends in means and medians give a sense of whether average housing conditions have changed. Average space per capita increased only slightly over time and was driven more by a declining

Table 4.1   Trends in housing inequality, urban Russians age 21–40

	1991	1995	2000	2005	2009
Housing space per capita					
Mean	NA	14	15	16	16
Median	NA	13	14	15	15
Coefficient of variation	NA	0.53	0.49	0.49	0.51
Gini coefficient	NA	0.25	0.24	0.24	0.25
Rooms per capita					
Mean	0.65	NA	NA	0.68	0.71
Median	0.60	NA	NA	0.67	0.67
Coefficient of variation	0.49	NA	NA	0.49	0.50
Gini coefficient	0.24	NA	NA	0.25	0.25
Percent having					
Separate apartment[a]	45	44	40	36	35
Separate room[b]	NA	65	67	65	68
All utilities[c]	74	72	68	75	75

Source: GSS–USSR 1991; RLMS.

Notes: GSS–USSR contains only living space, not comparable to total housing space.

[a] Nuclear family in owner-occupied dwelling; not dorm, communal, or rental.

[b] Separate room = at least as many rooms as generations in the household.

[c] Central heat; sanitation; hot and cold water.

population than an enlarging housing stock. The coefficient of variation and the Gini coefficient measure the extent of inequality.[2] According to these indicators, the distribution of space did not become more unequal during this time period.

The third section of the table displays trends in housing tenure and housing quality. The only significant change indicates a *decline* in housing conditions. The percentage of young adults having a separate apartment fell from 44 percent in 1995 to 35 percent in 2009 (this change is statistically significant at $p <= 0.05$ level). I also measured the number of rooms compared to the number of generations in the household, to see whether each generation could have its own room. Two-thirds of survey respondents lived in dwellings with at least as many rooms as generations throughout the study period. Finally, the proportion of dwellings having all major utilities—central heat, hot and cold water, and sanitation—increased slightly, but 25 percent of young adults still lacked at least one of these features as of 2009.

Growing inequality more likely manifests in the quality of interiors, which the RLMS does not measure. Income differences that are not adequate to alter core features of the home—size and property rights—likely suffice to make renovations such as replacing windows or redoing kitchens, since such upgrades can be readily purchased in the market and accumulated with smaller transactions over time. However, property rights over an apartment

(a)

(b)

FIGURE 4.1 Renovated kitchens: (a) kitchen in an inherited Soviet apartment, (b) kitchen and dining area in luxury post-Soviet apartment. (a) Photo by author, (b) photo by Anastasia Smirnova.

with sufficient space is a necessary condition for making such improvements. The small size and awkward layout of the typical Soviet-era apartment yields limited room for improvement. Figure 4.1 shows two kitchens. Panel (b) is a luxury apartment purchased and renovated by the owners. They take great pride in the open design of their kitchen.[3] Panel (a) is a kitchen in an inherited Soviet apartment, constructed in the early 1980s. (See also figure 5.2 for an image of a khrushchevka kitchen). Even though the owners renovated, they simply do not have the space for an open design.

In short, little appears to have changed, at least in the overall quality of the housing stock and its distribution. The most important change is declining access to separate apartments. Of course, difficulty getting a separate apartment is not new. In the Soviet period, many young adults also lived with their parents or in-laws well into adulthood. The difference is that Soviet youth knew that if they waited long enough, the government would give them an apartment. Now younger cohorts can no longer count on help from the state, but find themselves shut out of underdeveloped, unaffordable markets.

Evidence of Housing Mobility

Another way to look at the structure of inequality is to ask about its fluidity. How much movement is there up and down the housing ladder? Residential mobility in Russia appears to be low in comparative perspective, based on traditional measures that equate moving addresses with mobility (Andrienko and Guriev 2004). The Western literature on the life course typically treats departure from the parental home as the key transition to housing autonomy.

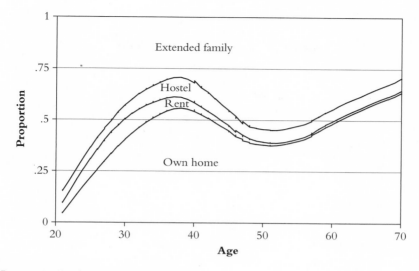

FIGURE 4.2   Housing tenure by age, 2009
Source: Data from RLMS 2009 urban cross-section.
Note: Results for loess regression (N = 4,592). Hostel category includes worker hostels, student dormitories, communal apartments, and roommate shares.

Physically moving does not necessarily signify upward mobility, however. People may move into better, worse, or similar housing conditions. In Russia, however, leaving the parental home is a poor measure of autonomy. Of the 60 percent of Russians age twenty-one to forty who were not living with their parents in 2009, only 70 percent had moved to a separate apartment (59 percent as owners, and 11 percent as renters). Fifteen percent were living with in-laws, 7 percent with other relatives, 7 percent in dormitories, and 1 percent with roommates. Furthermore, some people transition to autonomy without ever leaving the parental home; instead their parents may have moved out or died. Such "in-place adjustments" are common in postsocialist societies (Mandić 2001).

If we conceive of housing mobility in social rather than geographic terms, then the rate of change in housing conditions among contemporary Russians is significant. For this study's purposes, I define housing autonomy in terms of local understandings of the separate apartment: living only with nuclear family members (alone or with a partner and/or minor children) and having secure property rights (either a privately owned dwelling, or a state-owned dwelling that one has the right to privatize). Based on this definition, many young Russians do manage to acquire separate apartments. Figure 4.2 depicts housing tenure by age in 2009. By the age of thirty-five just over half owned separate apartments. Extended family arrangements resurge between ages forty and fifty-five, when people's own children become young adults still living at home. Renters and hostel dwellers, a small fraction of the population, occupy an in-between state of semiautonomy, not living with the extended family but also not having secure property rights.

The Logic of Unequal Allocation of Housing

So which young adults will acquire a separate apartment? Research on post-socialist housing mobility is sparse, but the comparative literature offers a point of departure for formulating hypotheses.

Economic Explanations

People are sorted into unequal positions in markets based on their capacities to realize their preferences. Some may be content with what they have even if in theory they could afford more; others may wish for better but cannot afford to move. The question is not whether Russians face constraints in general, but what is the nature of those constraints? Do economic factors influence mobility in Russia in ways that we would expect in a market?

Ideal typically a housing market has three features. First, housing should be privately owned. Second, it should be a liquid commodity with prices set by markets. And third, market position should determine housing chances. Labor market income should be the main component of market position for young adults, although inherited wealth and parental transfers are also factors. Successful market transition should therefore tighten the connection between income and housing conditions.

Most housing in Russia is now privately owned, meeting the first criterion for a market. However, as chapter 2 demonstrated, commodification is weak due to high housing prices and restricted credit markets. Therefore I expect little effect of income on housing autonomy. However, commodification may vary over time and across regions as housing affordability fluctuates. The miniboom in the mortgage market that occurred from 2005 to 2008 might have lent income new importance as a path to housing, but only for those with sufficient income to qualify.

Inheritances and other interfamily wealth transfers also influence housing trajectories in advanced capitalist societies (Hamnett 1991; Kurz 2004; Helderman and Mulder 2007). Inheritance and gifts are especially important where mortgage access is low and liquidity constraints are high, such as Italy and Israel (Guiso and Jappelli 2002; Spilerman 2004). Inheritance should therefore be a significant path to a separate apartment in Russia.

Demographic Explanations

Forming partnerships and having children are important triggers for leaving the parental home and becoming a homeowner in many countries, and are standard controls in the comparative literature. These major life events likely also motivate transitions to autonomy in Russia, with the precondition that resources suffice to realize aspirations to autonomy. However, the transition to adulthood in first world societies has become longer and less linear (Furstenberg 2002). As the life course becomes more complex, so do housing careers, leading to interesting cross-national variation. Some attribute this variance to differences in beliefs about the right time to leave home (Holdsworth 2000). Others point to market constraints that prevent people from converting preferences into reality (Mulder and Wagner 2001).

Comparative studies classify postsocialist housing regimes as resembling the southern European countries of Italy, Spain, and Greece, which have high homeownership rates but delayed leaving of the parental home, as well as low fertility rates (Schwartz and Seabrooke 2008). These patterns are attributed to traditional family values combined with constrained housing markets and minimal state assistance (Rossi 1997; Iacovou 2001). Yet traditional values are not keeping young Russians in the parental home. Almost all Russians prefer to live independently, as we shall see in the next chapter. Which of them will realize this preference is a joint function of material resources and subjective priorities.

Based on qualitative findings (presented in chapter 5), educated youth especially value having a separate apartment, lending support to the theory of the second demographic transition (SDT). According to SDT theory, values in modern societies have shifted toward individualism and gender egalitarianism. This weakens the traditional institution of the family, leading to delayed marriage and fertility, an increase in nonmarital cohabitation, and more out-of-wedlock births (van de Kaa 1987). Young people may delay departure from the parental home to invest in themselves, concentrating on education and careers before starting a family. At the same time, youth no longer consider marriage to be a prerequisite for leaving the parental home (Lauster and Fransson 2006). In SDT theory, "education can be used as a proxy for ideational change, with the most highly educated women being the first to adopt the new behaviors associated with SDT" (Perelli-Harris and Gerber 2011, 319). The separate apartment is emblematic of the values of individualism and self-realization underlying the SDT. Therefore, other things being equal, educated youth should be more likely to transition to autonomous housing.

Education may also interact with the life course. If traditional values mean staying home until marriage, then SDT might lead unconventional, educated youth to form their own households when they are single. On the other hand, Roberts et al. (2003) found that educated Russians remain single at home longer, but are more likely to live on their own after they form families. The authors attribute this finding to cultural convergence with the West, although they do not test the finding with longitudinal, multivariate modeling techniques.

In sum, the literature suggests a range of possible hypotheses. Whether income drives housing prospects depends on whether Russia has a true housing market or, as I argue, it is a case of property without markets. Inheritance should play a major role after mass privatization of family homes. The possible influence of demographic factors is also unclear. On the one hand, life course transitions likely matter, other things being equal. On the other hand, if markets are truly constrained, it may be impossible for youth to move. Further complicating life course explanations is the second demographic transition hypothesis, which suggests that educated Russians will place a priority on moving, but again, their ability to convert their preferences into reality is uncertain.

Bivariate Correlations between Housing, Income, and Family Structure

Table 4.2 compares housing conditions for the richest and poorest income groups among young adults, measured in terms of the top and bottom quintiles of household income (adjusted for household size). Young adults in the wealthiest households (the top quintile) do have a bit more housing space on average, but the differential does not increase over time. As for a separate apartment, a small but significant difference in 1991 persisted but did not grow by 2009. Both wealthy and poor saw a decline in their odds of attaining a separate apartment from 1991 to 2009.

Setting aside the key measure of housing tenure, significant gaps between rich and poor exist in quality of life at home, as measured by presence of utilities and access to a separate room. Young adults in wealthy households were more likely to have all major utilities and to have a separate room (for themselves, or for themselves and their spouses, if they were married). However, these differentials already existed in 1992 and did not increase with time. Furthermore, having a separate room could be a function of delayed or foregone fertility. Young adults from wealthier households, who are more likely to have higher education, may choose not to start families if it would mean living in one room with their children. In that sense, young people have some control over housing density, even if they cannot afford to change their place of residence.

Figure 4.3 provides another view on the question of whether market versus demographic forces drive housing conditions. The figure depicts housing

Table 4.2   Housing quality by income quintile, urban Russians age 21–40

	1991	1995	2000	2005	2009
Space per capita (median)					
Richest 20%	NA	14	16	15	16
Poorest 20%	NA	11	12	14	14
Rooms per capita (median)					
Richest 20%	0.74	NA	NA	0.67	0.67
Poorest 20%	0.56	NA	NA	0.67	0.60
Have separate apartment (%)					
Richest 20%	47	50	45	40	40
Poorest 20%	39	44	40	33	36
Have separate room (%)					
Richest 20%	68	74	76	68	75
Poorest 20%	47	56	59	62	66
Have all utilities (%)					
Richest 20%	78	81	74	85	86
Poorest 20%	67	65	60	56	67

Source: GSS–USSR 1991; RLMS.

Note: Income is total household income, adjusted for household size.

tenure of young Russians by wage quintile and family structure, indicators of market position and demographic status, respectively. Panel (a) shows only a weak correlation between wage income of young adults (and their partners, if present) and housing tenure in 2009.[4] Unsurprisingly, those with no wage income (because they are either unemployed or not in the labor force) are far more likely to live at home. But among young adults who are working, wages have little association with housing tenure.

Panel (b) of figure 4.3 shows that people with partners and children, especially in combination, are much more likely than others to live separately. Still, the Russian case is notable for the low rate of autonomy among singles and the high rate of extended family living among those with partners and/ or children. In the United States, by contrast, intergenerational households and living at home after marriage are rare (Goldscheider and DaVanzo 1985; Ruggles 2007). Countries from the former Soviet bloc, including new EU member states, also stand out within Europe in the high rate of coresidence (Billari et al. 2001; Mandić 2008; Philipov and Jasilioniene 2008). Thus figure 4.3b offers limited support for the hypothesis that life course transitions drive housing trajectories.

However, a true relationship between income and housing tenure could be masked by confounding variables, or conversely the apparent relationship between family structure and housing tenure might be spurious. In multivariate analysis, income was not significantly associated with housing

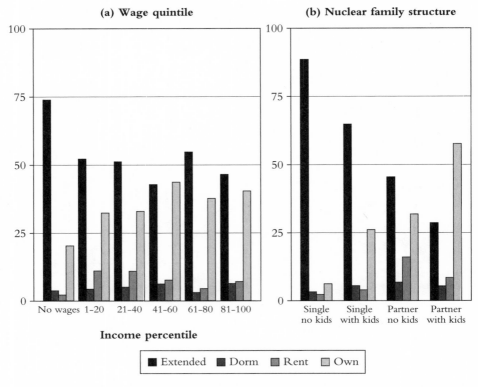

FIGURE 4.3   Housing tenure by family structure and income, age 21 to 40 in 2009
Source: Data from RLMS 2009 urban cross-section (N = 2,119).
Note: Singles include divorced and widowed; partners include married and cohabitating. Income adjusted for family size.

status in any year, after controlling for education, occupation, marital status, region, and presence of children.[5] Marital status and number of children did retain their statistical significance in multivariate regressions. However, studying associations between these variables in a single year does not elucidate the mechanisms that produce housing inequality, because we do not know the circumstances under which better or worse conditions were obtained. Analysis of housing mobility over time is more informative than cross-sectional analysis of housing conditions at a single point in time.

Mobility without Money: Explaining Post-Soviet Housing Transitions

Examining the correlates of housing conditions at one point in time, while suggestive of hypotheses, does not reveal the mobility patterns that lead to an observed distribution of housing conditions in any given year. The statistical technique of "event history analysis" takes advantage of longitudinal surveys, which revisit the same individuals multiple times, to model which characteristics predict a *change* in a variable of interest. Event history analysis is a standard technique in the scholarly literatures on transitions out of the parental home and into homeownership and is well suited for modeling transitions to separate apartments in Russia. The RLMS provides the necessary data structure, with its large sample size and many waves of data over time. After adjusting for missing data, 2,432 individuals (with a total of 7,683 person-periods) in the age range of interest participated in the study at least twice and so could be observed over time.[6]

Table 4.3 presents selected coefficients from the best-fitting model for transitions out of extended family arrangements into separate apartments.[7] As expected, partnerships are an important predictor of transitions to autonomy. When single people acquire new partners, their odds of transitioning increase by a factor of nearly thirty compared with those who stay single. This odds ratio is reflected in the bivariate relationship: 31 percent of cases with new partners move to independent housing within a year, versus only 1.4 percent of singles. People who have "old partners," with whom they have already been living along with extended family for some time, are less likely to transition, but their odds are still seven times higher than those of singles. The presence of children has a more modest effect, raising the odds an estimated 38 percent compared with respondents without children. The effect of children was approximately constant across partnership statuses.

A higher education does not appear to improve respondent's housing chances, contrary to SDT's predictions. The table presents the effect of education broken down by partnership status (the weak relationship between education and housing transitions also holds in a simplified model without this interaction term). Educated singles are an estimated 40 percent more likely to attain housing autonomy than less-educated singles, consistent with the image of Western-oriented youth defying convention. However this effect is not statistically significant, as the wide confidence interval indicates. Estimates are unstable because so few moves for singles are observed overall. We can be more confident in the finding that education does not improve the prospects of living autonomously with a partner.

What of the hypotheses on income and wealth? Do monetary resources improve housing chances, as would be expected if housing is a market commodity? And does success in labor markets improve housing chances? The answer on both counts is no. The reference category is the bottom quintile for wage earners; respondents with no wages (or whose partners also have no wages, if they have a partner) are categorized separately. The odds of

Table 4.3   Event history analysis of transitions to separate apartments, urban Russians age 21–40, 2000–2009

Partnership status			Nuclear family wages		
(Single)	1		(0 = not working)	0.48*	(.35, .65)
Old partner	6.8*	(4.4, 10.6)	1–20%	1	
New partner	27.3*	(18.7, 40.0)	21–40%	1.23	(.84, 1.81)
Higher education			41–60%	1.19	(.80, 1.78)
Single	1.38	(.69, 2.76)	61–80%	1.32	(.87, 2.02)
Old partner	1.09	(.73, 1.62)	81–100%	1.06	(.66, 1.70)
New partner	1.17	(.66, 2.07)	Death in household	3.21*	(2.10, 4.91)
			Have children	1.27	(.92, 1.74)

Note: Entries are odds ratios, with confidence intervals given in parentheses. (*) indicates a coefficient is significant at p <.05. Nuclear family wages includes wages of the respondent alone if single, or is the average wage for a couple if the respondent has a partner. Other variables in the model not shown here include age, gender, occupation, income of the extended family, and controls for time period and regional housing affordability.

transitioning to a separate apartment are practically identical (1.06) for the top quintile compared with the bottom quintile of earners. This result holds up even when comparing the top and bottom deciles. The top few percentage of earners probably do have improved housing chances in an economy geared toward luxury construction and cash transactions, but they are so rare as to be undetectable in this survey.[8]

The only significant difference observed for income is between those that have any wages and those with no wages at all. The odds of attaining independent housing are halved if there is zero wage income, compared with wage earners in the bottom quintile. Employment status is therefore important, although the level of wages is not. This has more to do with the costs of running a household than the cost of housing. People with no wages are not able to pay for everyday expenses, even if they have access to a separate apartment. Extended family may be more willing to help young people without jobs by keeping them in the family home than by supporting the full cost of establishing a separate household. In additional models, these findings were consistent over time. Neither wages nor extended family income have gained significance since 2005 despite government efforts to stimulate mortgages and construction.[9] Where material resources clearly matter is via inheritance. The odds of attaining housing autonomy triple if there is a death in the household.[10]

In sum, property without markets aptly describes Russia's housing regime. Neither wages nor education predicted young Russians' moves to separate apartments. Housing transitions were driven by life course events such as marriage and childbearing, and by inheriting privatized property from the extended family. Youth lacked control over their housing destinies, and yet life course events had strong effects. How is this possible? First, extended family is probably more willing to help adult children set up autonomous households: for example, by trading a large apartment for two smaller ones, once youth form families of their own (chapter 6 examines familial housing networks in detail). Second, there may be a reciprocal, anticipatory effect— youth may delay forming partnerships or having children until they feel assured that they will soon have a separate apartment (chapter 7 provides support for this hypothesis).

Inequality in the Regime of Property without Markets

Ideal typically, the transition from socialism to capitalism should shift the housing sector from state control to market allocation, from hierarchy based on rank to stratification based on market position. In the regime of property without markets, the labor market plays only a minor role. Neither education nor wages improve the housing chances of most young Russians, whose best hope for independent housing is inheritance. These findings are consistent with the conclusion of a market research report on a survey of the Russian middle class: "The size of housing has a very weak correlation with key characteristics of respondents: their age, income, or social status. This constitutes indirect evidence of the rigidity of the housing market and of the low geographical mobility of the population."[11]

To the proponents of market transition, Russia's mismatch between housing wealth and income signifies market failure. A UN report concluded: "Cost-free privatization has resulted in many property owners who are actually poor. . . . It is therefore possible in Russian mixed public housing to find a relatively comfortable 'tenant' living next to an indigent 'owner.' It will take many decades to eliminate this mismatch between economic circumstance and housing tenure" (UNECE 2004, 99).

Russia thus provides a negative case confirming Ruggles's (2007) economic development hypothesis on changes in household structure. If in the United States "the decline of intergenerational co-residence resulted mainly from increasing opportunities for the young and declining parental control over their children" (964), persistent coresidence in Russia is due to the lack of opportunities for the young and heavy dependence on extended family.

This unique housing regime resembles the southern European model but has one key difference: the insignificance of labor markets. A study of departures from the parental home found that in southern Europe, where credit is not readily accessible and the welfare state is weak, "The effect of one's own performance in the labour market becomes more important" (Aassve et al. 2002, 269). In Russia, the cost of housing in the fledgling market is so high as to make wages nearly irrelevant.

Russia's distinctive housing regime also highlights the importance of distinguishing between private property and markets in theorizing capitalist transitions. Privatization without institutions to support exchange—in particular, credit for both producers and consumers—turns housing wealth into a frozen asset. Russia is not unique in having had a prolonged phase in which housing wealth existed in the absence of fully functioning housing markets. A comparative study of thirteen former Soviet territories found that many countries initially achieved high levels of homeownership, but retained low levels of market-based production, transactions, or mortgage finance (Buckley and Tsenkova 2001). Similar patterns have also emerged in China and Viet Nam (Tran and Dalholm 2005; Davis and Feng 2008, 13).

This high-ownership/low-commodification housing system has strained the Russian state's legitimacy as well as the economy. Russians, who prefer to live autonomously, face mobility constraints that neither education nor earnings help to overcome. Many young Russians do manage to acquire apartments with the help of family transfers of privatized assets, particularly if they marry or have children. Nevertheless, as the next chapter will show, dependence on family and inability to earn housing leads young Russians to experience the post-Soviet housing order as arbitrary and unfair.

PART II

The Meaning of Housing in the New Russia

 CHAPTER 5

Disappointed Dreams

Distributive Injustice in the New Housing Order

A preoccupation of everyday life, housing is a lens through which Russians evaluate the legitimacy of the transition to capitalism. Most Russians perceive the housing system to be in crisis, according to surveys and focus groups commissioned by the Russian government. Unmet demand for housing remained high. In 2006 just 20 percent of city dwellers had moved in the previous decade, whereas half wished to do so but did not think they could. In 2007, two-thirds of eighteen- to thirty-five-year-olds reported they needed better housing conditions, but only one-third had plans to move within the next few years.[1]

This sense of crisis is compounded by a sense of injustice. Under the conditions of property without markets, success at work does not necessarily convert into better conditions at home. Interviewees highlighted the disjuncture between work and housing chances, leading them to characterize the present system as unfair and the Soviet housing order as more just. In evaluating distributive justice, less-educated respondents typically framed housing as a universal right for all workers. Respondents with higher education endorsed justified inequality, feeling that more skilled and valuable work should, but does not, result in higher living standards. Both perspectives lead to similar policy conclusions: the state should compensate for injustice and control the market.

Conceptualizing Distributive Justice in Russia

The ideology of market transition promised capitalism would raise living standards and distribute consumption opportunities according to merit. The architects of housing market reform regretted that Russians did not perceive real or immanent progress. Raymond Struyk, the director of the HSRP, wrote that "the 'housing shortage' is a mirage," and that families in the post-Soviet region were well housed compared to countries with similar incomes per capita (2000, x). He wrote in his final report to USAID:

> Overall the record of the Russian Federation in housing sector reform is very respectable.... Efficiency in the sector *is* improving, choice is expanding, and residential mobility increasing. Nevertheless, with massive cuts in national and local subsidies for the housing sector, most households are almost assuredly worse off now than under the old regime if their condition is measured by the share of their income they must devote to housing.... In such conditions the typical family may be forgiven for not recognizing the progress achieved to date. (1997, 9)

Russians, however, use a more complex set of criteria to evaluate progress than simply the "share of income they must devote to housing." And they focus less on where Russia stands in relation to other countries with similar incomes per capita than on where Russians stand in relationship to one another and to the Soviet past. In drawing comparisons, Russians question whether housing inequality has become more meritocratic. Most believe that privilege and chance, not hard work, drive the contemporary housing order. The desire for a meritocratic relationship between work and rewards has origins in the Soviet discourse on "necessary inequality" but is also compatible with capitalist ideology. According to Robert Lane (1986), the core ideology of market capitalism is market justice. A just market is open to all and rewards hard work. Kluegel and Mason (2004) build on Lane's theory to measure fairness in terms of distributive justice and conclude that perceptions of fairness drive judgments of the legitimacy of market reform in Russia and other postsocialist countries.

Scholarship on perceptions of income inequality supports my claim that Russians equate distributive justice with rewards for valued work. Inequity, not inequality, drives discontent in other postsocialist societies as well (Lee 2008). Tolerance for income inequality actually grew after the collapse of communism. But perceived inequality grew even faster, widening the gap between perceived and legitimate inequality (Kelley and Evans 2009). Russia ranked the highest among twenty-nine surveyed countries in 1999 in the "average discrepancy between perceived *actual* and perceived *fair* incomes" (Osberg and Smeeding 2006, 460). There was little consensus in Russia on what the wage distribution should look like or how to value specific occupations (Kelley and Evans 2009).

Normative support for wage inequality is higher among highly educated people across the ex-communist world, who typically think they should earn more than they do. One study attributes this tendency to the "greater knowledge and understanding that well-educated Central-East Europeans have of economics, and the intellectual predominance of market economy ideas in the public discourse" (Kelley and Zagorski 2005, 346). However, support for education-based inequality does not necessarily reflect support for markets. Education was also valued under socialism. Furthermore, support for inequality could exacerbate discontent among people who believe they should be on top of the wage distribution, but are not. In work on perceptions of fairness in China, Martin Whyte (2010a, 2010b) concludes that the lower classes are less likely to question market reform or the growth in inequality it produced. Likewise, support for market reform is only weakly associated with either economic or educational status in Russia. The mechanism is different in Russia, however. In China the poor are the most optimistic, perhaps because their living standards have risen dramatically. In Russia, lower social classes are not optimistic; they are simply more resigned and have lower expectations and aspirations.

Although the literature on perceptions of postsocialist inequality focuses on income, housing is also significant for subjective assessments of inequality because it visibly marks the consequences of privatization and inheritance. Housing also evokes capitalism's promise to enable average families to earn the "American dream" of homeownership. When work cannot be converted into housing, people are bound to think extant inequality is unfair. And when housing defines what it means to "live normally," this sense of unfairness is compounded by despair. Good housing encourages a general sense of well-being, confidence in the future, and trust in social institutions (Gilroy 2005). Insecure housing, by contrast, brings psychological distress (Cairney and Boyle 2004). The next section documents what kind of housing young Russians feel they need to live normally. Then I analyze how perceived barriers to normative housing de-legitimate the postsocialist housing order.

Dream Housing: Craving a Home of One's Own

Most young Russians would rather live on their own. A 2007 national survey asked respondents about the best living arrangements for a young family, defined as a married couple under age thirty. The question read: "Some people think that it's best for a young family to live separately from their parents from the very beginning. Others think a young family should first live for a while with the parents of one of the spouses. Which point of view is closer to yours?" Among respondents age eighteen to thirty-five, 86 percent agreed that young families should live separately from the beginning; 83 percent of thirty-six- to fifty-five-year-olds and 75 percent over age fifty-five also agreed (FOM 2007c). A strong preference for living separately also emerged in the qualitative interviews. Although we did not directly ask respondents about this preference, 78 percent referred favorably either to living separately (*otdel'no*) and/or having a place of one's own (*svoi*) at some point in the interview. The issue often arose when we asked people to describe their housing conditions, and then to tell us to what extent they are satisfied with them.

Separateness: A Place and a Room of One's Own

What does having a place of one's own mean in Russia? Chapter 1 documented the emergence of the "separate apartment"—a state-allocated apartment for the nuclear family—as the normative Soviet housing arrangement. Cultural standards of separateness escalated during the late Soviet period as living conditions improved. Russians came to expect not only a separate apartment for each nuclear family but also a separate room for each child. Many of today's young adults would feel cramped in a two-room apartment with multiple children. Chapter 7 presents evidence that some Russians delayed having multiple children, or chose not to have them at all, due to housing conditions. As one respondent put it: "A child needs his own room to develop normally."

Aspirations for separate space within the family, and not just for the family, increased during the post-Soviet period. Even among Russians with relatively good housing conditions, the living room often doubles as a bedroom for the parents. Many respondents said that they would like to have an extra room so that bedrooms would not have to serve multiple functions. Lena, a divorced mother living with her own mother and grandmother in a two-room apartment, said wistfully: "I've always dreamed of having a parlor in which no one sleeps, a room where we simply sit and watch TV or have a drink with guests."

However, separate rooms for children, let alone a separate living room for the nuclear family, are secondary aspirations. What matters most is getting a separate apartment. To qualify, a dwelling must satisfy three desires: autonomy from extended family, security of property rights, and the right to transform the interior and make a place one's own. For many young Russians, this primary problem of getting a separate apartment, of any kind, has yet to be solved.

Autonomy: Mastering Space without Extended Family

Most respondents in the Kaluga study who were living with extended family said they would rather live on their own. Ludmila, an accountant living with her husband and child in her mother's apartment, complained, "Of course I'm not satisfied. But we have no realistic alternative. I dream of having my own home, but I don't know when or if it will come true. Every year things are getting worse. Before we all complained about communism, but my mother got her own apartment when she was twenty-six. Now I'm twenty-six and I don't expect anything in two or even ten years." Ludmila's mother had worked in a regional party organization, which perhaps skewed her sense of how easy it was to acquire an apartment in Soviet times. The average waiting period in Soviet queues was around ten years. Ludmila, however, did not expect to "get" an apartment even within a decade.

Although Soviet-era avenues to pursue a separate apartment have narrowed, the expectation that a separate apartment is necessary for a normal life has not faded. If anything, it has intensified. Even single young adults now aspire to live on their own. In the USSR, singles were not considered families and were not entitled to separate apartments. However, most single respondents said they would prefer to live apart from their parents. Exceptions included young single men who found it convenient to live with their mothers, who cooked and cleaned for them, and single or divorced women with children, who often relied on their parents for childcare. More than 80 percent of the twenty-six singles in the study who were not in one of these categories asserted that they would like their own apartments.

Single and childless, twenty-nine-year-old Mikhail was living with his mother in a two-room apartment. After his father died, he dropped out of college due to financial strain. He earned twelve thousand rubles a month working as a sales manager in a grocery store. When he said he wanted to live alone, he signaled his awareness of the lingering stereotype that singles don't need to live separately. "In theory, there are two rooms for two people, right? So one could judge my situation as satisfactory. In my opinion, however, my conditions are not satisfactory, because I really want housing of my own. It's high time that I lived separately. It's just not financially possible." When asked to describe the best housing among his acquaintances, Mikhail told of a friend whose parents gave him their three-room apartment when

FIGURE 5.1   Room shared by a couple and their child. The sofa folds into a bed for the parents. The apartment's other room is occupied by the man's parents. Photo by Anastasia Smirnova.

they retired to the countryside. "It's in an old, prefabricated building and is far from the city center. All the same, a three-room apartment for one person is great."

Youth living with extended family often expressed the desire to live separately in terms of mastery of space. Living separately meant having control over the spatial and temporal organization of the home. Figure 5.1 is a photograph of a room occupied by a couple with a child. They spend most of their time at home in this small room, which includes a "child's corner," a crib, and a sofa that converts into a bed for the adults. Effort has been made to keep floor space clear for the child to play, and clothing is stored in cabinets in the hallway. The sofa and child's chair convert into beds. They live with in-laws in a two-room apartment (his parents occupy the other room). While the child often visits with her grandparents, the young couple and the grandparents typically only meet in the kitchen and the corridor.

The problem of "two women in the kitchen" is a common cliché capturing the younger generation's craving for spatial mastery in extended-family households. The eldest woman is usually considered the "mistress" (*khoziaika*) of the home, and younger women are supposed to defer to her. Figure 5.2 depicts a woman in her small kitchen, over which she has a clear sense of ownership, but which she shares with her daughter-in-law.

FIGURE 5.2 Grandmother in the kitchen she shares with her daughter-in-law. Her husband received the apartment in 1982 from his Soviet employer. Photo by author.

In some cases, the two women in question share formal property rights. When Soviet apartment were privatized, shares went to each person officially registered in that apartment, provided they had not previously privatized a share elsewhere. Nevertheless, most coresidents with extended family believe the apartments they inhabit belong to the older generation, regardless of who holds title. Formal ownership, when shared, does not provide the control that young Russians crave. For example, Svetlana, a divorced mother of two, was living with her children, her mother, and two adult sisters in a four-room house. She was a legal coowner of the home that she described as her mother's.

SVETLANA: I want to live separately. When multiple families are living together and there are four women in the kitchen, of course there are constant scandals.

INTERVIEWER: And what does your mother think?

SVETLANA: Naturally mama would also prefer for us to live separately. Mama is the owner; she earned all of this, so to speak. This home is her and papa's achievement.

For respondents who have managed to acquire their own apartments, this problem is solved. In figure 5.3, we see a family in the main room of their

FIGURE 5.3   Main room in a two-room apartment occupied by a nuclear family. The couple sleeps in this room on the convertible sofa. Their daughter has her own room. Photo by Anastasia Smirnova.

two-room apartment, acquired with the help of extended family. Although they lack a separate parlor (they sleep in the pictured room on the convertible sofa), they are delighted that their daughter has her own room and that they have their own place.

Respondents with separate apartments often spoke of the significance of separateness when they talked about their housing trajectories. Roman, a twenty-six-year-old scientist, spent seven years shuttling between the homes of in-laws and rentals. He was delighted to inherit a modest apartment from his grandmother. The apartment's separateness is its most important quality: "At last my wife and I live separately. In these times, to have a two-room apartment is marvelous. Therefore we are completely satisfied. We don't complain. It's on the ground floor and there is no balcony. But the important thing is that we got our own apartment." Similarly, Irina, a twenty-eight-year-old market researcher, has lived in the same apartment since birth. The apartment became her own when her parents moved out, via a complex exchange of extended family properties. "The building is old, from the 1950s. But at least it's a separate apartment. In general everything here is old, but it works. The apartment is quite cold, but we get by. Overall it's normal." By contrast, Larisa's extended family was unwilling or unable to help her get a place for herself, her husband, and child. She felt like a guest while living with her grandmother, and finally took out a mortgage to get her own space. "I felt like unwanted clutter. Here I get to be the mistress of my own domain. Even though it's small, I feel comfortable. It's mine (*svoi*), and that warms the soul."

Security: Why a Rental Is Not a Place of One's Own

If living with one's parents is the key problem, why don't more young Russians rent? According to the RLMS, just 8 percent of urban Russians age twenty-one to forty were renting in 2009. In other capitalist countries, moving from the parental home into a rental is celebrated as getting "one's own place." This is not true in Russia. Most respondents in Kaluga named either renters or hostel residents when asked who among their acquaintances had the worst living conditions. When explaining why renting was so awful, respondents spoke of extreme expense, poor physical conditions, and insecure property rights.

In Kaluga, as in most Russian cities, the rental supply is very limited and expensive relative to incomes. The average monthly price of a rental (twelve thousand rubles) approached average wages (thirteen thousand rubles) in 2009. Only about one-third of interviewees who were living with extended family could have afforded to rent even a one-room apartment, had they been willing to spend up to half of their wages on rent. Even those with apparently sufficient earnings did not perceive it as affordable. For example, Ludmila and her husband earned about thirty-five thousand rubles a month. In many market economies, paying one-third of one's salary for rent is par for the course. But not so to Ludmila. Renting, she said, would be worse than living with in-laws, because "rent would eat up so much of our salaries. I can't imagine how we would live."

Although rentals do provide autonomy from extended family, they do not satisfy the cultural criteria for a separate apartment. There is little autonomy from the landlord, which interferes with two other meanings of the separate apartment—security and possession. Renters in our study did not describe the apartments they inhabit as theirs. Instead, they typically felt vulnerable and constricted. When asked what they would like to change about their housing conditions nearly three in four said they wanted their own apartment. Most chose to rent out of a sense of necessity. For some, the necessity was material: they had no family locally with whom they could live. Other renters could have lived with extended family in theory, but the desire to live separately outweighed the cost and insecurity of renting. Renters, when asked to describe the worst housing conditions among their acquaintances, told stories of people living with in-laws. Pavel, an engineer renting with his wife and daughter, said, "I know one family with a husband, wife, their three children, and their parents. All seven of them live in a three-room apartment. It's like a communal apartment."

Whether living with extended family feels tolerable depends on personal relationships, but also on the nature of the space and the structure of the extended family household. When people living with extended families described their living conditions, they emphasized the importance of having one's own room, or at least not sharing with anyone other than partners and small children. The worst situations involved multiple generations living in the same room, particularly grown siblings sharing with each other, or adults sharing with their parents or grandparents. Some renters in the Kaluga study were escaping such situations. For example, Boris and his wife rented a single room in a four-room apartment (the other three rooms were used as storage by the owners, who had moved to another city). Boris was twenty-five years old and working as a prison guard in 2009. Six years earlier, his parents had received a voucher to purchase an apartment through a government program for military officers. The voucher only sufficed to pay for a two-room apartment, although the family had two teenage children at the time. Each family member received a one-quarter share of legal ownership. Since then, Boris's father passed away and Boris met his wife. They moved in together before they got married and rented from the beginning. Although the payments were a hardship and the apartment was far from ideal, they preferred those privations to the discomfort of sharing with his family.

> BORIS: How could the four of us live in a two-room apartment? When my father was alive it was okay, two parents and two siblings. But now it would be awkward with my girl, my sister, my mother, and me. It would be inconvenient to have three ladies in one kitchen.
> INTERVIEWER: You would have three. Usually there are no more than two.
> BORIS: Three is overkill!

Although many renters preferred their circumstances to living with family, most were still deeply dissatisfied with their housing conditions, due to insecure tenancy and the feeling that the place was not their own. Few renters in our study had a formal rental contract or a propiska registration at their rental address (exceptions were renting company-owned apartments). Renters worried that they could be evicted at any time, for any reason. Given the limited supply of rental housing in Kaluga, eviction caused extreme hardship. Several renters intimated that this legal and practical insecurity rendered them *bomzhi* (an acronym for persons without a registered address, which also means "bum").

Natasha was renting a one-room apartment with her boyfriend. She described renting as insecure independence: "At the moment, renting is our best option, because here we're not dependent on anyone. It's better to live where no one steps on my soul, to live separately from my parents and build my everyday life with the person with whom I'm planning to settle down." However, she still longed to own her own apartment and worried about not being able to afford the rent. Secure housing, she said, is imperative "to start a family and to be a proper, normal person in this society, and not, to put it bluntly, a bomzh who wanders from apartment to apartment."

Insecure tenure also inhibits place making. Most rental properties are owned and managed by individuals who either inherited them from extended family, or have moved to a new address and maintained their former home as a rental. Furniture and wallpaper are often in poor condition, but tenants are usually not allowed to upgrade them, and if they do, they risk the landlord raising the rent or finding an excuse to evict them in exchange for new tenants who will pay more. For example, Tamara, a single mother, rented a room in a worker's hostel. The rent was half her salary, and the conditions were very poor, but she needed to leave her mother's home to escape her abusive, alcoholic stepfather. She got some pleasure out of control over her tiny kitchen. "I always had problems with my mother in the kitchen. Either I didn't put a spoon in the right place, or I didn't wash something right away, or I was using the stove at the wrong time." She moved out so as not to "destroy my nerves." Nevertheless, the room was in terrible condition and did not feel like her own. Although she worked as an interior decorator, she had done nothing to fix up the room she inhabited. "Absolutely nothing. Because when it's not your housing, you don't want to expend any money or energy on it. If you fix it up now, the next time the landlord stops by and sees how much nicer it is, he might suddenly 'discover' a relative who needs housing and order you to leave."

Place making is also inhibited by landlords' incursions. Landlords often use rentals for storage and fill them with their own things, not only furniture, but also decorations, books, clothes, and chipped dishes. Tenants have to fit their own things around those of the owner. Inga, who lived with a large extended family in a run-down house, explained why she would not want to rent, even if she could afford it.

It's offensive that after you move into a rental, you want to live there and fix things up, but the owners will say: "Pardon me, but don't touch our wallpaper. Pardon me, but we don't want to remove that rug. Pardon me, but leave our books on the shelves. As if they were still living there. In the West, if you rent an apartment, you can make yourself at home. But here you feel like you've come to stay with some auntie and you're underfoot. She's given you permission to stay with her, and charges a fortune for the privilege.

In sum, renting is a choice between different types of constraint, either of which fails to provide a meaningful separate apartment. To stay in the family home is to remain subordinate in the organization of the household. To rent provides autonomy from the extended family, but at a high price, with little security, and without the opportunities for place making that young adults desire.

Housing Aspirations among More- and Less-Educated Young Russians

The preference for living separately is nearly universal. However, interviewees with higher education were more likely to emphasize this issue during the interviews. I classified respondents as prioritizing housing autonomy if they mentioned it unprompted at least three times during the interview, or if they categorically insisted a separate apartment is necessary, for example, to get married, have a child, or have a normal life. Among respondents living with extended family, a separate apartment was a priority for 79 percent who had attended or completed college, versus just 46 percent of those who had not. The trend was similar among owners: 68 percent versus 39 percent. Educated respondents described a separate apartment as a means to independence, self-realization, and even brain development. They were also more likely to say it is a prerequisite for starting a family.

Zina typifies this disposition. At the time of the interview she was twenty-two years old, finishing up a law degree, and living with her parents. Their apartment, built in Stalin's time, had three large rooms and was in good condition. When asked what if anything she would like to change about the apartment, she replied, "I don't want to change it; I simply don't want to live in it. I'd like to exchange that apartment for two smaller ones so I can live separately. But my parents have renovated their apartment, they put their souls into it, so naturally they don't want to move." She returned to the issue when asked about her relationship status.

> ZINA: If I have a family it will be in a rental or not at all. I categorically refuse to start a family living with parents—his or mine. I'm single, but if I meet someone I'll try to improve my housing conditions, and only then have children.
> INTERVIEWER: How would you try to improve your housing conditions?

ZINA: First I'll try to talk my parents into exchanging their apartment. Or perhaps my future husband will have his own apartment. That seems to be the only hope a woman has in Russia today.

To realize her dream Zina was counting on help from her family or a future husband. She did not sense any opportunity to earn the apartment she so desired: "In Soviet times one could earn an apartment through honest work," she claimed. "Now it's impossible to earn an apartment honestly."

Less-educated respondents living with extended family tended to be more resigned to their circumstances. When asked what they would like to change about their housing conditions, just one-third volunteered (unprompted) that they wanted to live separately. Ksenya, a stay-at-home mother, was living with her husband, toddler, and husband's grandfather in the grandfather's two-room apartment. She said they dream of a separate bedroom for their child but did not mention a separate apartment. Edward has no local family and was renting a one-room apartment with his wife and teenage son. He said, "In principle I'm satisfied. Of course if I think about it I'm not satisfied. So I try not to think about it since there's no way to change it." Anastasia, a twenty-three-year-old sales clerk, was more concerned about property rights than living separately. She and her daughter were living with her mother. Her mother had not yet privatized the apartment, which made Sofia nervous. When asked if she is satisfied with her housing, she replied, "I haven't really thought about it. I'm used to it. Probably I'm satisfied. When I lived with my ex-husband's family there were three of us in one room, and now I share a large room only with my daughter. So I'm satisfied with that. If only I had security and if I knew that this space belonged to me, then I would have had everything I need."

Not only did more educated respondents tend to crave separate apartments more; they also had higher aspirations for housing quality. We asked respondents to describe their dream homes, if money was no object. The majority, regardless of education level, dreamed of a detached home. However, highly educated people tended to describe their dream homes more vividly and to emphasize luxury. Among educated respondents, 58 percent said they dreamed of a luxury detached home and an additional 10 percent wanted an elite apartment. For the remainder, 22 percent wanted a modest house, and just 15 percent a standard apartment. Among respondents with less education, 33 percent dreamed of a luxury detached home, 40 percent a simple house, and the remaining 27 percent a standard apartment.

The benchmark for luxury is a large, modern, detached home, a so-called *kottedzh*. Although the word *cottage* in English conveys a small and cozy

FIGURE 5.4 A detached luxury home. Many respondents described such a home as their dream house. Photo by Anastasia Smirnova.

home, in Russian it denotes Western luxury. Such homes have developed on the outskirts of Kaluga; figure 5.4 shows an exemplar. These homes differ from the "New Russian" villas of the 1990s described by anthropologist Caroline Humphrey (1998); the homes in her study were designed for the external gaze by nouveau riche who rarely lived in them. I visited homes in Kaluga's new suburbs several times during the first decade of the new century. They are indeed occupied, typically by well-off families composed of a working husband, a stay-at-home wife, and at least two children. In showing me around, the owners invariably asked me whether their homes matched American standards and proudly pointed out that you could hardly see or hear the neighbors.

Pavel dreamed of owning such a home. He wished for "a large private house in a prestigious location with a beautiful environment: trees, sunlight, and fresh air. The neighborhood should be on the outskirts of the city, where you don't hear your neighbors. My wife and I would like to have a minimum of three children, so the house should have six bedrooms, one for each of us and one for guests. I would decorate my room in 'high-tech' style. My wife doesn't understand that style, so her room would have a classical style." Pavel was already renting to live separately from in-laws. He also wished for separation from the city and his neighbors, and even a separate room from his wife.

The Western-style kottedzh is also distinguished from its Soviet counterpart—the rural home (*chastnyi dom*)—by the absence of a vegetable garden. Marianna, owner of an inherited three-room apartment, described her dream home as a three-story kottedzh, "not a palace, but for a normal family with European-style amenities." The interviewer asked her if the house would have a yard. She replied, "Of course, but not for growing potatoes! There would be a lawn for leisure only: for barbecues, flowers, and children's play."[2]

By contrast, respondents with lower-class origins, lacking higher education or prestigious occupations, typically dreamed only of what the Soviet government had promised to everyone. If they spoke of a house, they more often referred to a modest rural home than a *kottedzh*. For example, Roxana hoped for such a house, with an indoor toilet rather than an outhouse, and a large kitchen, "since I'm the family cook and that's where I spend most of my time." The rest of the house would preferably be small and easy to clean.

Boris dreamed not even of a detached house, but of a "standard apartment." He was more concerned with quality of construction than size or style.

BORIS: I'd like an apartment close to the city center in a new, brick building. It shouldn't be a corner apartment, and should be located between the second and fourth floors. Three rooms would be ideal. The building should be in normal condition, with good heating. Preferably the apartment would already be renovated so we wouldn't have to do it ourselves.
INTERVIEWER: What style would you like for the interior?
BORIS: I'm not sure. It should be simple. Not too rich, but attractive.
INTERVIEWER: Did you forget you have unlimited means?
BORIS: Even if you have money, what's the point of luxury? Coziness is what's important. You can't construct coziness with expensive floor lamps and ornate furniture.

Boris's pragmatic concerns stem from his history of living in dilapidated housing. His distaste for corner apartments derives from the Soviet tendency for such apartments to be poorly insulated and awkwardly laid out. The passage also reflects Soviet dictums on taste, which valorized simplicity, attractiveness, and coziness.

Boris's lower aspirations indicate what Pierre Bourdieu (1984) calls "the taste of necessity." When asked about dream houses, some respondents said it was unlucky to dream for much more than one could hope for. Less-educated youth do not embrace extended family living; in opinion polls most say living separately is better in theory. But the mismatch between ideal and reality appears to trouble them less. Educated youth, by contrast, crave autonomy and are unhappier without it. This stronger preference, however, did not raise their chances of gaining separate apartments, as chapter 4 showed, leading to frustration among the social class that was supposed to be the vanguard of capitalism.

To Each According to His Work? Distributive Justice in Past and Present

Both socialist and capitalist governments in Russia promised to distribute consumption opportunities according to merit at work. Yet work played a minor role in the housing trajectories of participants in the qualitative interviews, consistent with the statistical findings reported in chapter 4. Most— 93 percent—said they could not afford to buy an apartment at the moment. Among owners without mortgages, 55 percent received their apartments outright as a gift or inheritance. An additional 27 percent used a gift or inheritance as starting capital to purchase an upgraded apartment, while 18 percent claimed to have purchased their apartments without family help. Only 11 percent of respondents living with extended family and 17 percent of renters expected to obtain an apartment through their earnings alone, without an inheritance, family help with a down payment, or a fortunate marriage. A few held out hope for free or subsidized government apartments. Even mortgage holders, who qualified for loans based on their salaries, did not necessarily view the labor market as a realistic path to housing. Twelve out of fifteen borrowers got their down payments by selling privatized apartments they had received from family.

Post-Soviet Luck, Not Merit

Post-Soviet housing trajectories were attributed mainly to fortune, not fortitude. Imagery of luck, chance, and fate were common in the interviews. The most important form of luck was timing: where a person was living when the great giveaway of 1992 began. Mikhail recalled his family's sense of good fortune in 1992 when they got an apartment through the waiting list at his father's factory. "We got one of the last free apartments. At that time, everything had started to fall apart and there was great uncertainty. We were so happy that we finally got our apartment. It turns out that was literally the last chance to improve our housing conditions." Ludmila had the opposite experience: "If you weren't in the right place at the right time, then you didn't get an apartment. Privatization slipped through our fingers."

Luck could come later in the guise of wealthy parents, as Pavel explained: "My friend's parents work for a construction company and helped him get his own, spacious, three-room apartment. He's very lucky to have such parents. I don't know anyone else who has had such good fortune." Inheritance was another form of luck. Lena, divorced and living with her mother and grandmother, characterized her friend's inheritance as follows: "On the one hand I envy her: she lives in a nice, large two-room apartment. She is the sole owner, although her husband lives there too. But I don't envy how she got it. Her parents simply died. It's not as if she could have gotten it on her own."

One might expect mortgage holders to describe their apartments as earned, given that they typically pay the mortgage out of wages. But most instead employed imagery of chance or fate when explaining how and why they took out a mortgage. For example, Polina said that eviction from her rental apartment set the wheels in motion, and she just "happened to be in the right place at the right time" to find an affordable apartment and a low-interest loan. "I am grateful to my landlady for evicting me when she did, otherwise I never would have played the mortgage game because it always seemed too risky." Vera also attributed her loan to fate. She still preferred the guarantees of the past to the uncertainty of the present. "Before you had to wait in line. But everyone got an apartment, especially if they had a child. Now you still have to wait, and you may get nothing. You wait for someone to die. Or you wait for good luck, to fall into a good job, but realistically you probably won't find one."

Some respondents were more optimistic about the possibility of earning an apartment when speaking in general terms than when speaking of their personal prospects. Toward the end of the interviews, we asked respondents the following question: "Which of the following statements better describes the situation in our city? (A) If a person is capable and works hard, he can earn an apartment; (B) No matter how hard a person works, he cannot afford to buy an apartment." Forty percent selected option A, 44 percent option B, and 16 percent gave ambivalent responses. The distribution of responses was similar across education groups and housing tenures.

Responses to an open-ended follow-up question, however, reveal systematic variation in how respondents interpreted the question. Among educated respondents who said it is possible to earn an apartment, two-thirds spoke in ideological terms about how they wished things to be, rather than how they actually were. The following passage exemplifies this discourse.

MARINA: The first option is better. One must account for the human factor.

INTERVIEWER: So you prefer the first option. Does it describe the situation in Kaluga today?

MARINA: I can't think of a concrete example. Most of my acquaintances got their apartments from their grandparents. But I lean toward the first response because I believe in it. For now.

Less-educated respondents answered the question more literally, with sixty percent describing what they perceived to be the reality of a distant elite. For example, Kira observed, "Lots of businessmen are earning lots of money. Look at how many mansions have appeared in the suburbs. Look at the new elite apartment buildings in town. Curtains are hanging in the windows, so someone can afford them. How they got the money is another question."

In neither case does the response reflect the respondent's own experience. Optimistic responses to a general question on the possibility of earning a separate apartment were incongruent with respondents' descriptions of their personal histories and prospects. Even the most seemingly optimistic respondents tended to be ambivalent. As Roman said, "I like to think that it's possible to earn an apartment. It is if you earn a high salary and you are very frugal. But how many people can be on the high end of a skewed salary distribution? The fact is, only a few families can buy housing on their own. That is why most Russian families—it sounds awful to say it—are counting on their grandmothers to die so they'll receive an inheritance."

For a few respondents, earning an apartment has been a reality. Ten claimed to have bought their apartments with no inheritance or family help. Seven of these ten maintained that others who did not manage to earn an apartment were lazy, poorly organized their budgets, or suffered from a Soviet mentality. For example, Zoya, a stay-at-home mother of three whose husband owns a construction company, described her circle of acquaintances as "people who have a high standard of living. Our friends all work hard and they earned their apartments. Because today in Russia, if you want to work, you will own something. If you don't work, then you won't get anything." To most respondents, however, this statement would better describe the Soviet housing order.

The Ease of Earning a Soviet Apartment

Market transition was supposed to make labor markets the arbiter of inequality. Yet most young Russians believe that work was more relevant to housing outcomes in the Soviet period. Respondents were asked to describe the Soviet housing system and to compare the pluses and minuses of past and present. Seventy percent offered that Soviet housing was given out in exchange for work. One recalled the slogan: "'He who works will eat.' He who worked was given an apartment. That's how it was in the USSR." Ivan, a factory worker with a secondary education described the system in more detail: "People were guaranteed housing if they worked at a factory for some period of time, say ten years. Every factory had its own housing stock and they gave it out. You might suffer for a while living with your parents after you got married. But it was easier because you were queuing for your own apartment and you knew you would get it. My parents did."

This sense of ease, predictability, and stability in the Soviet Union was a common theme in interviews. Examples of this discourse included: "The housing question was simpler then"; "There was stability so, even if things weren't always easy, at least you knew what to do to get an apartment"; "Any worker could get an apartment, unlike today when one is rich and ten are poor." Survey evidence confirms that this opinion is widespread: in 2003 three-quarters of Russian survey respondents said that housing problems had grown more difficult to solve over the previous decade. Even among young adults age eighteen to thirty-five, only 20 percent said the housing question had become easier to resolve (Petrova 2003).

Many respondents spoke of the Soviet system not just as simpler, but also as fairer, because people could earn their own apartments. For example, Ksenya claimed, "In the Soviet epoch it was possible to earn an apartment. People stood in line at their enterprises. It was hard but it was achievable. Now it's not realistic to earn housing, except for a very small minority." Although respondents were too young to have adult memories of Soviet-era allocation, most implicitly equated Soviet allocation with ownership. Dmitri made this point explicit by stating that the previous system was better because the government "gave people their own property (*sobstvennost'*) for free." Now, he said, it is much more difficult to acquire property. He also asserted that the Soviet system was more efficient because it incentivized work. Enterprises could attract employees by offering housing, and workers had more loyalty and there was less turnover.

Interviewees drew few positive comparisons of the present with the previous housing order. Even those who noted the long queues, low quality, and corrupt distribution in the Soviet period sharply criticized the present. At best, the situation had not worsened because it had always been unfair. A focus group participant in a study of the Priority National Projects said, "Those who had parents in power could get an apartment. That was the situation in Soviet times, and it remains the situation now" (FOM 2007c).

The dominant discourse about the present is that is that it is impossible to acquire an apartment through honest work. Highly educated Russians are vociferous on this point. Nearly three-fourths of respondents with higher degrees indicated that education and skills are not adequately compensated in contemporary Russia. The Soviet system on the other hand took care of "young specialists." For example Tatyana, a curator at a local museum, earned a modest salary. She was living with her boyfriend in a dilapidated hostel at the time of the interview. With her advanced degree and cultural specialty, Tatyana felt she would have been better off in the past with respect to housing.

> The Soviet Union only had pluses in this regard. When a person gradu-
> ated from university, he was given a job and housing for which he
> didn't pay. My parents got a dorm room during college, and then a
> room in a communal apartment for a little while, and finally a three-
> room apartment after I was born. And now? No one will give a student
> a decent dorm room. After graduation no employer will give him an
> apartment. And if you have children it's even worse, because you could
> never earn enough to buy an apartment. Not even with mortgage
> credit, which doesn't work in Russia, unless you are wheeling and deal-
> ing in private business. But not all of us should have to be businessmen.
> We need doctors and teachers and artists and scientists. Therefore I
> don't see any pluses today. Only that they are building higher quality
> housing. But I can't afford it.

The Illegitimacy of Housing Markets in the New Russia

Housing markets function poorly in Russia. Proponents of market transition might argue that the solution is to fix the market by building supporting institutions: a stable currency and banking system, clear and enforceable property rights, and macroeconomic growth to raise incomes and make housing more affordable. However, market failure led many Russians to the opposite conclusion. Most interviewees believed that government should control construction and prices to make housing more affordable, and redistribute housing to deserving youth in order to redress market injustice.

Controlling the Market

In a 1999 survey, 93 percent of Russians agreed that it is the government's responsibility "to provide decent housing for those who can't afford it."[3]

Interviewees in Kaluga in 2009 proposed a mix of possible policy solutions, including public construction, price controls, and housing subsidies in cash or in kind.

About 60 percent suggested that the government should either build housing or compel enterprises to build for their employees. Although this resembles Soviet policy, there was a post-Soviet sensibility to calls for a renewed government role. Respondents often labeled government subsidies as "starter homes" or "starting capital." For example, Emma, a twenty-three-year-old student, was content to live with her parents and sister for the time being. But she worried about what she and her sister would do in the future when they formed families. The government, she maintained, should provide starter homes to those left out by privatization or inheritance. "My family has two siblings. One of us will eventually inherit this apartment, but what about the other one? Two families aren't going to live in one apartment. So the government needs to help young people get starter homes in today's economy. Maybe they could give out small apartments like they used to, but not control them so strictly. If you manage to earn a good salary, you could sell the first apartment for starting capital to buy a better one. If not, at least you have some kind of separate housing."

Most Russians support private ownership and the right to buy and sell housing. Privatization was popular because it resonated with the sense of de facto ownership Soviet citizens already had over the apartments they inhabited. A survey of urban Russians in 1993 found that only 16 percent opposed housing privatization on principle, whereas over half agreed that privatization was essential to solving the country's housing problem (Dolgova et al. 1993). However, nearly two decades later, few trusted markets to set prices for this privatized property. In our 2009 interviews, we asked people whether the market or the government should regulate prices, and why. Seventy-four percent of respondents called for price controls, 14 percent were ambivalent, and just 12 percent supported free market prices. Likewise, most believed that the government should control interest rates on mortgage loans.

Proponents of price controls appealed to two principles: setting prices in relationship to incomes, and setting prices in relationship to costs. "If the government is going to decline to give out housing like it did before," Polina said, "at the very least it should ensure that private housing is affordable. That means capping prices in relationship to regional salaries." While recognizing that private builders need to turn a profit, many objected to profit maximization in the housing sector. Marina warned, "If limits are not set, prices will rise to the cosmos. I'm not opposed to private builders earning money, but they shouldn't be so brazen. They charge ten times more than it costs them to build. What have they done to merit such profits? It's wrong. The government should restrict the percentage they can charge above their costs."

Advocates of price controls were asked a follow-up question: "By what means can our government actually regulate prices, given the conditions of today's market economy?" Some denied that a market even exists or described Russia's variety of capitalism as "wild." Others rejected housing markets on principle. Lucia argued, "Not everything should be regulated by the market. Market prices are not always affordable, and most of it goes into the pockets of entrepreneurs who currently control the housing market. The government should control the market for such an essential good." Tatyana, the museum curator introduced earlier, also rejected markets on principle: "The economy should not be a command economy, but it should be regulated by the government. A pure market works according to the ancient principle: he who is strongest will survive. But the best people do not always survive." In her view, markets by nature lead to an unjust distribution. So who deserves assistance when the market fails them?

Compensatory Justice

The leaders of market reform had promised that markets would be fair. Yegor Gaidar, chief architect of shock therapy, asserted that suffering was justified because everyone shared in it, just as everyone would have a share in the opportunity to prosper. "I think the justice of reforms has been brought home to people. . . . The burden sits equally on every shoulder. . . . The privatization option we have chosen is a truly popular option with everyone getting an equal share."[4]

However privatization shares, of housing as well as of state enterprises, were not equal. Although public interest in privatization was high, especially among those with something to gain, 91 percent of Russians surveyed in 1993 considered it essential to compensate those with subpar housing conditions through vouchers or cash payments. This endorsement of compensatory justice is consistent with broader attitudes toward the government's duty to mitigate inequality (Dolgova et al. 1993). For example, 61 percent of Russians in 1996 supported a guaranteed subsistence income, and only one-third agreed that the government should not set ceilings on income—attitudes that strengthened during the first post-Soviet decade (Shlapentokh 1999).

In 2009, young Russians were still concerned about the unfairness of privatization, which in turn led to unequal inheritances. When asked what, if anything, the government should do about the housing question, about two out of three owners and three out of four nonowners in the Kaluga study proposed that the government should help anyone who did not own a separate apartment. Inheritance was an unfair principle for determining the haves and have-nots. Regina, a thirty-year-old homemaker who inherited a room in a worker's hostel, framed compensation for those who did not inherit anything as a matter of justice. "Few Kalugans can afford to participate in housing markets, except for a few people who inherited several apartments from their grandparents and aunts and uncles. And now those people are 'living in chocolate': they live in one apartment, rent out another, and sold the third one to live off the profit. It's not based on merit. They simply got lucky. The government should give an apartment to everyone who doesn't already have one; that would be justice."

Nelly cited inequality within her own family to make a similar argument. "My sister is eight years older than me. She managed to get her own apartment in time, in 1991. Meanwhile I'm still living with my parents. I don't blame my sister for her good luck, but I feel that I should also be given starting capital. Although others got their apartments for free, I am prepared to work for it. If the government would pay half the cost of an apartment and give us an affordable loan for the rest, we could pay out of our salaries."

Many respondents emphasized their willingness to work for an apartment. In this discourse, working people deserve apartments, and if the market does not reward work, then the government should. Russians strongly equate work with moral worth. In the Soviet period, work and housing had been closely linked, so that one necessarily implied the other. Housing signified the worthiness of the worker, and homelessness was the ultimate sign of worthlessness. The homeless in the post-Soviet period demonstrate the lasting power of this cultural equation. In an ethnographic study, homeless Russians took pains to distinguish themselves from worthless homeless others by describing themselves as exceptions who were at least willing to work (Höjdestrand 2009, 47–48).

In the Kaluga study, nearly everyone thought housing should be a reward for work, but they differed on what types of work should be best rewarded. Less-educated respondents typically appealed to the principle of housing as a universal right for work. Anna, for example, is a salesclerk with a high school education. In 2009 she was living alone in an apartment given to her by her grandmother, who had recently retired to her ancestral village. As a single twenty-two-year-old, Anna was fortunate to have her own apartment. Nevertheless, she disapproved of the housing system. "People are living in hostels with children, and they have no way out. It's not right." In Soviet times, she said, "They gave out apartments to everyone who worked. The apartments were similar and people didn't strive to stand out and they were happy. Let them give everyone who works now a simple apartment. If that's not good enough for somebody, let him try to improve it in the market." Likewise, Dennis said that Soviet society lacked such distinctions between rich and poor. "Everyone worked according to their abilities, unlike today where one worker has an apartment and another one does not, for no apparent reason. It was a lot simpler and fairer in the USSR."

Educated youth, by contrast, were more likely to endorse policies that would privilege skilled, white-collar specialists. Feeling that human capital is undervalued in today's Russia, about half of educated respondents suggested that housing subsidies could redress that injustice. Tatyana proposed low-interest, subsidized mortgage loans for young specialists that would be paid for by "taking profits from natural resource extraction and spending them to help develop the nation's human capital." Dmitri, a computer programmer living with his wife's aunt, suggested that housing should be allocated proportionate to the value of specialized labor.

> I know doctors and professors and military officers who live in terrible conditions despite their skills and experience. It's offensive. The government must organize normal work, with normal salaries and normal housing. We could take some elements from the Soviet system, by distributing housing at work. But they shouldn't give free apartments to everyone. Instead they should give people the opportunity to merit an apartment though work in one's profession. They should determine square footage in part based on family size, but also in proportion to the quality of a man's work and his value to the enterprise.

Expectations of the State

Although respondents differed on exactly who should be compensated how, they agreed that the housing system is broken and the government must fix it, not by stimulating markets, but by controlling them. This sense of distributive injustice and its remedies varied little by housing tenure. People who inherited apartments did not view the system as fairer than did those who rented or lived with their parents. What matters is not simply what people got, but how they got it. Nearly the only supporters of a liberal market economy for housing in the Kaluga study were those few who had managed to buy an apartment outright. Such positive market experiences are rare, not only in this qualitative sample, but also in the population at large. This creates a legitimation problem for a government that continues to advocate markets as the ultimate solution to "Russia's tight housing knot." Medvedev has argued repeatedly that controlling prices or interest rates would backfire and make housing less affordable.[5] This position, which is consistent with the Washington Consensus on market reform, surely fails to resonate with Russians accustomed to market failure.

Nevertheless, Russians' concrete expectations of the state are low, due to poor opinions of state capacity and cynicism about state corruption. In a 2007 survey only 4 percent of young respondents who said they were planning to move within the next two years believed the national projects would assist them. In 2008, just 3 percent of surveyed eighteen- to thirty-five-year olds reported having received help with housing through the affordable housing initiatives of the PNP, while 16 percent knew someone who had (FOM 2008).

In the Kaluga interviews as well, respondents were pessimistic that current housing policies could help them or young Russians in general. When we asked respondents what they had heard about the young families program, most responded skeptically, or at best indifferently. Many criticized the new "youth settlements," government-sponsored developments of prefabricated detached homes on the outskirts of Kaluga. Eligible purchasers of the homes (who numbered fewer than five hundred as of this writing) could receive a 30 percent grant as a down payment and finance the rest with personal funds or a subsidized mortgage. Respondents described these developments as unrealistic and a scam. Critiques ranged from frustration with eligibility limitations to suspicion that the authorities were appropriating housing subsidies for their own friends and families rather than giving them to truly needy applicants.

Several respondents tried to apply for a housing subsidy through the YFP (only one was successful). Their experiences suggest that skepticism is well founded. The waiting list was very long and barely moved. And getting on it was very difficult. If applicants already occupied more than eleven square meters per capita, or if they owned any housing space, even just a share of a parent's apartment, they were disqualified. If both spouses did not have a local propiska, they were also disqualified; as we shall see in chapter 6, this was a common problem. Those who did finally get a subsidized home found they had paid a high price for very low quality construction and poor neighborhood amenities.

Said one respondent: "All our so called national projects are for the rich. For the rest of us, there are no projects, there is only hope in oneself." Even those who had managed to move into better housing viewed the sector as corrupt, with remarks such as: "Prices are formulated in the interests of builders or others, but not in the interests in citizens"; and "In principle there should be government control over producers and prices, but our government is incomprehensible." Those few who were more optimistic spoke of the government's orientation toward the problem rather than specific hopes: "It's significant that the government recognizes housing as a national problem"; and "It's good that the government has been thinking about this problem and has returned to face the people."

Although most Russians no longer anticipate help from the government with housing, most still believe that the government should help, and in ways that defy market logic. Ninety percent of national survey respondents in 2007 agreed the government should subsidize families who need to improve their housing. Nearly as many, when asked an open-ended question about what could be done to improve housing conditions, said that the government should control prices, either by selling housing "for what it actually costs," or at least by establishing a "fair relationship between cost and price" (FOM 2007a). The coexistence of high expectations with low confidence in government creates a legitimation problem (Reutov 2006). As Olga Shevchenko concludes in her study of crisis discourse in Moscow, people blamed the state for "the most trivial and diverse phenomena, from postal mistakes to currency fluctuations" (2009, 6). If the government was blamed even for everyday minutia, even more was at stake in placing blame for housing, one of the most profound problems Russians face in daily life.

My findings on perceptions of distributive injustice in the housing sector also call into question the extent to which educated or affluent young Russians endorse market economics. Housing woes make even well-paid youth ambivalent toward market transition. As Dmitri exclaimed: "My salary is fairly good by Kaluga's standards. I work hard and my specialty is in demand, and I am compensated for that. We don't economize on food, we buy quality clothing and laptop computers, and we vacation in Egypt and Spain. Nevertheless, even if I was very frugal, I could not fulfill my family's most basic need on my salary—I can't buy an apartment! This market is completely idiotic." The sense of unfairness and exclusion in the housing sector has led most young Russians, even those with higher education, to reject housing markets in principle. This may not generalize to other kinds of markets. I suspect that most young Russians enjoy markets for things like clothing and cosmetics, in which just about anyone even with modest wages can afford to participate. Housing market outcomes, on the other hand, are categorical, with clear haves and have-nots.

Despite their sense of the futility of working for housing or hoping for help from the government, young Russians are resourceful in their quest to improve their living conditions. The next two chapters examine young

Russians' strategies for coping with the regime of property without markets. Chapter 6 analyzes family-based strategies for getting an apartment, including inheritance, swapping, and marriage. All involve a form of exchange, but none resembles activity in a liquid housing market. These strategies demonstrate the continued salience of the propiska, which is now based more on a practical sense of secure property rights than a legal claim to ownership. Chapter 7 investigates whether Russians calibrate their family sizes to their housing conditions. Both qualitative and quantitative evidence suggest they do. Fertility restriction is a strategy for keeping one's living conditions tolerable in the absence of a clear path to a separate apartment for the nuclear family and/or separate rooms for each child.

CHAPTER 6

Mobility Strategies

Searching for the Separate Apartment

How do young Russians try to obtain separate apartments under the conditions of property without markets? The vast majority turns to extended family for help. Most have little hope of buying their own homes with their own means. Renting is realistic for some, but as we saw in chapter 5, does not qualify as a place of one's own. Opportunities to borrow are also limited, and mortgages do not provide a full sense of ownership, as we shall see in chapter 9. Thus home buyers usually either pay in full at the time of purchase or invest a significant down payment in a building under construction, with the remainder to be paid off when construction is completed (these installment loans qua investment schemes are called *rassrochki*). In either case, to purchase an apartment requires significant starting capital, which for most young Russians cannot be saved from wages. Their best option, then, is a gift of housing capital from extended family.

The property rights of most owners today can be traced, directly or indirectly, to privatized socialist housing. The generation I studied, who were born between 1974 and 1988, were too young to have received separate apartments from the Soviet government. By 2009, recent acquisitions were sometimes three or four times removed from the original privatized property, which had been swapped or sold. To leverage privatized wealth, young Russians needed either the cooperation of older family members who were still alive, or an inheritance from those who had passed away.

This chapter concentrates on the logic of practice: how do young Russians try to improve their housing conditions, and what cultural dispositions guide their strategies? Although many young Russians participated in privatization and share legal ownership with their parents, de facto property rights remain in their elders' hands. Young adults therefore depend on family to help them acquire a place of their own. But they are also strategic in how they negotiate with extended family, spouses, and in-laws over property rights. To diversify their possible routes to a separate apartment, and to secure those rights in case of divorce, young Russians exploit a perceived disjuncture between the residence, based on the propiska, and ownership, based on title, as the basis for legal claims to property.

The Cultural Logic of Property Rights

Practical versus Legal Property Rights within Families

Privatization rights were transferred in equal shares to all persons, including children, with a propiska at a given address in 1992. Therefore, many young Russians share title with their parents to privatized properties. However, the older generation retained more control over property rights in practice. They could make decisions on behalf of minor children about when and under what circumstances to privatize, and whether to exchange or sell property privatized in their children's names.

The older generation also has a moral claim to these apartments, even if they share title with their children. The generation who initially received these privatized units acquired them through their workplaces in Soviet times and developed a sense of deserved ownership. These original recipients maintain a sense of entitlement to control the property, to which their children usually defer (and when they do not, a family scandal may ensue). Throughout the interviews, respondents routinely described the apartments inhabited by their parents and grandparents as belonging to elders. This was true even though respondents were often registered (had a propiska) with their parents, and/or owned a share of the property. The following exchange illustrates filial deference within extended-family households.

INTERVIEWER: Tell me about your household. With whom do you live?
NELLY: My husband and I live with my parents. We would like to get
    our own place, but we can't imagine it will happen any time soon.
INTERVIEWER: So your parents live with you. You don't live separately.
NELLY: No. My parents don't live with *us*. We live with *them*.
INTERVIEWER: Where are you registered?

NELLY: I am registered at my parent's apartment, as is my sister, who lives with her husband in his parent's apartment. My husband is registered with his parents.

INTERVIEWER: OK. So who are the legal owners?

NELLY: The apartment was divided into four shares when it was privatized, between my parents, my sister, and me. But as for whose apartment this will be, I don't know who will get it. Probably I will, because my husband's brother is already living with his parents, so we couldn't go there. But my sister is unhappy living with her in-laws, so it's a painful question in our family. My parents are trying to sort something out. Maybe an auntie will help them to find a way to get an apartment for each of us.

This logic of deference over familial property rights goes back at least to the Soviet system, in which the person who received an apartment had the right to register others or to transfer it, and retained property rights following divorce (Attwood 2004). The rank ordering of rights within the extended family may also have earlier origins in the peasant household and resembles the Chinese "logic of the family estate," which "articulated property claims within a web of family relationships and emphasized the right of parents to divide a family estate with regard to the particular needs of surviving descendants and expressions of filiality" (Davis 2010, 467). The logic of the family estate works best when younger generations do not expect autonomy. However, the cultural norm of a separate apartment for the nuclear family produces a sense of suffering and abnormalcy for youth living with extended family, who deploy various strategies for escaping the family home.

The Propiska as a Property Right

In the introductory chapter I described the theory of legal "transplant effects," which derive from the gap between law on the books and local meanings and practices. This gap is evident in young Russians' strategies for maximizing their chances of inheritance. When the American model of property rights was transplanted to Russia, not only laws, but also cultural sensibilities, were exported. In a capitalist economy, holding title to a privately owned property confers rights of use, transfer, and profit. These new conceptions of property were superimposed onto preexisting sensibilities, in which the propiska conferred formal rights of use and transfer (and informal opportunities for profit).

Deborah Davis, in work on discourses on residential property in China, draws on the comparative literature on changes in property rights in Latin America and Eastern Europe to understand how people make sense of market transition in the housing sector. "New property regimes imposed from above are revised and resisted by the larger population in order to protect and assert their own immediate interests" (2004, 289). Chinese people "were able to invoke both the logic of family justice and the logic of the regulatory state even as they accepted the rights of individual ownership and market exchange" (293). In Russia as well, all three sets of claims are at work, but the "logic of the regulatory state" has a peculiar twist. It is based on the legacy of the Soviet internal passport system, in which a propiska conferred long-term property rights (the Soviet propiska is detailed in chapter 1).

Changes to the propiska system in the post-Soviet era eased its coercive elements and affirmed its significance for acquiring rights in the new property regime. In 1993, the propiska was legally abolished by the "Law on the Right of Russian Citizens to Move Freely and Choose Their Place of Sojourn and Domicile within the Borders of the Russian Federation" and replaced with a less restrictive registration system. The propiska had codified the limited freedom of movement that Soviet citizens had. The new registration system required only that people notify the authorities of their place of residence, not that they gain governmental permission to move (Katanian 1998, 53). It is also now possible to legally own a property (and even multiple properties) without being formally registered as living there.

Nevertheless, in popular vernacular, the term *propiska* is still widely used. In our interviews, we used the verbal form of propiska to ask people, "Where are you registered?" No one objected to the term, and everyone understood what we meant. The propiska's persistence was predicted by Cynthia Buckley in 1995: "Since the passport and *propiska* system have come to symbolize an official guarantee to state-subsidized housing and a link to official systems of distribution they may be difficult to dismantle given the social continuity that the restrictions provide" (915).

Continuities also persist in the social rights that propiskas provide. Outside Moscow, a propiska is no longer essential to get a job or to migrate. Nevertheless, as of 2009, registration at a permanent address was required to exercise most civil rights and social benefits, from school enrollment to medical insurance. As Höjdestrand put it, the propiska is the "only indisputable criterion for social exclusion in Russia" (2009, 5). In 1999 at least a million people were estimated to be residing in Moscow without a propiska. Many more were registered at some other place than where they actually lived. These people are "effectively non-persons in the eyes of the law" (Schaible 2001, 344; see also Tikhonova 2004). A qualitative study of internal migrants to Moscow evidenced numerous challenges. Employers illegally demanded local permanent registration as a condition of employment, and those without permanent registration could not get any form of credit. Landlords required them to prepay utilities and banks refused to give them accounts or loans

(Blitz 2007, 392). The police interfered with the registration process and punished people for not being registered, especially ethnic minorities. The vicious cycle of the Soviet period persisted: you had to have a place of residence to register, but you could not get a place to live without registration.

Propiskas also continue to define housing rights, but in new ways. Legal title was supposed to replace the propiska as the arbiter of property rights. Yet the propiska remained important due to its role in privatization. The government gave all persons with propiskas the right to claim an ownership share over housing units eligible for privatization. Unprivatized units remained part of the municipal housing stock. Registered residents of unprivatized units retained the right to privatize at any time (provided they had never privatized in the past), blurring the boundary between unprivatized and privatized housing in practice.

The persistence of the propiska also contributes to renters' insecurity. Most renters cannot get a propiska at their rental addresses. Landlords used to be motivated mainly by tax evasion. More recently, even though renters and landlords were increasingly signing contracts (which protect landlords more than tenants), landlords still declined to offer renters a propiska, because they worried this could complicate eviction by providing the tenant with permanent residency rights that bordered on ownership.

Many Russians do not live where they are officially registered, register relatives at their addresses who do not live there, and may not even register at properties in which they live and to which they hold title. When I first began this research, I thought that this state of affairs signified the declining importance of the propiska. Indeed, respondents who felt secure about their property rights often did not bother to transfer their propiskas to their current addresses. However, the interviews made clear that registry patterns reflect systematic strategies to diversify potential property rights. Young Russians often registered with extended family in hopes of a longer-term claim to the property.

De jure, the propiska may not confer the rights that many people expect, suggesting a cultural lag in understandings of the law. The post-Soviet housing code is full of contradictions, which impeded the development of housing markets and especially mortgage markets (UNECE 2004). Until recently, a propiska made it virtually impossible to evict either a tenant or a mortgage holder in default, if the tenant owned no other housing space. Although those laws have since been clarified in favor of owners versus legal residents, how these new laws will be applied in practice is unclear, as test cases were just beginning to work their way through the legal system as of this writing (Guseva 2009). In any case, to understand the logic of practice, we need to investigate how people decide whether and how to codify their property rights, and not just what the law says those rights are.

Patterns of Residence, Registration, and Ownership

Just over half of respondents in the Kaluga interview study were registered where they lived. Permutations of propiska status, legal title, and household structure produce diverse patterns of bundled property rights that provide more or less security. Table 6.1 shows the distribution of respondents' property rights where they lived at the time of the interview (it does not reflect rights over other dwellings in which they were not residing).

People living with extended family had the greatest range of forms of property rights. About 30 percent were on the title, but most of these shared title with someone other than a spouse—usually with parents or grandparents. Another 18 percent had the potential to become future owners through privatization, which could only move forward if all who share in the rights at that address agreed to the transaction. The remainder had few meaningful property rights. Forty percent were registered in the homes of extended family, but the home was already privately owned, and not by them. Some of these joined the household after it had been privatized, for example, by moving in with in-laws. Others had switched their propiska registration to properties of other extended family such as grandparents in hopes of expediting inheritance. Renters had the weakest property rights. Not only were they (by definition) not titleholders, but most did not even have propiskas at their rental addresses (exceptions included people living in dormitories or hostels or in rental housing provided by their employers).

Table 6.1 Property rights and registration patterns in the Kaluga interview study

Property Rights	Extended Family	Renters	Owners	Mortgagors
Name on title				
Full titleholder	7%	NA	42%	NA
Partial titleholder	23	NA	NA	91%
Name not on title				
Registered with right to privatize	18	0%	13	NA
Registered without right to privatize	39	22	17	0
Unregistered	14	78	28	9

Notes: Property rights in this table pertain only to the dwelling where the respondent resided at the time of the interview. Full titleholder means the respondent is the sole titleholder or shares title with a spouse. Partial titleholder means someone other than a spouse is also on the title, or that there is a lien on the title due to a loan. Registered means having a propiska stamp with the address where the respondent actually lives.

The proportion of "owners" with partial or no property rights is striking. When we drew the sample, we classified as owners anyone who was living only with the nuclear family in a dwelling that was either privately owned or eligible for privatization. Among these, nearly half lacked title and/or a propiska where they lived. These were mostly people living in apartments owned by their partners. When one spouse inherited an apartment, the other usually remained registered with his or her parents. In most cases in which spouses were registered together, they had sold an inherited apartment and pooled resources to buy something better.

Among mortgagors, none had secure property rights. Based on local definitions of security, a lien on one's home renders ownership inherently insecure. Most were legal owners with valid propiskas. A few still had not managed to register where they were living, even though they had already started paying a mortgage, because their buildings were technically under construction and it was impossible to register a place under construction as one's legal address.

Figure 6.1 illustrates the mechanisms by which these diverse patterns of property rights emerge. Strategies for claiming shares of potential inheritances or swaps can generate complex networks of property relations. The diagram depicts the network surrounding Aurika, a twenty-two-year-old with a secondary school education who was on maternity leave from her job as a sales clerk at the time of an interview. Her network is prototypical in its registration and ownership patterns. The apartment at the center of this network is of the last generation of *stalinkas,* spacious apartments in baroque buildings constructed in Stalin's time. The apartment, built in the 1950s, has ten-foot ceilings and three large rooms of nearly twenty square meters each. The apartment also has a lot of auxiliary space: there is a large corridor, the rooms all have separate entrances, and the kitchen is nine square meters. One room serves as Aurika's parents' bedroom; the second is the room of Aurika, her husband, and two-month-old baby, and the third is reserved as a parlor. A small dog and cat round out the family.

Aurika's parents got the apartment in 1989 through familial machinations reminiscent of those described by Yury Trifonov in the novella *The Exchange* (1973). Aurika's father had received a two-room apartment through his enterprise. When his father's (Aurika's grandfather's) health was failing, the elder man agreed to combine housing resources, swapping his one-room apartment and his son's two-room apartment for a three-room apartment. "Grandfather was elderly, and so as not to lose his apartment, they combined them through an exchange. Because he understood that there were two children in our family, and that's how we got this apartment."

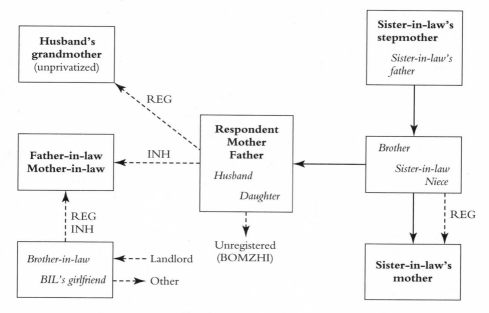

FIGURE 6.1 Prototypical property network
Notes: Boxes represent dwellings; people are placed in the dwellings in which they reside.
BOLD: registered and (partial) owner at residence;
Ital: registered and/or owner elsewhere;
Solid arrow: dwelling where registered and (partial) owner;
Dashed arrow: nonowner (REG registered; INH inheritance rights).

Aurika was registered where she lived, as were her parents. Her brother, who lived elsewhere with his wife, was still registered at his parents' home as well. She said of her brother:

AURIKA: His father-in-law helped him get an apartment.
INTERVIEWER: So they have their own apartment.
AURIKA: Well, it's still registered in his father-in-law's name, but they are living there.

Aurika's brother's father-in-law owned and was registered at the apartment; meanwhile his father-in-law lived elsewhere with his new wife. But as he had no property rights at his second wife's apartment, he declined to transfer rights to his own apartment, either ownership or registration, to his daughter (Aurika's sister-in-law). She in turn was registered at and part owner of her mother's privatized apartment, where she had also registered their daughter (Aurika's niece).

As for Aurika's own immediate family, she planned to register her daughter with her parents as well, but had not gotten around to doing the paperwork, and joked that her daughter was a *bomzh*. Her husband owned a share of his parent's privatized apartment, in which he grew up. However, he was registered at his grandmother's apartment, which remained unprivatized. Aurika explained why.

> There are some nuances. We are all spinning around trying to solve the housing question! First of all, my husband's brother is renting a place right now, but he also has a claim to their parent's apartment. All four of them have shares: father, mother, and two brothers. But the two brothers aren't going to be able to live in a two-room apartment with their wives and children. So they decided to split things up. My husband registered at his grandmother's so he can inherit it. She is nervous about privatizing it; you know how old people can be! But even if she doesn't get around to privatizing it, he will still have the right to the housing space because he is registered there. We can privatize it later, and maybe sell it to get our own place. Her apartment is run-down and tiny, so it won't be enough to buy something good, but maybe if we got that, and we could persuade my parents to exchange this apartment, we could get a two-room apartment.

Several themes emerge from this story. First, everyone among the younger generation was counting on some form of inheritance. There was no discussion of working and saving for an apartment, let alone taking out a mortgage. Second, there was implicit distrust between generations within families. The grandmother's refusal to privatize protected her from potential pressure from her children or grandchildren to sell before her time. In my interviews in 2002, I heard many stories, both personal tales and apparent "urban legends," of elderly people, usually grandparents, being tricked out of their housing space by distant cousins or selfish grandchildren.

Third, spouses and in-laws mistrusted one other. Registration stayed strictly within kin networks, especially when spouses did not own a place together. Aurika's sister-in-law had received neither a propiska nor a legal share of ownership of her father's apartment, which he was apparently keeping in reserve in case things did not work out with his new wife. Meanwhile, Aurika and her husband, as well as her brother and his wife, were registered as if they were living apart. In both cases, the purpose was to keep options open for claims to property rights within the extended family, and also to prevent potential claims from in-laws.

Counting on Family

Nearly all respondents who hoped to acquire an apartment described help from the extended family as essential. Even respondents who appeared optimistic that they could earn an apartment usually clarified that they would need some help from family. For example, when asked whether it is possible to earn an apartment in Kaluga, Pavel replied, "Both yes and no. I think that if I work really hard, I'll be able to buy an economy-class apartment. My employer is doing well, and if they manage to land a profitable contract, there's a good chance I'll get a raise. Therefore I think in a year or two we might be able to buy an apartment, although probably only with help from our relatives."

Respondents often described having a propiska at an unprivatized residence of extended family as a path to inheritance. For example, Olesia, a renter, had recently transferred her registration from her parents to her grandparents. They offered to register her, she explained, "because they are of sufficient age to be thinking about the question of inheritance." The apartment was unprivatized, but Olesia believed she would be able to privatize it after their death based on her propiska. Likewise, Irina, who was living in an apartment owned by her husband, was registered with her father (her parents were divorced). She stayed registered there "just in case" so that she could privatize the apartment to herself, presumably after her father's death. Elder generations often prefer such arrangements, which secure their control over property as long as they are alive.

Many respondents also believed that a propiska could provide an inheritance claim to a privatized property (whether this is true is unclear and depends on whether there is a will, and whether there are competing claimants to inheritance). For example, Veronica bought a tiny room in a hostel to get away from her violent, alcoholic father. Nevertheless, she remained registered at her parents' privatized apartment, which she hoped to inherit. "Just in case something happens to them, I want to be able to stake a claim to that apartment. I give them money to cover the extra cost of utilities.[1] We don't get along, but all the same I'm not going to give up my inheritance." Likewise, Margarita, a renter, registered her propiska with her parents, but only her parents held title to the apartment. Her brother, who was living with them, also had only a propiska. The interviewer said, "It seems you are not counting on inheriting it." Margarita replied, "Why not? I'll get my share because of the propiska. I'm not worried about it."

Sometimes registration patterns reflect hopes of qualifying for government assistance, although most youth perceive these programs to be empty promises. Propiskas matter both to document housing need and to establish region of residence to qualify for municipal subsidies. For example, Vladimir, who ultimately managed to get a subsidized mortgage through the Young Family's Program, transferred his registration to his wife's grandparents' home to create the illusion of extreme crowding (in fact, they were living in another, less crowded property owned by extended family). This entailed a significant risk for him, since by removing his propiska from his own grandparents' unprivatized apartment (in another city), he gave up the right to privatize it in the future. In another story reminiscent of Soviet housing strategies and constraints, Faina's parents were de facto divorced, but continued to stay married and registered in one apartment in hopes of eventually getting a housing voucher off of a long waiting list for military families. Conversely, Yana's parents got a "fictitious divorce" to give the impression that they required another apartment, in a desperate but probably futile attempt to move up on a municipal waiting list on which they have been standing since 1990.

Inheritance strategies frequently lead spouses who live together to register at different addresses. This practice also serves as insurance for extended family against losing familial property to in-laws, a serious concern given Russia's high divorce rate. This makes property rights unequal even within the nuclear family. Among respondents living with partners, 65 percent had unequal property rights. Neither gender was disproportionately disadvantaged, a finding that initially surprised me as I had expected women to be worse off compared to their male partners. Under the condition of property without markets, birth order, family size, and property networks of both extended families matter most for which side of the family provides a couple with housing. Spouses with superior property rights usually claimed some prospect of inheritance to justify why they did not offer their partners registration or ownership. Yet in interviews with people who were disadvantaged with respect to their spouses, these inheritance prospects often appeared unlikely.

Unequal property rights within nuclear families, while pervasive, are an uncomfortable topic. The subject was generally spoken of indirectly, in coded terms, in the interviews. For example, Albert was not registered in an apartment his wife owned. Their starting capital came from his wife's family. They had also taken out nonmortgage loans for housing and appliances, but always in her name. So everything "they" owned was in her name, although his salary went to pay off their loans. When asked where he is registered, he said, "Her family decided it's better to register me and my son with her great-uncle." When asked why, he replied, "I don't think anyone is interested in my opinion." An immigrant from Ukraine, he had no family of his own in Russia with whom to register. He implied that his wife's family only let him register at the great-uncle's apartment, in a faraway city to which he is unlikely to move, so that their grandson could also be registered there (children must be registered with a parent) for a potential inheritance. Implicitly, he was also registered there because he had not been invited to register at his wife's apartment.

Likewise, Irina did not share ownership of her husband's apartment, which he had inherited from his parents. Irina talked about how happy she had been to move in with her husband and how wonderful it was to have her "own apartment" after living with her parents until the age of twenty-five. However, she and her two-year-old son remained registered with her parents. When the interviewer asked why, she answered:

> IRINA: It would be a lot of paperwork. It's just inconvenient to stand in line to change our registration!
>
> INTERVIEWER: And how did you decide the question of where to register your son?
>
> IRINA: Well, naturally a child should be registered with his mother.
>
> INTERVIEWER: And who owns the apartment?
>
> IRINA: Technically it's the property of my husband.
>
> INTERVIEWER: Excuse me for the delicate question, but does this arrangement concern you at all?
>
> IRINA: One doesn't want to think of unpleasant subjects. Of course one has to be realistic. If something were to happen between us, I still have housing space in my mother's apartment.

Conversely, Vitalii owned an apartment where he had neither registered his wife nor offered her ownership. The interviewer asked where she was registered. He replied, "There are some nuances," code for a sensitive family situation about which one does not wish to speak openly. The interviewer guessed at his meaning: "It is a question of inheritance?" "Yes," he replied, "because some of her relatives also aspire to take over her family's apartment, so it's safer for her to stay registered there."

Developing networks of property claims and inheritance prospects across both sets of extended families can improve a young couple's housing chances. But these tactics may also generate tension, conflict, and inequalities within families. In fact, moving in with a spouse sometime puts the other party at a disadvantage within their own extended families, because their housing problem has been at least temporarily solved. Other siblings or cousins might get priority over familial properties that open up for inheritance. Unequal outcomes could then lead to estrangement among siblings. For example, Klara managed to consolidate control over her father's unprivatized three-room apartment. By the time of her father's death, she was the only one among three siblings who was still registered there. Her parents had arranged for her sister to register with her grandmother and her brother to register with an aunt in order to provide each with a path to inheritance. Klara was the last to get married, and so the last to remain in her parents' home. Her brother, who had been living in an apartment owned by his wife's family, got divorced, at which time he moved in with his aunt. He asked Klara to give him half the value of the apartment when she privatized it, but she refused, arguing that he could count on his aunt (who seemed unlikely to die anytime soon). Her enraged brother stopped speaking to her.

The evidence suggests that marriage is not necessarily a path to housing autonomy or security. Nevertheless, unmarried and divorced respondents, both male and female, often mentioned a good marriage match as one possible solution to their housing woes. Among the worst housing conditions we encountered were those of Diana, a twenty-four-year-old single woman who shared a one-room apartment with her parents and her twenty-year-old brother. Although they had set up a partition to create two tiny rooms, there was little privacy, and the family was so poor that they lacked alternatives. Diana's brother was away serving in the army, which relieved the extreme crowding temporarily. But they worried about what to do when he got out of the army. "My parents keep telling him: Find a nice girl. But only one with an apartment!" Her only hope of a "normal life," she said wryly, "is to fall in love with someone with an apartment. That's why it's important that I always look my best when I go out. You never know when you could meet someone with living space!" From Diana's point of view, a place to live and start a family would have been far better than her existing prospects, even without a propiska or an ownership share. However, the experience of other couples suggests that marriage may not provide long-term security and a place that is truly one's own.

Counting on family can also have negative economic consequences. One study of working-class provincial youth found that their tendency to rely on inheritance for housing inhibited geographical mobility, and therefore earnings potential (Walker 2010). Youth who believe propiska registration confers permanent property rights may also be mistaken, given recent revisions to housing law. In the past, propiska rights made lenders wary because they made it very difficult to foreclose. Weakened propiska rights, while directed at the tiny sliver of the housing economy occupied by mortgages, may have long-term consequences for family networks and the trajectories that spouses and siblings follow when conflicts arise.

In conclusion, complex networks of residency/ownership reflect both the importance of inheritance and uncertainty about the meaning of ownership. The propiska system initially impeded a mortgage economy because lenders feared that residency rights would supersede contractual rights to property. Mortgage law reform has since clarified the distinction between residence and ownership, but these legal changes have not translated into changes in registration practices. The disjuncture between de facto residency, de jure residency, and legal ownership enables youth to diversify their portfolio of potential property claims. But it may exacerbate inequality within families and impede access to social benefits tied to residency permits. The disjuncture also impedes cultural consensus on the meaning of private property, a prerequisite for functioning housing markets.

 CHAPTER 7

Rooms of Their Own

How Housing Affects Family Size

Most young Russians define normal housing in terms of Khrushchev's promise of a separate apartment for the nuclear family. Many also believe that parents need a separate room from their children, and ideally each child in the family would have his or her own room. As chapter 6 showed, Russians rely on extended family networks for help with housing. How do they make do when neither family nor market can provide them with the housing they feel they need to live normally? Restricting family size is one strategy for keeping one's living conditions tolerable, when a separate apartment and/or a separate child's room remain out of reach. However, little is known about how housing affects fertility, in Russia or elsewhere. This chapter asks: do housing conditions actually influence how many children Russians have?

Few existing studies systematically explore the causal relationships between housing and population. The dearth of research on this question is striking in relation to its policy implications. A report by the United Nations in Russia urges the government to devote special attention to "programs that provide young families with improved housing... as a key tool in an effective demographic policy" (2008, 22). Policy recommendations include increasing housing subsidies by the number of children, and completely writing off housing debt after the birth of a third child. According to the report, "Studies suggest that housing conditions are the most important socio-economic factor influencing reproductive behavior" (22). However, the report does not cite any supporting studies. The maternity capital policy is based on the unsubstantiated assumption that housing constraints are driving down the birthrate. Putin suggested as much in his 2004 annual address to the Federal Assembly: "The fact that young families are unable to afford housing of their own affects their plans to have children, and it is still common to find several generations all having to share the same apartment."[1]

To an ethnographer on the ground in Russia, the claim that housing influences fertility has face validity. I first became interested in this hypothesis while conducting fieldwork in Kaluga in 2002. I was struck by how often people talked about the relationship between housing and family size as if it was self-evident. As one young woman said to me in 2002, "We'd like to have a second child. But we are still living with my parents. We want to live normally, in a separate apartment of our own."

I also noticed behavior that suggested people were adjusting family size to fit their housing conditions. In 2002 I met a twenty-eight-year-old woman named Oksana. She, her husband, and her six-year-old daughter shared a spacious three-room-apartment with Anna, Oksana's mother-in-law. Anna's deceased husband had received the apartment via his high post in the Soviet energy industry. Oksana and Anna were close, and Oksana was grateful to have live-in childcare, as she worked full-time. Oksana wanted another child but said the apartment was too small. They had no prospects for getting a separate apartment in the near future. Her own parents had already exchanged their privatized apartment for two small ones to help Oksana's older sister, who gave birth to a second child soon after moving to her own place. In 2006 Anna died of cancer. Shortly thereafter, Oksana, then thirty-three years old, stopped using birth control, and a year later gave birth to her second child. Anna's former room was converted into a nursery.

This chapter moves beyond anecdote to systematically examine the relationship between housing and reproductive behavior. In the next section, I draw on the demographic literature on fertility to formulate hypotheses on how housing might, or might not, influence childbearing. My qualitative analysis of discourses on having children elucidates possible cultural mechanisms that could link housing to reproduction. However, these discourses may be post hoc and justificatory, as people have children for complex reasons and their decisions may not be consciously deliberative. In the final section, I use survey evidence to formally test hypotheses on how housing tenure and housing space affect the odds of having a second child.

The interviews indicate a cultural consensus that a separate apartment for the nuclear family, and a separate room for children, is requisite for a normal family life. For most Russians, both men and women, the desire to have at least one child outweighs housing conditions. In other words housing does not influence whether Russian women have at least one child (although it may affect the timing of first birth). In describing their housing and family histories, many respondents indicated that they had calibrated their decisions on second and subsequent births to their housing circumstances. I noticed some variation by education in expressed housing needs in the qualitative sample. Respondents with higher education tended to consider both a separate apartment and a separate room for each child to be essential, whereas less-educated women were more concerned with space than separation. These findings are partially confirmed by statistical evidence presented in the last section of the chapter.

Theorizing the Effects of Housing on Reproduction

Analysts of Russia's fertility decline offer a range of hypotheses to explain fluctuations in the birthrate: from economic crisis and recovery, to changes in family policy, to shifting cultural preferences for small families, to long-standing trends in the population's age structure. Research based on demographic surveys in Russia finds that economic factors such as income, employment, and wage arrears have null or counterintuitive effects on births (Kohler and Kohler 2002; Maleva and Siniavskaia 2006; Roshchina 2006; Zakharov 2008), perhaps because having children is a way to counter uncertainty (Friedman et al. 1994). These studies, however, do not consider housing conditions as a potentially independent cause of low fertility, despite the policy emphasis in this direction.[2] The demographic literature on this question in other countries is also sparse. Clara Mulder, a housing scholar who is one of the few to have tackled this question, notes, "The lack of attention to housing in population research stands in unjustified contrast to the routine attention paid to education and socioeconomic status" (2006b, 410).

Demographers may hesitate to take up this question because it is difficult to determine the direction of causality, that is, to know whether changes in housing circumstances motivate expanded family size, or whether plans to expand one's family lead people to upgrade their housing conditions. In general, research on housing effects is plagued by the problem of selection effects, whereby unobserved attributes of people influence both housing and the outcomes it is purported to affect. As Sandra Newman argues in a review of scholarship on housing effects, "The overarching issue with this hefty body of literature is failure to identify causation" (2008, 901). However, scholars have not hesitated to ask how demographic transitions such as marriage and childbearing affect housing transitions, and usually assume the causal direction to be from the former to the latter.

According to Ström's (2010) review, the small literature on housing and population processes does point to some potential effects of housing, although effects vary widely cross-nationally (Mulder and Lauster 2010). At the macrolevel, nations with high barriers to housing market entry for young people have very low fertility rates (Mulder and Billari 2010). At the microlevel, housing affordability affects family formation and couple stability in Sweden (Lauster and Fransson 2006; Lauster 2008). Housing space, but not tenure, is positively associated with first births in Sweden (Ström 2010) and with third births in Finland (Kulu and Vikat 2007). Homeownership could have negative effects, because homes may compete with children for a couple's financial and emotional resources (Mulder 2006a). Housing expectations also influence fertility: changing conceptions of affluent women's housing needs correlate with changes in reproductive behavior over the past century in the United States (Lauster 2010).

The Russian context presents an opportunity to isolate housing's effects. Selection bias in predicting housing effects is severe where housing is attained via markets (Galster et al. 2007). The Russian context mitigates this problem because market processes play a limited role in housing allocation. Soviet housing allocation principles, rapid and unexpected housing privatization, and persistent post-Soviet barriers to housing market entry mean that housing circumstances—particularly space and ownership—are largely beyond the control of young Russians. Although, as we saw in chapter 6, young Russians are resourceful in trying to diversify their potential paths to inheritance, they control neither the timing of housing gifts nor the qualities of the apartments that they receive.

Why Housing May Affect Fertility

We can derive hypotheses on how housing might affect fertility in Russia from the demographic literature on the effects of socioeconomic status (SES), security, and subjective well-being on fertility. Nearly all quantitative research in which fertility is the dependent variable includes a measure of socioeconomic status as a control variable, even if it is not the main focus of the research. Housing is a household's most expensive and significant durable good, and homeownership is an important component of permanent income or household wealth. Therefore it is reasonable to postulate that, if SES influences fertility, so should housing. Most demographic analyses of fertility either do not measure housing at all, or at best treat housing as an indirect measure of SES (Bollen et al. 2002). However, housing may have a direct effect in its own right. I conceptualize housing not as a proxy for SES, but as a distinct determinant of a household's material and subjective well-being. This distinctiveness is pronounced in the regime of property without markets.

Housing may also have an effect through the sense of security it can provide, especially in uncertain times. Housing is, according to Bourdieu, "a wager on the future or, more exactly, a biological and social *reproduction project*" (2005, 21). When the future seems uncertain, people may defer or forego having children. Risk aversion may explain fertility decline in countries whose social safety nets have been eroded by neoliberal policies embraced by the Washington Consensus. Demographers have identified an association between subjective uncertainty and delayed or foregone reproduction in low-fertility societies (Blossfeld et al. 2005; McDonald 2006). One study of fertility in Russia found that subjective well-being predicted fertility more strongly than did formal employment or income (Perelli-Harris 2006).

If housing tenure influences one's sense of security, then we might expect housing to affect fertility as well, since having a child is a lifetime commitment, and housing is one of the key long-term problems that young families must solve. The issue is confidence: "Delay of family formation is based not so much on experienced economic outcomes but, like any other investment, on the degree of confidence that potential parents have about their capacity to undertake family formation while not placing themselves at economic risk or at risk of falling short of their individual aspirations" (McDonald 2006, 495). The kind of housing people need to feel secure is culturally and historically specific. For Russians, security derives from long-term usage rights more than legal title.

Housing is also significant for Russian definitions of a normal life. The Soviet promise of a separate apartment for every family is still the standard by which Russians judge the adequacy of their housing conditions. Russians commonly cite housing problems to account for why many women have only one child. Reducing family size in accordance with escalating expectations for living standards is also consistent with the theory of the second demographic transition (SDT). SDT theory has been applied in Russia to explain low fertility, which is often attributed to crisis but is most pronounced among educated women (Maleva and Siniavskaia 2006; Philipov and Jasilioniene 2008; Zakharov 2008). Housing autonomy and separate space for each family member may trump other values, such as having multiple children, and may be a prerequisite for educated youth before they are willing to grow their families.

Why Housing May Not Affect Fertility

It is plausible that housing does not affect fertility, especially in Russia. Almost all Russian women have at least one child, and most do so young, without regard to whether they have established independent households; the same is true in the Ukraine (Perelli-Harris 2005). Russia's fertility rate plunged not because of fewer first births, but due to postponing or foregoing second and further births (Perelli-Harris 2006). If Russians are willing to have one child while living in cramped, multigenerational housing, perhaps housing also plays little role in decisions regarding the second. This does not mean that housing is unimportant for subjective well-being. Rather, the cultural imperative to reproduce may outweigh the cultural ideal of having a separate apartment for the nuclear family.

Housing autonomy could even depress fertility. Kohler and Kohler (2002) found that Russians are more likely to have children when they face unemployment and wage arrears and experience subjective uncertainty. They argue that fertility serves as an "uncertainty reduction strategy" (256), following Friedman, Hechter, and Kanazawa's (1994) argument that children are a global strategy available even to those with uncertain prospects in labor or marriage markets. This could also weaken the relationship between housing and fertility among educated youth. Rather than having additional children to provide security, they may prefer to invest in their careers and homes.

Personal Accounts of Reproductive Behavior

The belief that economic conditions impede childrearing is widespread. A participant in a focus group commissioned by the Russian government remarked in 2007: "Many youth have to live with their parents, and this naturally does not help with the healthy formation of a family." Such general statements were also common in the Kaluga interviews in 2009. We asked participants whether and how housing conditions influence the number of children people have. Most—77 percent—asserted that there is, or should be, a strong connection.

For example, Darya was divorced and living in two rooms with five other people—her mother, daughter, sister, and two nieces. She said, "If a couple has a normal apartment with an adequate number of rooms for children—not just for themselves, but also for their children—then naturally they can permit themselves to have not just one child, but as many as they like. But if they are living in a one-room apartment, they can't allow themselves to have more than one child under any circumstances." The same was true for her personally when she was living with in-laws. "We were three people living in one room. It wasn't realistic to have a second child. Regarding the first, we wanted a child, and so we had one in any case."

The belief that housing impedes childbearing also emerges in national surveys of young adults. A 2008 survey of women age eighteen to thirty-five asked if they were planning to have more children. Of the 22 percent of respondents who said they were not planning more children, half said the main reason was that they could not afford kids or did not have adequate housing. Half of the women in the survey also felt that economic conditions in Russia are not conducive to having children (Mendelson and Gerber 2008). In an August 2010 survey, respondents (both men and women) were asked which factors could influence whether they decide to have another child in the next two to three years. Among twenty-five- to thirty-nine-year-olds, just 16 percent said their decisions would be unconditional. By contrast, 33 percent said further childbearing would depend on improving their housing conditions. Among other conditions, 39 percent named a good salary, 35 percent confidence in the future, and 27 percent government support for families with children (Levada Center 2010).

In the Kaluga interview study as well, most respondents asserted that material factors had or could have constrained their fertility behavior. Almost half (including 31 percent of owners and 64 percent of renters) claimed housing conditions had prevented them from having more children. Another 20 percent said their housing conditions sufficed for the number of children they desired, but they would have had fewer kids had things been different. Only one in four did not consider housing conditions to be relevant to their reproductive histories and aspirations.

In discussing their personal histories, men in the qualitative sample were more likely to cite housing as an impediment to having a second child than were women (59 percent versus 44 percent). Women more often mentioned other impediments to having children, such as a stable relationship or access to adequate childcare. Women appear to be more unhappy living with extended family while single than are men. Interest in housing increases for men relative to women once they start a family. For example, Boris explained that he and his wife were delaying having children because they were renting a one-room apartment. He referred to his father as the standard against which he measured himself. "In our family, when my father worked in the military, he was given a three-room apartment. That's how I was raised. So I could only imagine raising two children if I also had my own three-room apartment." Even Igor, who was content living with his mother for the time being ("Mama cooks for me!"), said that when he finds someone with whom to settle down, they would not have children until they got their own place with at least two rooms.

One Child Is Natural, Two Children Are Questionable

When discussing how housing has affected their childbearing decisions, respondents distinguished sharply between having one child versus multiple children. A few childless respondents (12 percent) said they would not even have a first child unless their housing conditions improved. These were almost all people with higher education, who were living in rentals or with extended family. Most however said that housing conditions had not been, or would not be, the deciding factor in having a first child. In a 2007 national survey, 86 percent agreed that having children is very or extremely important to a happy life (Mendelson and Gerber 2008). Most Russian women would likely be more troubled by being childless than by having cramped housing conditions.

Diana, for example, was engaged to be married, and she and her fiancé were planning to live with her parents. She was concerned about feeling crowded, but felt they had no other choice. Regarding children, she was planning just one.

> DIANA: We will be living in one room together. It would be difficult to have two or three children under those circumstances. Although our president is paying out 250,000 rubles in maternity capital, you have to wait so long to get it and who knows if it will be useful by then.
>
> INTERVIEWER: What about having one child? Do housing conditions matter?
>
> DIANA: Probably not. Because a family should have a child. You can have one under any circumstances. You have it and you are happy about it. For example, my cousin lives in a two-room apartment. She and her husband and daughter live in one room, and her mother lives separately in the living room. And it's fine. Her husband doesn't get along so well with her mother, but it's okay.

Several interviewees framed caution about a second child as a moral imperative. For example, Yana reported that her first child was not planned, but she has been more careful about avoiding a second pregnancy. "With the first, you're young and in love and not thinking things through. But now you have a child to think of, and it would be wrong to have another child if you don't have the space. Because how will that affect the child that you already have?"

Lena initially said it would be wrong to base decisions on material conditions. "In Soviet times people lived in hostels and they had kids all the same. Of course, then people had more hope of eventually getting free housing. Nevertheless, the desire to have children should not depend on material conditions. I'm against that mentality." Living conditions, she claimed, did not influence her decision to have her first child. However, when asked how many children she would like to have ideally, she said, "Only two. And only if I meet a good man, and hopefully he will come with housing space! Otherwise no, because in my present housing conditions there is just no room for a second child. Some people have only one room and they have one child after another, from five to seven children. I think that's wrong, because every child needs the chance to be alone sometimes."

The Significance of Security

Respondents had various visions of what type of housing is necessary to have a second child comfortably. But almost everyone could agree that secure property rights are essential. Most renters and mortgage holders (70 percent) felt constrained in their personal fertility aspirations, versus 47 percent of those living with family or who owned their apartments outright. This concern was clearest in interviews with renters, many of whom hesitated to have a single child, let alone a second. For example, Margarita and her boyfriend were renting an apartment together. She decided not to have children after witnessing her friend suffer.

> MARGARITA: We will only have children when our living conditions permit it. Because we won't have children in a rented apartment.
> INTERVIEWER: Not even one, right?
> MARGARITA: Not even one, of course. We wouldn't survive; we are barely making it now. One of my friends had a child in a rental. Now they have to constantly ask their parents for help. It's terrible with a child. I observe her and understand that I could never have a child in a rental apartment. Because it's very difficult. First of all, it's a small, one-room apartment. Secondly, you have to pay rent, but you also have to feed and dress the child. There's no money left for shopping. She can't even go to the hairdresser. She had to let her hair grow out.

The cost of renting was only part of the problem. She also feared eviction. "We would have a child immediately if it wasn't for our living conditions. If only this was our own apartment. It's very scary that at any time the owner can order us to vacate within two weeks. Plus I can't afford to take maternity leave because we have to pay rent." Security predominated her vision of her dream home, which she described as "a two-room apartment, a three-room apartment. I don't care, just so long as it's my own."

A few renters in our study had two children, but these children had either been unplanned and the impetus for moving into a substandard rental, or were still fewer than the respondent wanted ideally. For example, Olesia had two children while living in a rental apartment. "I wanted two no matter what. Housing did not play a role." But she would have liked a third. "If I could buy a three-room apartment and have normal housing, I would happily have a third child. But it would have to be my property, that is, without a mortgage."

Mortgages were considered too insecure and too expensive to permit having more children. Six out of nine interviewees who held mortgages claimed that financial stress had led them not to have a child they would have otherwise wanted. Larisa explained her hesitance: "Spiritually we are already prepared to have another child, and we have the space. But right now it's impossible, because we have so much mortgage debt and I can't afford to take maternity leave. We can't afford to risk it because even if we were to live frugally while I took leave, what would happen if my husband suddenly lost his job? The bank would take the apartment away." Maria, who also had a mortgage, but no children, believed that security was necessary for psychological as well as material well-being. When asked about her dream home, she said, "The apartment should have eighty square meters, with three rooms and nice balconies. I need to get married and have children, so I'm thinking of my future family. We would own it outright, so we could raise our children without having to worry about housing. We could put our energy into other things."

Both mortgagors and renters, when asked about the pluses and minuses of the Soviet housing system, praised the security that the Soviet housing provided. Raisa, a renter, said, "Then, if a person had three children, as far as I know, he was given an apartment. A person worked for some government organization, waited some period of time and received an apartment in accordance with family composition. So of course people would have two or three children, knowing that the government would help them. Now, it's too risky. It's very difficult to decide to have multiple children, knowing that you won't get such support."

A Room of One's Own

Owning an apartment is, in most Russians' opinion, better for starting and growing a family. However, even some owners hesitate to have more children due to overcrowding. Said Regina, the owner of a tiny apartment converted from a dorm room: "Speaking of my dream house, I would like to move to a two-room apartment on the second story of a five-story brick building, with a large kitchen and rooms with separate entrances. Because if we could solve our housing problems, then we could have a second child. My husband and I would live in one room and our children in the other one. Housing is the only thing holding us back." The number of rooms was more important to her than the number of square meters. "As long as we are three people living in one room, a second child is simply not realistic."

At a minimum most respondents required at least two rooms, one for parents and one for children, before they would consider having a second child. A nuclear family of four in an apartment with two rooms is not unusual in Russia. According to the RLMS, 47 percent of families composed of a couple with two children had two rooms in 2009. Respondents in the qualitative study with such living arrangements considered them tolerable. Irina had recently been given a two-room khrushchevka, with small rooms and leaky pipes. Still, she and her husband were considering a second child (they already had one). "I think that if you have your own apartment, then you can easily have two children. In Russia, to have a two-room apartment is an enormous plus, it's the minimum that you need to be able to turn around. If we had continued to live with my parents, then we would have ruled out a second child. Because people are private, they want some separation. Every person wants to have his own corner, where he can go to be alone."

Respondents with less education tended to have lower expectations for what they needed to live comfortably with children (likewise their dream homes were also more modest; see chapter 5). For example, Lena was divorced and living with her daughter in one room of her mother's apartment. When asked about her dream house, she simply dreamed of an extra room "for my daughter. In principle everything else is okay. It would also be nice to be on a lower floor, not on the fifth floor, but that's not essential. I haven't really thought about what it would be like to have something different, a new apartment for example, because it would never happen in my lifetime." She also remarked that, if she ever got remarried, she would only require a two-room apartment to have a second child. By contrast, respondents with higher education were twice as likely to speak of wanting or needing separate rooms for *each* child. Pavel, who was renting two rooms, explained that he would like to rent a place with more rooms because "then we could consider having another child. Here, unfortunately, it's already crowded with one child. He needs to do his homework; he needs to have his own space."

FIGURE 7.1 Children's rooms. (a) Room of an adolescent boy. He and his parents live in his grandmother's three-room apartment. (b) Baby's room in a renovated separate apartment. The room is rarely used as the baby sleeps in her parent's bed. Photo by Anastasia Smirnova.

Figure 7.1 shows two children's rooms for apartments belonging to parents with higher education. Panel (a) depicts the room of a teenager in a three-room apartment; his parents occupy the second room, and his grandmother the third. His parents decided not to have a second child, although they claimed they would have liked one had they had an additional room. But they did not want their son to have to share such a small room with a sibling. Panel (b) shows a baby's room in a three-room apartment. This apartment, inherited and renovated, is occupied by a couple with two children. Before they inherited the apartment, they lived with in-laws and had a single child. Within two years of inheritance, their second child was born.

Normal Housing for Modern Families

Most respondents linked their reproductive histories and aspirations to their material living standards. However, they varied by education in how they talked about why housing conditions matter. Those with lower education spoke concretely about their living conditions and incomes in explaining their fertility plans. Respondents with a higher education related their reproductive decisions to the demands of modernity or civilization (out of thirty-seven interviewees employing this discourse, 84 percent had a higher education).

Lucia's case exemplifies the latter discourse. At the time of the interview Lucia was working in advertising and living with her boyfriend in a one-room rental. Age thirty, she explained why she did not have children as follows:

> Finances are very important to me. I would want my children to be better off than I am, so that they would feel confident in all regards. Here, a normal and comfortable life would not be possible. Intimate moments would disappear if a child was to live in the same room with his parents. I would not put myself in that position. Some people do have children in one-room hostels. It's a nightmare.
>
> My mother is surprised that I'm still waiting. Maybe before people didn't worry as much about the future. But times have changed and there are no guarantees. To be frank, I don't want to descend into utter poverty. Everyone is pressuring me about my age, it's time to have kids, blah blah blah. They haven't achieved the correct mentality. In Europe everyone can have as many children as they want and no one worries about these questions. But in Russia things are different. If I had better conditions, financially and with regard to housing, I would probably have waved my hand and already had children. But now it's impossible.

Similarly, Zhanna, a single, high-income woman with a mortgaged apartment, felt that it was old-fashioned and abnormal to have children in over-crowded conditions.

> To allow oneself to live with a child in a one-room apartment, or in an apartment where others are living—grandma, grandpa, etc.—I think that influences a child's development and ruins his character as well as the nerves of his parents. Yes, one can say in the abstract that people even had children during the war. But we are not at war, and we shouldn't judge ourselves from the standpoint of previous centuries. Therefore it's very important for me to pay off this mortgage as soon as possible so that when I get ready to have a child, the housing question will not weigh on our souls.

These qualitative findings are consistent with the hypothesis that housing influences reproductive decisions, and that the nature of these effects varies by education. However, there are limitations to interview data for assessing this hypothesis. First, in this particular interview study, respondents knew that the study's focus was on housing for young families, and this probably led them to focus their answers to general questions about reproductive decisions on the role of housing. Respondents did mention a range of other influences on childbearing—from the high cost of children's food and education, to the risk of unemployment, to relationship instability, to a preference for investing more energy into one child versus diluting one's emotional and financial resources to have two. I am not arguing that housing is determinative, only that it is influential.

Second, we should be cautious in inferring behavior from discourse. As the UN report warned, "A significant portion of respondents in household surveys cited financial or housing difficulties as well as uncertainty about the future as factors limiting their desired number of children. However, these answers do not always reflect respondents' true preference but are sometimes cited as a socially acceptable explanation for not having children" (United Nations in Russia 2008, 20). Therefore, I turn now to RLMS data to formally test hypotheses by tracing the relationship between changes in people's housing conditions on the one hand, and their reproductive histories on the other.

Statistical Evidence That Housing Matters

The qualitative evidence suggests that housing may delay but does not impede having one child. Housing appears to matter more for deciding whether to have a second child. In this section, I statistically model how housing influences the odds of bearing a second child. Focusing on decisions to have a second child is also advantageous because second children are far more likely to be planned than are first children. This is evidenced by the extremely low rate of birth of a second child outside of marriage, high rates of abortion of unwanted pregnancies, especially at parities higher than one, and interviewees' discourses about their decision-making processes for first versus second children. Of course, even "planned" pregnancies involve a complex series of decisions, and discourses may reflect post hoc rationalization rather than thinking at the time. My aim in this section is to test whether available survey evidence, despite its limitations, is at least consistent with the hypothesis that housing influences childbearing decisions.[3]

RLMS data can be used to formally test the following hypotheses. First, I expect that women who have a separate apartment—that is, a home that they own and occupy only with the nuclear family—are more likely to have a second child. Second, more spacious housing will increase the odds of having a second child. Specifically, having separate rooms for parents and children or better yet, a separate room for each child as well as for the parents, will be associated with childbearing.

The effects of housing tenure and housing space may be interactive rather than additive. The effect of a separate apartment may vanish if that apartment is a studio with only one room. And extra rooms may not influence people who are living with extended family. Therefore, I expect having a multiroom, separate apartment to dramatically raise the probability of having a second child.

All of these factors could matter more for women with higher education. Qualitative evidence suggests that highly educated women particularly crave a separate apartment and separate bedrooms for each child. If such housing conditions are truly a priority for educated women, they are likely to restrict their fertility until they have achieved this goal.

Figure 7.2 depicts the strong correlation between housing conditions and childbearing in Russia in 2009. The graph shows the percentage of women age twenty-one to forty having zero, one, or two or more children, compared by their housing conditions and their level of education. Housing tenure and housing space are cross-classified into four categories, based on whether or not the person owned a separate apartment and lived only with the nuclear family (own versus not own), and whether or not the apartment had more than two rooms (big versus small). Higher education is defined as those who either have a college degree or are currently enrolled in college (this latter group is included to avoid confounding educational attainment with age).

People with their own, large apartments were about twice as likely to have two children as were others. About half of women had two children if they had their own apartment with three or more rooms, regardless of level of education, and nearly all had at least one child. The difference by education level in the correlation between housing conditions and the tendency to be childless is striking. Educated respondents without their own apartments were far more likely to have no children, regardless of size. Although the difference by education in the correlation between housing conditions and having a second child is less dramatic, it is still statistically significant.

This snapshot of correlations in one year tells us little, however, about the causal relationship between housing and the number of children. The apparent difference in having one child by education is likely a tempo effect: most women with higher education eventually have a child, but they wait longer. Furthermore, this delay could be driven by waiting to complete school, instead of by waiting for a separate apartment. Regarding having a second child, the direction of causation is unclear. People might move to independent housing or a more spacious apartment because they have already decided to have a second child. These patterns also do not control for potentially confounding variables such as age, income, and marital status.

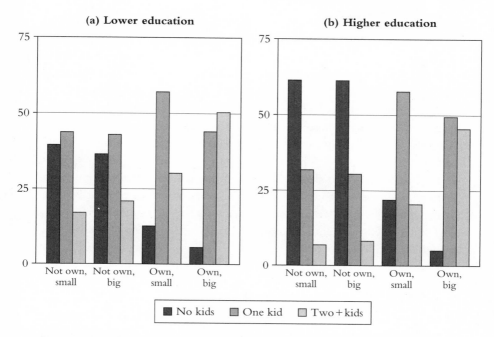

FIGURE 7.2   Number of children by housing type and education, women age 21 to 40 in 2009.
Source: Data from RLMS 2009 urban cross-section.
Note: Own nuclear family with secure property rights. Small one or two rooms; large three or more rooms.

Measurement and Modeling Strategy

To test hypotheses in multivariate models leveraging longitudinal data, I conducted an event history analysis of the odds of having a second child. The technique is the same as that used in chapter 4, but this time housing conditions are treated as a cause rather than effect. The outcome of interest is birth of a second child. The unit of analysis is the "person-period": each spell during which each individual is "at risk" of having a second child. I define the risk set as including urban women between eighteen and forty years of age who already have one child and are married or cohabiting with a partner. I exclude women without partners because Russian women rarely have more than one child while single (Perelli-Harris 2006).[4] I also exclude men from the statistical analysis, as is standard practice in demographic research, because attributes of couples are highly correlated, and women are ultimately the ones who bear children.[5] Finally, I drop renters from the analysis due to small sample size and likely endogeneity (renters are market participants and are more likely to have acquired housing because they had decided to have a second child).[6]

To define the "event" that comprises the dependent variable, I subtract eight months from the date of birth, so that the model measures the effect of housing conditions (and other covariates) at the time of the likely decision to go through with a pregnancy (Whittington et al. 1990; Perelli-Harris and Gerber 2011). Therefore, the dependent variable is whether a woman becomes pregnant with her second child during any observation year (that is, a child whom she later bears, so this excludes terminated pregnancies).

After adjusting for missing data, 1,489 women were observed with one child and a partner/spouse at some point between 2000 and 2008, and so were eligible for analysis of the probability of a subsequent birth by the end of the study in 2009.[7] Of these, 16 percent experienced the event of interest, that is, had a second child, 32 percent dropped out for unknown reasons, 8 percent turned forty without having a second child, 14 percent became divorced or widowed (without remarriage by age forty) before having a second child, and 30 percent had not had a second child by 2009, the last year for which data were available.

I use two criteria to measure housing conditions relevant for birth of a second child. The first is the measure of "housing autonomy" developed in chapter 4: living only with nuclear family members (alone or with a partner and/or minor children) and having secure property rights. My second measure of housing quality is number of rooms. Many other studies treat housing space as a continuous variable, measured in square meters. However, the number of rooms better captures how Russians conceptualize housing space in relationship to the actual or desired size of the family. Recall that when Russians speak of a "one-room" versus a "two-room" apartment, they are counting the total number of rooms, excluding auxiliary space such as kitchens and bathrooms, not the number of bedrooms, as is typical in the United States. As of 2002, 23 percent of Russian homes had only one room, 41 percent had two rooms, 29 percent had three rooms, and 7 percent had four or more rooms. Newly constructed flats tend to be bigger; 50 percent of apartments constructed in 2001 had three or more rooms (UNECE 2004, 33–34). The models also control for time elapsed since the first child was born, respondent's age, respondent's education, household income, and employment status of both respondents and their partners.[8]

Results of the Event History Analysis for the Odds of Having a Second Child

Table 7.1 compares results for models run separately on women with and without higher education,[9] to see whether the relationship between housing and reproduction varies by education. Housing status has been transformed into a five category variable to aid interpretation of the interaction between housing tenure—whether the woman was living with extended family or had her own home—and number of rooms—whether the woman's housing sufficed to have a separate room for children. For women living only with the nuclear family, I also distinguished between those who had one versus two separate rooms for children (having more than one additional room for children while living with extended family was rare and so not distinguished here).

The groups differ on several key coefficients. Among those living with extended family, having a separate room for children nearly doubled the odds of having a second child for those without higher education, but had no significant association with childbearing decisions for respondents with higher education. The only housing circumstance that significantly increased the odds of a woman with higher education to have a second child was possessing her own apartment with at least three rooms (so that there could be a separate room for each child). This arrangement was also associated with higher odds for women with lower education (p <. 10). A small apartment of only one or two rooms did not significantly increase the odds of having a second child.

In short, having more space for separate children's rooms while living with extended family apparently only has an effect for less educated women, while space matters to all women with their own apartments. How should we interpret this finding? As chapter 4 demonstrated, educated young Russians place a higher value on housing autonomy, but because of economic constraint they are not more likely to achieve it. They are also more likely to say that each child

Table 7.1　Event history analysis of birth of a second child, by education

	Lower Education		Higher Education	
Tenure by space (extfam, no kids' room)	1		1	
Extended family, separate kids' room	**1.75***	(1.19, 2.59)	1.24	(.64, 2.39)
Separate apt., one room	0.70	(.27, 1.81)	0.61	(.26, 1.42)
Separate apt., two rooms	1.00	(.45, 2.2)	1.08	(.53, 2.20)
Separate apt., three rooms	1.92	(.94, 3.94)	**2.19***	(1.05, 4.58)
Years since previous birth	**1.28***	(1.08, 1.52)	**1.42***	(1.08, 1.86)
Years since previous birth squared	**0.985***	(.974, .997)	**0.98***	(.96, .99)
Age group (21–25)	1		1	1
26–30	1.2	(.61, 2.36)	0.9	(.31, 2.43)
31–35	0.8	(.43, 1.6)	0.9	(.32, 2.82)
36–40	0.54	(.17, 1.69)	0.86	(.24, 3.03)
Income quintile (0–20%)	1		1	1
21–40%	0.84	(.47, 1.50)	0.47	(.15, 1.54)
41–60%	0.88	(.47, 1.67)	1.02	(.36, 2.91)
61–80%	0.84	(.46, 1.56)	0.78	(.32, 1.91)
81–100%	**1.97***	(1.02, 3.78)	1.24	(.45, 3.43)
Respondent employed	0.91	(.53, 1.56)	0.82	(.40, 1.71)
N	2,484		1,737	

Note: Entries are odds ratios, with confidence intervals given in parentheses. (★) indicates a coefficient is significant at p <.05. Regional controls were also included in the model.

should have his or her own room. Once they achieve the first goal of having their own apartment, they are likely to settle on having one child—even more likely than those who are still living with extended family if they must all live in one room—unless they have a separate room for each child, that is, at least three rooms total. I speculate that women who have second children while living with the extended family have given up hope on ever getting a separate apartment, at least during their fecund years. Those who have their own apartment, having achieved a key milestone for a "normal" family life, will then set even higher standards for the space needed to expand a family.

The effects of income and employment are also noteworthy. Other things being equal, higher incomes have a weak but positive effect on the chances of having a second child, and employment status does not have a significant effect in either direction. This contradicts Kohler and Kohler's (2002) finding that fertility is a form of insurance or an alternate life strategy for those who are unsuccessful in the labor market.

Low fertility is not just a demographic issue; it is also an issue of social justice. At least in Russia, restricted reproduction appears to be a function of constraint, not preference. Internationally, very low fertility rates are contrary to individuals' preferences. "In expressing higher 'ideal preferences' on average, women are effectively commenting on the nature of the social-institutional setting in which they consider having children. They are saying that, in a different institutional setting, they believe they would have had more children" (McDonald 2006, 485).

It is not natural or inevitable, of course, that a separate apartment for the nuclear family, or a separate room for children, should be requisite for reproduction. People throughout human history have reproduced in materially inferior circumstances to those faced by most Russians. Housing has particular meanings in Russia—of normalcy, autonomy, and stability—that makes it profoundly important for deciding whether and when to have children.

Establishing the link between housing and fertility in Russia, while important for policy evaluation, does not mean that the maternity capital policy will succeed. Ten thousand dollars does not suffice to purchase an apartment without significant additional capital. Most Russians do not qualify for mortgage loans, and even if they do qualify most do not want them due to a strong aversion to long-term debt (see chapter 9). But even if maternity capital will not actually raise the birthrate, the government, by acknowledging frustrated fertility aspirations, would seem to have found a way to achieve another goal of social policy: to enhance the state's legitimacy. Nevertheless many Russians react negatively and cynically to the government's efforts in this direction. The next chapter explains why.

 **C H A P T E R 8**

Children Are Not Capital

Ambivalence about Pronatalist Housing Policies

Housing influences decision making about second births, as chapter 7 demonstrated. How have young Russians reacted to government policies that seek to stimulate birth by investing in the housing sector? Housing-based baby bonuses could potentially influence the birthrate, through two mechanisms. The first mechanism is straightforward: if maternity capital improves housing conditions, and housing conditions determine reproductive behavior, then maternity capital should lead to higher fertility. The second mechanism is political. Russia's fertility decline symbolizes the decline of the nation after socialism. If maternity capital helps to legitimize the transition to a housing market, this could improve women's confidence in the future, which would incline them to have more children. This mechanism was suggested to me by a middle-age woman I interviewed in Kaluga in 2002: "When you walk around the city, you hardly see babies anymore. On a weekend during the Soviet era there would be hundreds of women with babies in city parks, and now there are hardly any. Maybe such women exist, but they stay home because of crime. But probably women just stopped having children. The people have lost confidence in the future, and so they aren't producing the next generation."

Maternity capital is likely to fail on both counts, as either housing policy or a legitimation strategy. As we saw in chapter 3, the value of these certificates as of 2009 was insufficient in most regions to help the average working family purchase an apartment even with a mortgage, let alone buy one out-right (see figure 3.1). This chapter demonstrates that maternity capital has also backfired as a legitimation strategy.[1] Young Russians are well informed about maternity capital. More than 90 percent of both male and female respondents in the Kaluga study had heard of maternity capital, and about two-thirds knew the ruble value of the certificate and were familiar with the restrictions on how it could be used. About one in three personally knew someone who had received a maternity capital certificate, and many others mentioned that they had read about it or heard about it on television. Yet knowledge about the policy did not lead to greater support for government or confidence in the future. To the contrary, reactions to the policy were overwhelmingly critical and cynical. Only about 10 percent of respondents unconditionally supported the policy.

However, the majority of respondents shared three assumptions embedded in the maternity capital policy (see chapter 3 for a review): housing influences inclinations to reproduce (77 percent); the government should try to improve housing conditions so that women will have more children (72 percent); and pronatalist housing incentives should be targeted toward women (95 percent). The policy raised expectations that the government will help to house its citizens, but failed to make housing more affordable. The policy also put the cart before the horse by requiring women to reproduce before offering them any support. Although many respondents said they would have more children if they had better housing, they were offended by this requirement. There is something distasteful about overtly incentivizing birth. As Rosa put it: "Children should not be conceived of as capital."

Critical Economism: Maternity Capital Is Insufficient

Most Russians believe the nation's low birthrate is a serious social problem as well as a syndrome of the postsocialist order. In a 2007 national survey, 80 percent of Russian adults agreed that the birthrate is too low.[2] Like the government, most Russians attribute low birthrates to economic factors. Among survey participants, 83 percent named economic problems and/or poor social guarantees in response to an open-ended question on why birthrates are low in Russia. Few (6 percent) offered cultural explanations—for example, of a shift in values toward career or consumption and away from family. Economic framing of reproduction was also evident in the perception that living standards and birthrates are positively correlated: 55 percent believed, erroneously, that birthrates are higher in countries with higher standards of living.

The broad consensus on the sources of low fertility is congruent with the government's own framing of the issue. In the eyes of the public, the government is correct in its economic diagnosis and cure but has severely underestimated the dose of capital necessary to influence reproductive behavior in a positive direction. Russians are extremely dismissive of a baby bonus whose ruble value exceeds annual average wages. This derision derives from conceptions of what type of housing is needed for a family to "live normally," and from the Soviet legacy of government responsibility for housing, which has been reinforced by the maternity capital initiative.

Interviewees supported the idea that the government can and should incentivize birth. However, they criticized the government for setting up insufficient or improper incentives.[3] I call this discourse on maternity capital "critical economism." In the qualitative interviews, nearly two-thirds of respondents employed economistic discourses in their critiques of the policy. Just 15 percent thought it was not possible to incentivize birth, and 12 percent said this approach was immoral (the distribution of responses on this question was similar for men and women).

Roxana, a twenty-six-year-old midwife who was renting a room in a workers' hostel, employed the critical economism discourse in the following passage:

ROXANA: Maternity capital is a good idea, but it's been poorly implemented. The money is ethereal. People who would like to have a second child think twice when they find out about the conditions placed on maternity capital. It's very limited and difficult to use, and the amount isn't even enough for a down payment. If they would have given us 600 or 700 thousand rubles down, and the rest via a subsidized mortgage, then renters could afford to buy their own homes. And then of course they would have more children without any problem.

INTERVIEWER: Do you think maternity capital will affect the birthrate?

ROXANA: Well, some people have children out of stupidity. I hear about it at work. Women will say, "Now there is maternity capital." But then when they deal with the details, they come back and say, "Oh we were wrong to think it would help."

This example contains the core elements of the critical economism discourse: maternity capital is insufficient, difficult to use, and improperly incentivizes birth.

Critiques began with the ruble value of the certificates. The sum of 250,000 (or 300,000 after inflation indexing), the largest baby bonus in the

world relative to income, was deemed "miserly," "insulting," "pointless," and
"absurd." In evaluating the program, respondents most often compared the
amount to the total cost of raising a child, of buying an apartment, or both.
Several said it would only suffice to buy diapers. And many pointed out that,
at least in urban central Russia, it was not enough to buy an apartment, and
indeed not even enough to upgrade from a two- to a three-room apartment.
Some respondents did not expect the program to affect the birthrate precisely
because it did not make housing more affordable—implying that had the
amount been greater, it would have had effects. Vera explained her reasoning:
"It will not affect the birthrate. Personally, when I heard about the program,
I did not suddenly have a desire to give birth to a second child. Because it's
very little money with which to buy an apartment." Vera reluctantly took out
a mortgage after an unplanned second pregnancy (one of only three respondents with two children who said the second was unplanned). She hoped to
use her maternity capital certificate to pay down some of her mortgage, but
insisted it was not a deciding factor either for getting a mortgage or for going
through with the pregnancy.

Maternity Capitalism as a Scam

The mismatch between the amount of maternity capital and the full cost of
housing led many respondents to conclude that the government was making false promises so as to trick women into having children. Said Anastasia, a twenty-three-year-old sales clerk with one child: "We're prepared to
have more children, but the government needs to create realistic conditions.
Maternity capital provides no practical motivation to have a second child.
They want us to have more children and take out mortgages, but if you consider the actual cost of raising a child and paying for a mortgage, then you
realize it's a scam."

About half of respondents equated maternity capital to a scam or even a
conspiracy. Margarita called maternity capital "virtual money" and "hog-
wash." She speculated that the government was holding onto the money as a
money-laundering scheme, so that inflation would eat its value and corrupt
officials could pocket the difference. Many others were skeptical that inflation indexing would preserve the value. Furthermore, the bureaucratic process involved in converting the certificate into real resources was so complex
as to make the policy seem "ephemeral" (Olga) or "unreal" (Georgy). As
Galina put it: "Maternity capital is dead capital."

Not everyone impugned malign motives to the programs' design-
ers. Several described the program as "pleasant" but ineffective. Lyuba,

a divorcee with a child and a one-room apartment, said, "I don't think it will influence the birth of second children. Maternity capital—it would be very pleasant to receive it, if they give it out. But I'm not going to have a second child knowing that's how I'm supposed to improve my housing conditions."

Many critical respondents suggested that the program could raise the birthrate if only it were more generous. Suggestions included increasing the amount, indexing it to the cost of housing, distributing it in cash, and providing it for first as well as second children. In this discourse, the government's economic diagnosis and cure are correct in principle; only the implementation is problematic. This is consistent with findings from survey research as well. Most Russians, feeling that the birthrate is too low, agreed that the government should try to do something about it (85 percent in a 2007 FOM survey). One-third agreed that income subsidies for mothers and families with children would be sufficient to raise the birthrate. Among the 55 percent who disagreed, most proposed additional policies that are still economic in nature: 29 percent suggested housing subsidies (e.g., "free housing immediately after the birth of a child"), 25 percent highlighted the need for better employment opportunities and higher wages, and 20 percent mentioned the cost and quality of healthcare, childcare, and education.

Even the most approving respondents in Kaluga became more critical of the policy when speaking of their personal situations. Zina, a single student living with her parents, echoed official discourse when she described the maternity capital policy. "It's a really useful, needed measure. It's helping to improve the nation's demographic situation. It provides a foundation for having a child, by enabling recipients either to provide an apartment for the child in the future, or to save up for the child's education. In principle it's helping women to become bolder with respect to having a second child. Some kind of certainty is emerging. One senses the support of the government." However, she switched to critical economism when asked about her own plans. For her personally, maternity capital would not have an effect, she claimed, because it is not enough. "I'd need to be certain that I could afford a home for my child. It's not possible to buy housing with the money they are offering. A down payment is insufficient. I would need enough to buy an apartment outright."

Many respondents referred to their own circumstances when discussing whether maternity capital would raise the birthrate. Nearly half of respondents also generalized from their own situations to the policy issue earlier in the interview, before questions about maternity capital or the birthrate were asked. This tendency was more pronounced among respondents with higher education (56 percent versus 24 percent of those with lower education). Out of the cases who did so, nearly all related both personal and national reproductive trends to economic constraint. For example, Natasha, a renter and recent college graduate, said she would surely have one child, but the second would depend on whether she and her fiancé could buy an apartment. She then switched to talking about demographic trends in Russia. "Everyone I know is either waiting to have children or has had only one so far. In Russia in the past many people my age already had two or three children. But now people are more pragmatic because they have to buy housing themselves. They wait to have children until they can provide for them, or they have a maximum of one. They plan to have more children only if their housing prospects improve or both spouses attain stable incomes."

This discourse contradicts a study of discourses on fertility in Russia by Ken Roberts and collaborators (2003). They find that educated and affluent individuals are more optimistic when talking about their own lives and prospects than when talking about the country in general. The authors conclude that falling birthrates are a function of "young adults' lifestyle options and choices—new options and choices in some cases—rather than economic and housing conditions *per se*" (71). I did not find this to be the case. Instead, talk about gloomy personal prospects prompted discussion of the macrosituation, especially among highly educated respondents. Restricting reproduction, especially with regard to a second child, was framed as a form of self-control in the face of constraint, as opposed to people who, in a common turn of phrase, "reproduce without thinking." This discourse provides a strategy for respondents with aspirations to a middle-class identity to distinguish themselves from others and is especially common among those with higher education but low incomes and wealth, that is, what Pierre Bourdieu would call high cultural capital and low economic capital.

Maternity Capital Will Affect Other Mothers

Despite criticizing maternity capital as insufficient and ineffective, about half of interviewees in Kaluga thought the policy was having at least modest effects on the birthrate. In the FOM 2007 national survey as well, about half expected maternity capital to boost the birthrate. Very few respondents, however, suggested that maternity capital would be the deciding factor for their own reproductive plans (5 percent of women and 10 percent of men). In discussing the potential effects of maternity capital on reproductive behavior, respondents distinguished themselves from others along two lines: economic and moral.

Economic Distancing

Many respondents with limited resources, especially those who did not own apartments, expected effects to be limited to people who were already well to do. Maternity capital, they argued, would only help families with the wealth or income to convert the capital into more housing space. Raisa, a renter, said maternity capital could be useful to someone who already had an apartment. For example, someone who had inherited a one-room apartment could upgrade to a two-room apartment, with the help of maternity capital and a small loan. Anastasia, who was living with her parents, also viewed maternity capital as helping people better off than her. "Maternity capital will have no effect on me because I don't have an apartment to trade up. I own nothing. I have no starting capital. I think it might only affect someone who is almost in a position to get a mortgage, because even though it's not a lot of money, it's a significant amount for topping off a down payment."

Nika felt that maternity capital could help "normal" families, but would not help her as a single mother without property of her own. "I think that it's affecting the birthrate by helping to increase living space. Many families, including normal families that are more or less well to do, have a second or third kid so as to increase their living space. I saw several stories on television about mothers who are thanking the government. Thanks to maternity capital, they have their own apartments."

Others pointed out that maternity capital could have significant effects in small towns and rural areas farther from Moscow, where the cost of housing is much cheaper. Such respondents also implicitly accepted the fundamental premise of maternity capital—that birth can be incentivized via housing subsidies, as long as subsidies are adequate relative to housing prices.

Moral Distancing

Despite complaints that maternity capital is inadequate, many respondents asserted the paltry amount would still influence reproduction among the poor. In arguing that maternity capital would influence others but not themselves, respondents distanced themselves from what they considered to be lower classes, based on income, intelligence, or morality. In this discourse, only fools would be influenced by maternity capital, as opposed to people who, in Dmitri's words, are "intelligent," "capable of calculating the true costs of having a child," and "realistically understand the situation in the country." Marianna, who inherited an apartment, said poor people are especially vulnerable to the false promise of money.

MARIANNA: After the birth of a second child they give you some money, and they index it to inflation. Now it's about 300,000 rubles. But what the heck is 300,000? It's a pointless joke. As a result the people who suffer from poverty and need money will give birth, and such people will unfortunately produce the next generation.

INTERVIEWER: Do you know anyone personally who decided to have a child after finding out about the program?

MARIANNA: I don't have such acquaintances, but I have heard such stories about people who did. They didn't understand the details and thought they could cash in immediately. And it had a very negative result.

INTERVIEWER: Do you think it will affect the birthrate somehow?

MARIANNA: I think not, of course, among people who are capable of thinking first before deciding to have children.

Irina seemingly approved of the measure: "At first no one believed that they would follow through and give out such a large sum of money. But at last the government is having some good ideas." But when asked if it would influence the birthrate, she also contrasted the desperation of the poor with the sobriety of the middle class. "Unfortunately, I think it will mainly encourage the poorest of the poor to breed. Those who are in a hurry to get that money. It won't influence normal, well-off, middle-class people. I heard on television that all kinds of homeless people and drug addicts are starting to have children, because for them this money is significant." Likewise, Evgeny expected that some greedy people would give birth just to get the money, which would lead to "undesirable outcomes." Vadim was more direct about the negative effects: "Quantity is not quality. It will increase the birthrate among idiots, leading to depletion of the nation's gene pool."

An Immoral Incentive

In contrasting "normal" versus "abnormal" rationales for reproducing, a minority of respondents (about 12 percent) rejected the entire premise that the government should try to incentivize birth. They were not opposed to helping needy people with children, but they disapproved of encouraging people to think of children as an investment. Svetlana, divorced and living with her parents and child, said:

Maternity capital is an unpleasant concept. In addition to financial questions, one needs to consider the moral issues. I'm probably a bit old-fashioned in this regard. I don't think of children as a source of income. A child is a relative whom you love. Concerning effects on the birthrate, it all depends on the person. There are some people who might have a second child and then discard him, just to use him as a source of capital.

Birth incentives were morally problematic during the Soviet period as well. In the novella *A Week Like Any Other,* a group of female co-workers was asked to fill out a survey on time use and work-life balance. One claimed, ironically, that the authorities were not meeting their "production norms" for childbearing. One woman remarked, "Maybe there would be more results if they took a more practical approach. In France the government pays mothers for each child. Probably that would be better then all these surveys." Another exclaimed, "Pay? Like on a pig farm? You don't see a difference between pigs and people?" Said another, "Anyway, in France, there is capitalism" (Baranskaya 1989, 19).

Although birth incentives existed in the Soviet Union, the metaphor of "maternity capital" reinforces the notion that incentivizing birth is a specifically capitalist phenomenon. Maternity capital, like capitalism, brings out the worst in people, according to Polina: "Before, people had children because they wanted them, not as a source of income. Now people are starting to think of them as a way to earn money, and increasing the birthrate in that way of course produces negative moral tendencies."

Likewise Ludmila equated maternity capital to the moral degradation of consumerism. She claimed that when she was pregnant, she witnessed multiple women leaving the obstetrician's office to get an abortion as soon as the doctor told them they couldn't get the money for three years. "They decided to get pregnant without thinking it through. They thought, I'll get maternity capital and buy myself a car or go shopping. These were forty-year-old women, who already had children and suddenly decided to have a second or third because of the money." This story strains credulity, but is indicative of a broader moral panic over reproduction in Russian society. Ludmila still supported material support for mothers, but not as a birth incentive. "Help for mothers shouldn't be presented as a 'stimulus' for reproduction. It should help children who already exist and are in need. What difference does it make if they were born before 2007? There are families with four children living in one or two-room apartments. But no one helps them."

Others advocated reversing the causal flow of the logic of maternity capital: people should become interested in maternity capital when they decide to have as second child, and not the other way around. Kira, a married renter with one child, said of maternity capital: "I haven't looked into it. As soon as

I decide to have a second child, I'll find out more. One should not play with the life of a child over money. I'd rather be oriented toward the long-term future than receive that small change. That's not to say the government can't help. But some people will not use this aid for their children, but will use their children to get the money." Conditioning housing on having a child is, in the views of many Russians, an immoral policy as well as an abnormal logic for personal decisions about reproduction. "Give me an apartment," said Raisa, "and then maybe I'll think about having another child. I shouldn't have to have children before I can get help buying an apartment. It's wrong to think of children as a source of so-called capital."

We Need a Normal Country

The comparative demographic literature is pessimistic about the ability of governments to stimulate reproduction via economic incentives (the literature has little to say specifically about the effects of housing incentives). The track record for "baby bonuses" akin to Russia's maternity capital is particularly poor. Demographer Anne Gauthier, in concluding that economic incentives for reproduction do not work, states: "Popularity of baby-bonus schemes among governments is difficult to understand" (Balter 2006).

Russia's pronatalist policies are comprehensible if we understand economic rationality as a discourse and ideology, rather than a neutral scientific yardstick by which policies should be evaluated. Maternity capital's most important effects are in the field of politics, not demography. Gail Lapidus, writing about pronatalist measures in the 1970s under Brezhnev, predicted a discursive rather than practical effect: "Taken by themselves, these measures are too limited to have a substantial impact on current patterns of female employment or reproductive behavior. They are significant, rather, as indications of the high priority that the Soviet leadership has begun to attach to demographic and family policy" (1982, xxxix). The same could be said today.

The notion that people reproduce according to an economic calculus is attractive to governments like Russia's that recently converted to capitalism. What in the Soviet period was in public policy called "the human factor" is now termed "human capital." Women's bodies become a material input into the development of the nation's stock of human capital, and women's psyches the object of maternity capital as a birth incentive. The policy aims not simply to raise the birthrate, but to raise the state's legitimacy by framing reproduction as nation building in a market economy.

In a 2007 survey, more than half of respondents (56 percent) agreed that in principle it would be possible to raise the birthrate in Russia, while 20 percent disagreed and 25 percent said they did not know. Qualitative evidence however demonstrates that skepticism runs more deeply than this survey result suggests. Statements made during focus groups in several provincial cities in 2006–7, as well as the Kaluga interviews in 2009, indicate widespread doubt about the intentions and competence of government: "The leadership of the country are same people who got us into this catastrophic situation—they will not be able to take us out of it." "None of these programs will work because they will not bring stability to the country." "How are we supposed to reproduce on this maternal capital—when there is no normal healthcare, no normal education, in general nothing is normal in this country!"

Most respondents, both male and female, supported the policy's focus on helping women. We asked men an additional question about how they felt about the government's decision to allocate maternity capital to mothers and not to fathers or to both parents. All but two men in the sample (one of whom was recently divorced, the other of whom is a self-described feminist) supported the idea. Most either said that it's "natural" that women receive it because they are the primary caregivers, or that it's fair because women are more economically vulnerable if they take time off from work to have children, or following divorce. However, this had no bearing on their overall approval (or, in most cases) disapproval of the policy for all of the reasons enumerated in previous sections. Men and women's discourses in this regard were remarkably similar.

In social marketing advertisements, the Russian government has tried to appeal to Russians' sense of patriotism to encourage them to have more children. The economism discourse, however, resonates far more with Russians than does the civic-nationalist slogan that "Russia needs you to set records" (see chapter 3). Notably absent from the interview transcripts are references to reproduction as a patriotic action or duty. This is not because Russians are unpatriotic in general: in a 2007 national survey, 85 percent of Russians age eighteen to thirty-five described themselves as patriots. The few references in the interviews to the government's attempts to frame birth as patriotic were ironic and cynical. For example, Martha, a single mother living with her own mother, recalled that when she heard about maternity capital, she joked with a friend: "Wow, 250,000 rubles, let's get pregnant and go buy ourselves fur coats! The policy was clearly thought up by idiots. You can't do anything with this capital in reality. And they blame us that the birthrate has gone down. Come on girls, let's go, reproduce! Set a demographic record for Russia! It's a national pyramid scam."

The cynicism and distrust in government across the interviews is striking. Why are Russians so critical of a comparatively generous baby bonus?

Much of the frustration with the policy has to do with what it provides as a concrete resource. But popular discontent suggests a deeper legitimacy issue. Russians simply do not trust the government to have the competence or will to create the conditions they feel that they need to provide a normal life for their children. At the same time, they feel that it is the government's responsibility to do so.

After a decade of retrenchment of the welfare state, maternity capital has once again opened the door to raised expectations of what the government can and should do for the people. Yet Russians are primed to expect the government to disappoint them. Maternity capital has crystallized these tendencies, such that the policy is seen as both an economic and a moral perversion. The metaphor of capital also has a peculiar resonance in the post-Soviet context. Respondents in interviews were quick to distance themselves from it, saying things like "I'm not the type who would have a child simply to get some money." These women crave a sense of possibility and stability in the basic economic resources needed to have children: housing and income. But the government's overt attempt to "incentivize birth" is morally distasteful.

Maternity capital, in undermining the government's legitimacy, has also backfired as a civic-nationalist project. Talk about Russia as a nation throughout the interviews is overwhelmingly critical. The nation is referred to as "a difficult country," "an unstable place," "uncivilized," "wild," and "inhospitable to families." Rather than viewing reproduction as a means to build the nation, young Russians suggest that the government needs to build a nation in which people will want to reproduce. As Flora put it:

> The maternity capital policy is unjust. Of course, they are clever and cunning in how they try to motivate people to increase the birthrate. But I think that it should not depend on the quantity of capital. Instead of trying to stimulate people with this money, the government should simply create the conditions under which people will want to have children. Give us fair salaries, give us stability, and people will have children without this so-called capital.

 CHAPTER 9

To Owe Is Not to Own
Why Russians Reject Mortgages

Most analysts attribute mortgage market failure in Russia to material conditions: high interest rates, high housing prices, an unstable currency, and macroeconomic instability. This chapter analyzes a critical but little-studied factor that undermined the emergence of the market: the lack of consumer demand for mortgages. This is not to deny the significance of supply constraints: most Russians as of 2009 would not have qualified for a mortgage even if they had wanted one (see chapters 2 and 3). Yet the problem was not simply one of tightened supply, as credit crises are usually understood. Credit can only flow if potential borrowers want it. Most Russians would not have wanted a mortgage even if they could have qualified for one.

President Putin in 2003 pointed to the demand side of the problem:

Mortgage loans must become not only accessible but also habitual, operating as the norm and not as an exception. Assessments vary, but most experts believe that many families with stable incomes can afford to take out a mortgage loan, provided of course, that incomes grow steadily.... I think you would agree with me that so far the word "mortgage" mystifies our citizens. We must... explain the substance of this procedure, the essence of this mechanism. It is necessary that people come to believe that it can be used to solve the acute problem of housing.[1]

The state's efforts to promote mortgages successfully explained them but failed to generate belief in them. In 2000 only 7 percent of surveyed Russians said they knew what a mortgage was, 21 percent had heard the word but were not sure what it meant, and over 70 percent had never even heard the word or had difficulty answering the question. By 2006, 38 percent of surveyed Russians said they knew what a mortgage was, and another 38 percent had at least heard of it. Yet by 2007, just 3 percent of Russians had home loans. Only 22 percent said they would consider a mortgage if they needed housing; that proportion shrank to 9 percent in 2009. Among eighteen- to thirty-five-year-olds, only 25 percent in 2008 said they would consider a mortgage if they were planning to purchase a home (FOM 2006a, 2008, 2009a).

Low demand for mortgages is striking given high unmet demand for housing. More than half of urban Russians age twenty-one to thirty-five were living with extended family in 2009. The quest for a separate apartment preoccupied young Russians in the Kaluga study, as most believed one was necessary for a normal family life. Most also indicated low expectations of concrete help from the government. Why, then, have not more Russians turned to mortgages to solve the housing question?

This deep aversion to mortgages is evident in the primary metaphor that Russians use to describe them: they are called *kabala,* which means "debt bondage." A crude cultural explanation might attribute this disposition to premodern objections to usury, or to general hostility toward foreign financial instruments. Such explanations fall short, both theoretically and empirically. Russians do not object to all forms of interest payment. As Alya Guseva (2008) shows, Russians quickly adopted credit cards when they were offered on terms that resonated with post-Soviet understandings of fairness and trustworthiness. Nor do they object to home loans in general: *rassrochka* investment schemes, in which consumers coinvest with builders in a property in exchange for deferred payment at a discounted price, have proven quite popular, if risky.

I argue that Russians reject mortgages due to conceptions of ownership, risk, and fairness that developed in the crucible of postsocialist transition. The locus of three major financial crises in two decades, Russia gives both banks and borrowers good reason to be skeptical of long-term loans. But low demand for mortgages is only partially about risk; it also derives from Russians' sense that mortgaged homes are not owned, and that secure housing should be a right, not a gamble.

The conditions of postsocialist crisis invert the cultural logic that has legitimized mortgages in the United States, at least until recently. American mortgagors consider themselves homeowners, but Russians insist that the bank owns the home. Whereas in the United States borrowing to buy a home is seen as a virtuous investment compared to credit cards, in Russia a mortgage entails unconscionable hubris on the part of both the borrower and the bank, while small-scale credit is considered banal. And while to Americans, decades worth of interest payments are take for granted as a cost of ownership, Russians, by contrast, are outraged by the prospect of paying many times over for the deferred promise of owning a home—a good they consider a basic right.

Mortgages as a Cultural Transplant

The theory of the "transplant effect" posits that laws must be locally meaningful to be effective (Berkowitz et al. 2003). Mortgage law in Russia presents a clear case of legal transplant effects, as Yulia Guseva (2009) demonstrates in her study of Russian mortgage legislation and case law. In this chapter I broaden the concept of transplant beyond the law to consider the cultural meanings that support a mortgage system. Though American mortgage institutions were formally transplanted to Russia, they neither have been fully institutionalized nor acquired a "taken for granted and routine character" (Stryker 2000). A mismatch between foreign institutions and local understandings of ownership and property rights has impeded markets and undermined the legitimacy of housing policy.

To fully understand the cultural dimension of the transplant effect, we must first understand the culture that proponents of housing markets, American style, tried to transplant. What did mortgages mean to Americans prior to the recent subprime crisis? Unfortunately cultural studies of American mortgages are sparse. I triangulate across a variety of studies of culture and credit (not necessarily focused on the United States) to posit a theory of the core consumer beliefs that sustain demand in established mortgage markets. This theory is supported by comparison with the Russian case: Russians reject each of the beliefs about mortgages that Americans take for granted.

Most Americans believe that ownership begins at the moment they receive the keys to their mortgaged homes. Keys, for example, symbolize a happy ending in the reality television show *My First Place*. A buyer in one episode exclaims on opening his front door with his new key: "It's like we're opening up our future here. . . . Now we're homeowners and we know this is ours and no one can take it from us."[2] Scholarly and policy discourse also equate debt with ownership. Studies of housing mobility routinely define the transition to homeownership in terms of entry into a mortgage contract. Federally subsidized refinancing programs are called "Help for

America's Homeowners," a discourse that depicts foreclosure as the loss of something previously owned.[3]

Legally, a mortgagor does own the property, but it is not true that no one can take it away. A mortgage is a lien on a home's title as security for the loan. The borrower is also the owner as the holder of title. The lien, however, gives the lender the right to repossess the home in case the borrower breaches the mortgage contract.[4] Practically speaking, a lien makes ownership status ambiguous. The home buyer's practical sense of ownership requires misrecognizing this conditionality. By "misrecognition," I do not mean that borrowers are ontologically wrong. I borrow this concept from Pierre Bourdieu's theory of symbolic power, which he defines as the capacity of dominant groups to impose "the definition of the social world that is best suited to their interests" (1991, 167). The cognitive foregrounding of ownership over debt buttresses mortgage-based housing systems.

In the book *Credit Card Nation,* Robert Manning explains how Americans came to take debt for granted. He attributes the spectacular rise in consumer debt to "the erosion of the traditional 'cognitive connect,' or fiscal equilibrium between household income and consumption decisions. This behavioral calculus defines an individual's or household's standard of living based on *present* income (total earnings) and *future* (expected/unexpected) expenses.... [In the credit card nation] Americans' consumption patterns tend to be influenced by their perception of future economic conditions...rather than by current trends—even during periods of declining real wages or economic difficulty" (2000, 105–6, 127).

Though mortgages epitomize consumption today based on projections about the future, Manning says little about mortgages in his book on debt-fueled consumption. This omission reflects the extraordinary legitimacy that mortgages hold as a form of virtuous debt in the West. As two French economists note in their history of consumer credit: "Housing loans...are dignified by the wholesome utility of dwellings. Consumer purchases are seen as superfluous expenditure.... Property loans are the only loans which are spared this moral stigma" (Gelpi and Julien-Labruyere 2000, xi). The rise of home equity loans and refinancing also normalized housing debt by transforming the idea of a home from purely a dwelling into an investment. The expectation of rising prices and refinancing opportunities enabled subprime lending—a market of staggering risk—to appear rational and even virtuous (Smith et al. 2002; Jarvis 2008; Langley 2008; Cook et al. 2009).

The self-amortizing loan transforms interest payments into a taken-for-granted cost of homeownership. I view self-amortization as a case of the "purification" of money "to rub off the stigma adhering to money obtained through morally condemned activities" (Carruthers and Ariovich 2010, 64). The rise of consumer credit nearly erased the moral stigma on usury. However, charging interest can still seem immoral if the rate or amount is seen as excessive. The concepts of special monies and monetary taboos are helpful here. Interest is a special kind of money, which must be justified both by the consumer (is it wasteful? Is it worth it?) and also for the domain (is it proper to charge interest for purchase of a basic right?). A self-amortizing loan draws cognitive attention to the total monthly cost rather than to the amount of interest paid, because payments are held constant over the life of the loan, while the ratio of principal to interest in each monthly payment gradually increases over time. Although consumers can see the breakdown in their monthly payments, consistent payment amounts over a thirty-year period blur the distinction between principal and interest.

The virtue of housing debt was born of necessity in weak welfare states. Homeownership rates are highest where social spending is low, providing households with a source of security in old age (Conley and Gifford 2006). Because the cost of housing far exceeds annual incomes, young families without inheritances that wish to own a home must borrow. In the United States, low-income homeownership was achieved by deregulating access to mortgages rather than by subsidizing low-income households. The moral valence of mortgages thus helped legitimize state retrenchment from the housing sector.

In sum, the following beliefs buttress the American mortgage economy. First, consumers equate mortgages with ownership. This sense of ownership is enabled by the "cognitive disconnect" that calibrates present consumption to optimistic projections about future income and housing values. Second, mortgage debt is perceived as more virtuous than other types of consumer credit. And third, borrowing to buy homes is regarded as a reasonable alternative to state-subsidized housing.

Mortgages as Debt Bondage

As we saw in chapters 2 and 3, the Russian government sought to normalize mortgages as it transplanted the American model of housing markets. Yet Russians view mortgages as both risky and immoral. The most common metaphor for mortgages in the Kaluga interviews was the term *kabala*. More commonly known in English for its association with Jewish mysticism, the word in Hebrew also means receipt for a payment. The term developed negative and anti-Semitic connotations in Russia during the Imperial era in association with Jewish moneylending. The phrase *dolgovaia kabala* is the translation of the term *debt bondage* in the USSR's ratification of the United Nations 1956 Supplementary Convention on the Abolition of Slavery, which defines debt bondage as "the status or condition arising from a pledge by a debtor of his personal services or of those of a person under his control as security for a debt, if the value of those services as reasonably assessed is not applied towards the liquidation of the debt or the length and nature of those services are not respectively limited and defined."[5]

The following examples illustrate contemporary usage of the term kabala to describe mortgages.

> What is a mortgage? It is a kabala. It is to enter into slavery for thirty-three years, with the bank as your master. The bank, by charging interest, is earning money on the backs of human beings.—Alexei, thirty-year-old civil servant, married with one child, owner

> It's not realistic for us to get our own home. To enter into a kabala for twenty-five years by taking out a mortgage, when it's not clear what will happen in two years. Today I'm married, tomorrow is unknown. Who knows if I'll even be alive in five years. I can't hang a kabala on my child. What would happen if I paid off only half and then something happened to me? They'd take away the apartment, and they'd take away the comfortable childhood that I could have given him if I hadn't had to pay that debt. I can't hang a kabala on my child. It's abnormal.—Ludmila, twenty-six year-old accountant, married with one child, living with parents

> A mortgage is a kabala. There must be better options than to believe in the "radiant future," but to constantly worry that that at any moment, even tomorrow, you could have problems at work, your salary could go down. And then what will you do? Will the laws change tomorrow? Will interest rates change tomorrow? It only adds anxiety to one's life, nothing more.—Vadim, thirty-three-year-old civil servant, single, renter

> Mortgages in our country are a kabala. Our mortgage system is so underdeveloped and perverse, that a family who takes one on thinking they are simply taking out a housing loan has unwittingly entered into a lifelong kabala. One fine day he may not be able to pay, but he must pay. The bank will collect its interest even if it means you will have nothing left to eat, even if you have children. But we are constantly in crisis in this country, so people lose their jobs and can't pay. In the end the bank, which has risked nothing because it owns the mortgaged home, will take it away. A bailiff will come and say, "Goodbye, vacate

your housing space, you're not in a position to pay."—Klara, thirty-year-old journalist, married with one child, owner

Thirty percent of respondents in the Kaluga interview study used the term *kabala* spontaneously (interviewers did not suggest it). Although interviewees with mortgages did not use the term, eight of fifteen described their mortgages using related terms such as *shackle, yoke, slavery,* or *burden*—as did 34 percent of all respondents.

Aware of public perceptions, the news media often pose the question of whether mortgages are a kabala in their headlines.[6] A discourse on mortgages as an endless burden existed in the Soviet press as well. For example, lectures to prepare Soviet citizens for the American model home exhibition that was the locus of the famous "Kitchen Debate" between Khrushchev and Nixon in 1959 "stressed the burden of mortgage repayments" (Reid 2008, 893). An article in the newspaper *Pravda* in 1961 reported: "As a rule, [American] workers are not owners of the cars and homes they use; they are merely renters of these things. Credit makes a worker into a perpetual debtor, paying off his debt for his entire life."[7]

The notion of debt bondage arises from uncertainty about the possibility of repayment. Interviewees imagined catastrophic scenarios—from unemployment to sudden death—and worried that the terms, not only of a specific loan but also of the economic system, could change at any moment. The burden of debt overshadowed any sense of ownership.

Owing versus Owning

In established mortgage markets, I have argued, consumers misrecognize debt as outright ownership. Russians see things in the opposite light—they insist that the bank is the true owner, even if the mortgagor holds title. This disposition can be traced to the conceptual distinction between ownership and possession. In the Soviet period, people developed a sense of possession over the apartments they inhabited, describing their residences as "mine" (*svoi*), even though the government was the legal owner. Conversely, being an owner of record (*sobstvennik*) with a mortgage lien does not necessarily provide Russians with a practical sense of possession.

Russians without mortgages typically see borrowers as debtors and regard any sense of ownership as an illusion. Natasha classified mortgagors as closer to renters than owners: "To own a home is the ideal situation. Most of my acquaintances either have a mortgage (*nakhodiat'sia v ipoteke*) and are still working toward owning, or they are renting, or they are living with their parents." The expression "nakhodiat'sia v ipoteke," which translates as "to be situated in a mortgage," suggests a transient state. A renter with no prospect of inheritance, Natasha had looked into mortgages, but was wary.

> In theory, a mortgage is better than renting, because you have the feeling that you are paying for something that is yours, so it's easier to part with the money. But it's complicated. My friend and her husband had a baby and they decided to take out a mortgage and they got a subsidy from the Young Families Program. But still, her entire salary goes to paying the mortgage.
>
> Even if you get a subsidy, you only have yourself to rely on. The subsidies for young families are not insignificant, but they don't guarantee a stable job or sufficient income in the future. A mortgage is an enormous risk under any circumstances. The government doesn't insure your debt. You and not the government pay the interest and sign the contract with the bank. So if something changes for you, you will pay the penalty, and the bank will take away the apartment, which in reality was not yours. Plus they won't even refund the money you already paid.

Economic instability exacerbates Russians' sense of incomplete and uncertain ownership. Svetlana, desperate to move out of her mother's apartment, inquired about the Young Families Program and was disappointed by what she learned. "You have to be prepared to pay for practically the rest of your life. Everyone I know who looked into it ran away when they found out the conditions. Naturally, because the future is unclear. Unfortunately we live in a country where every time it seems that things have stabilized, a crisis appears. People are losing their jobs. And thus those with mortgages are losing homes that they renovated and invested in and mistakenly believed belonged to them."

The fear of instability extends to the banking system as well as to jobs. Raisa, who had also looked into a mortgage, explained why she decided against it:

> We applied for a mortgage, but when we understood it better, we decided that it's a lost cause. Anything could happen, our salaries could be cut, crisis or no crisis, and the situation in our country is inscrutable. Although you have to pay 30,000 rubles a month, in reality you have nothing. You don't even get ownership documents immediately, and if you are late with a payment, the bank will kindly ask you to get out. The amount that you already paid is automatically incinerated. As long as the bank is holding

the ownership papers, it's scary, because anything can happen with banks these days. The bank could suddenly go bankrupt or disappear. And then what? How will you prove to whom the apartment belongs?

The belief that foreclosure means automatic forfeiture of any previous payments, while incorrect, was widespread. Many suggested that their children, and even their grandchildren, would also be responsible for the debt if they could not pay it. Respondents had little conception of equity or the possibility that a mortgaged property could be sold if payments became unaffordable. They also had little faith in insurance. For example Vladimir, who had taken out a mortgage, claimed that insurance companies would always find a way not to pay. "You could be riding a bus and have alcohol in your blood because you had a beer beforehand. And the bus crashes, and you die, and they analyze your blood and deny your family's claim because you died while 'under the influence.'" While this sounds extreme, a study by AHML found that insurance companies go to great lengths to avoid payouts.[8]

Even respondents who were generally favorably disposed toward mortgages usually described ownership as beginning only after the debt is paid off. For example, Ruslan said, "Mortgages can be a normal option. One needs to consider the cost of renting versus a mortgage. I think there are a lot of people who don't have homes but have high incomes and are wasting their money on rent. For that money they could take out a mortgage and eventually receive their own apartment after ten to twenty years. After you pay the loan, you can finally become an owner." Ruslan and his wife were living with her parents, and he craved a home of his own. Nevertheless, when the interviewer asked if he would consider a mortgage for himself, he replied, "The interest rates are too high now, up to 30 percent. I don't want to get into a kabala. If one could get a mortgage for 10 or 11 percent, that might be realistic." In fact, interest rates were 12 to 13 percent at the time of the interview; far closer to his ideal of 10 to 11 percent than his perception of 30 percent. Ruslan's openness to mortgages dissipated when the discussion shifted to his concrete personal plans. By using the kabala metaphor, he effectively declared a mortgage to be out of the question.

My presentation of findings has emphasized the most common discourses on mortgages, rather than variation across socioeconomic groups, among whom I found striking consensus. To further evidence these shared meanings, I document similarities where one would least expect to find them: between those who did and did not have mortgages. Respondents who had taken out a mortgage did not equate their mortgages with homeownership, and rarely defined themselves as property owners. Three corrected interviewers who referred to mortgaged apartments as owned. For example, one interviewer said, "So you've been living in that apartment for a year. You have your own property now." Larisa clarified, "It was purchased a year ago with a thirty-year mortgage. It's not our property yet. I'm thirty-four now, so when I'm sixty-three, god permitting, it will finally belong to us. It's optimistic to think that will happen, but it was our only option."

When mortgagors did describe their homes as "mine," they typically referred to living separately from the extended family, more akin to a renter getting his "own place" than a buyer becoming a homeowner. Yuri remarked that the bank would own his mortgaged apartment "until we reach retirement age." But he expressed no regrets: "Some people will say, 'No way, I don't want a mortgage, it's not so bad to live with my auntie! But we had already rented and experienced what it's like to live separately. What's mine is mine [*svoi*]; it's good to be the master of my own domain [*khoziain*]."

For those struggling with payments, the burden foregrounds their debtor status. Vera, whose husband was laid off six months ago, explained:

VERA: Mortgages are not affordable for young Russians. But it's also unrealistic to save up and buy an apartment outright. The government should lower the interest rates. We have to overpay by triple the amount that we borrowed.

INTERVIEWER: Well do you like the apartment?

VERA: There's nothing special about it. It's small. But we aren't used to better conditions. It seems as if we live in our own apartment. I don't know.

INTERVIEWER: So do you at least have a sense of happiness that now you have your own place?

VERA: No. There is no joy. Because I always say that this apartment belongs to the bank, and not to us.

Vera contradicts the stereotype among Russians that mortgagors are wealthy and live in elite housing. Most respondents with mortgages in the Kaluga study were house poor despite their relatively high salaries, paying large portions of their incomes to live in mediocre Soviet housing. As Maria, who purchased a one-room Khrushchevka with a mortgage, said, "It was a shock when I realized how dearly I would have to pay, and how little housing I could get." Figure 9.1 illustrates the gap between expectation and reality. While most people who look into taking on significant debt to purchase a home hope for an apartment in an elite building like the one in the background in the photograph, they typically can only afford a secondhand Soviet apartment in a building like the one in the foreground.

FIGURE 9.1 A Soviet-era apartment building in the foreground, with a luxury post-Soviet apartment building in the background. Mortgagors are often disappointed when they find that they can only afford to borrow to buy the former. Photo by Anastasia Smirnova.

Such laments echo Pierre Bourdieu's description of home purchases as "one of the major foundations on which the suffering of the petit bourgeoisie is built":

> The aspirations that underlie the dissatisfactions, disillusionments, and tribulations... always seem to owe something to the complicity of the sufferers themselves.... By embarking upon projects that are often too large for them, because they are measured against their aspirations rather than their possibilities, they lock themselves into impossible constraints, with no option but to cope with the consequences of their decisions, at an extraordinary cost in tensions, and at the same time to strive to *content themselves*... with the judgment reality has passed on their expectations: they may thus spend their whole lives striving to justify misconceived purchases, unfortunate schemes and one-sided contracts both to themselves and to their nearest and dearest. (2005, 185–86)

The difference between the French case in the 1980s and the Russian case today is that Russian mortgagors must struggle even more to content themselves with a decision that is not taken for granted in the mainstream culture. To the contrary, mortgages remain highly illegitimate in Russia.

Russians' insistence that a mortgage is not a type of ownership leads to the question of why borrowers in the West believe that it is. If kabala is a metaphor in Russia, homeownership is a metaphor in countries where mortgages are taken for granted. Linguist George Lakoff defines metaphor as a cognitive mapping of a familiar source domain onto a less familiar target domain (1993). Equating mortgages with ownership maps the practical sense of possession onto more abstract financial arrangements. A qualitative study of mortgage holders in the United Kingdom asked respondents: "If your mortgage were an animal, what would it be?" Most chose domestic animals, reflecting how "mortgage finance is entrenched in daily life" (Cook et al. 2009, 138). Even risk-taking mortgage holders who routinely draw on home equity framed their mortgages as lively but domesticatable, like a dog that must be trained. I suspect that if Russians were asked the same question, they would choose a wild animal instead—just as they often call Russia's own variety of capitalism "wild" (*dikii*).

Mortgages versus Credit in a Culture of Permanent Crisis

Mortgages in the West are supported by what Manning calls the "cognitive disconnect" that leads households to make consumption decisions based on rosy predictions about the future. By contrast, the experience of repeated crisis inclines Russians to predict catastrophe. Unprompted, 44 percent of respondents used the term *crisis* at some point during the interview. Nearly 80 percent worried about possible personal misfortune such as job loss or death, and about two-thirds spoke of systemic instability, from economic implosion to the possibility of war. The sense of impending doom makes equating a mortgage with debt bondage comprehensible, since it seems impossible to predict how, when, or whether a debt can be paid. As Nina, a renter who owned a hair salon, put it: "In present conditions, a mortgage is a kabala. We have a financial crisis. Anything could happen. Maybe a few people already have other property or land they don't need that they could use as collateral. But if you start out dog poor and hang a mortgage around your neck when you don't know what you will eat tomorrow, I think that's very difficult. Especially during a crisis."

Few respondents linked the crisis in Russia to the ongoing global financial crisis when discussing mortgages. Instead, the problem of crisis was framed as either uniquely or extremely Russian. Max, one of the few who referred to the global crisis, framed Russia's crisis as more extreme. "Look at America. Everyone there took out mortgages and now we see the consequences.

Everyone is burdened by debt. It's dangerous to get into serious debt for a banal reason: you may not be able to pay. Especially in our country. Right now due to the international crisis, people everywhere don't know what will happen tomorrow. This is even more true of Russia." When asked in a survey which countries had suffered the most from the "global crisis," Russians ranked their own nation first (followed by the United States and Ukraine).[9]

Russians' conception of crisis, even in 2009, is captured by Olga Shevchenko's depiction of a culture of "permanent crisis," which she argues has pervaded Russian society since the collapse of the USSR. Crisis became a "symbolic resource, creating a situation in which people could most easily achieve trust through affirmation of universalized distrust" (2009, 9–10). The crisis framework "functioned as ways of self-presentation as much as they were coping strategies, for they performatively indicated that the subject was in control" (12). In the culture of permanent crisis, stability is paramount. "Change for them was almost never a good thing. Even those whose personal encounters with the reforms of the 1990s had been lucrative . . . did not consider such markers to be their main achievements. Rather, they praised themselves for being successful in the preservation of their families' peace and well-being" (8).

Following the 1998 ruble default, when Shevchenko conducted much of her fieldwork, consumption strategies were oriented around predictions of renewed crisis. Russians rushed to convert their cash into consumer durables, in case sudden inflation or unemployment should place these items out of reach. From the standpoint of 2009, a mortgage would have entailed an unacceptable loss of control, because rather than turning cash into durables, it makes one's most important durable possession depend on future cash flow. Ippolit, a married father still living with his mother, exclaimed, "Considering the instability of incomes, and of our Russian world of sustained crisis, to take on a project of twenty or thirty years is suicidal!"

If avoiding mortgages signified self-control in the context of crisis, then risking a mortgage was, in the views of many, an "absurd" strategy. In Russian, the word *absurd* has connotations of both irrationality and immorality; the term is used to describe mortgages as well as government policies that encouraged people to take them on. For example, Vadim said, "The government wants us to take out mortgages, but I don't believe in them. An apartment simply cannot cost so much in relation to salaries. It should cost no more than three years of my income. Maybe I'm a pessimist, but it seems absurd to decide to buy an apartment by projecting about my income over twenty-five years. I might not live that long."

Many respondents compared Russia to the West to explain why mortgages could not work. Recall that these interviews were conducted in 2009, at the height of an international mortgage finance crisis. Yet when they drew comparisons, most respondents said mortgages worked well in the West. By contrast, Russia was unfertile territory for mortgages due to systemic crisis and economic dysfunction. For example, Sofia declared mortgages for young families to be an endless kabala. "Furthermore," she said, "mortgages in the West and in Russia mean two different things. For example, our interest rates are much higher, they are enormous. If in the West, mortgages turn out to be simply installment loans, here they are truly mortgages with very strict conditions. That is, the bank can set the interest rates, which our government is incapable of regulating, because it is incapable of controlling anything."

Arkady, a wealthy entrepreneur who owned his elite apartment outright, foregrounded stability to explain why his perceptions of mortgages and ownership differed from those of his brother, who had immigrated to Germany.

A mortgage is when a person digs himself into such a hole that he will be trying but failing to dig himself out for the rest of his life. But on the other hand my brother in Germany took out a mortgage for 220,000 Euros and built a house. They get to live in it now but they have to take the payment from his salary each month. But their conditions are so stable that they just live in it and don't think about it. They openly say, "This is our house. We own this home." That is, they understand perfectly that if they are short even 20 rubles on a payment, the bank could take the house away from them. But things are stable, so it's okay. Here that's not the case. I think that if you don't have the money to pay, you should control your appetite.

If mortgages do not fit Russians' crisis-fueled cognitive connection between immediate income and consumption, how can we explain the explosion of other forms of consumer credit? Russians are increasingly using virtual forms of money. Bankcard use increased from just 10 percent in 2003 to 43 percent in 2010 (Levada Center 2011). According to national survey data presented in table 9.1, the percentage of Russians using credit for items other than housing more than doubled between 2003 and 2006, from 15 percent to 36 percent, and then dipped after 2007. Rates of use were even higher among young adults: the percentage age eighteen to forty-five who had used credit was 25 percent in 2003 and 50 percent in 2007. As of December 2008, 36 percent of eighteen- to thirty-nine-year-olds had an outstanding loan. Most used credit to buy appliances, consumer electronics, and computers, followed

Table 9.1   Russians who used consumer credit in previous two years (%)

	2003	2004	2005	2006	2007	2009
Housing	NA	2	3	2	3	2
Car	NA	1	2	4	5	7
Other	15	22	27	32	31	25

Source: Bondarenko (2009).

by furniture and cars. Consumer confidence in credit peaked in 2007 and then plummeted as the global crisis hit Russia. Still, according to a May 2009 survey, two-thirds of Russians were prepared to take out a short-term loan if they were to have an urgent need of cash. By contrast only 9 percent said they would consider a mortgage.[10]

Why is consumer credit accepted by so many, while mortgages are usually rejected? According to Alya Guseva in the book *Into the Red,* the fastest growing segment of consumer loans in Russia as of 2008 were "express loans" for specific retail purchases, such as microwaves, stereos, refrigerators, and tires (2008, 115). At first glance, these appear to resemble the frugal caution of installment credit in the United States at the turn of the twentieth century (Calder 1999). But Guseva argues that express loans evoke Manning's (2000) credit card nation more than they do Calder's Puritan ethos. Express loans were typically made by banks at kiosks inside retail establishments. Screening for creditworthiness was minimal, and the consequences of default relatively minor. Lending at the point of purchase led consumers to associate borrowing money with the goods they desired, which encouraged impulse borrowing and circumvented Russians' aversion to borrowing from banks.

Acceptance of small-scale consumer credit was evident in the Kaluga interviews, although we did not ask questions about nonhousing credit. A few respondents emphasized that they always pay for things in full and oppose debt on principle. But about half spoke favorably or matter of factly about credit. For example, Olga, a thirty-three-year-old seamstress, exclaimed, "Mortgage is a dirty word! The cost is simply thievery. You overpay so much. When you do the math, it's pretty unfair. The banks are unscrupulous. You pay and pay and pay and never know if you will ever finish paying. And even if you do, when you consider the interest, in the end you paid for three apartments, but you only own one." Later in the interview she said, "Credit is okay if it's for appliances. The stores give good loans, without too much overpayment. It's good when you want to buy something a little better, a little more expensive, for example, a digital camera. It's more convenient to pay five hundred rubles a month than pay all at once. You practically don't notice it in your budget. And it allows you to buy a better product. I have a lot of experience with credit and I am not afraid of it. It helps, so why not?" Consistent with Guseva's analysis, Olga's focus on the store and the monthly payment led her to downplay the interest buried in the monthly payment.

Another respondent named Martha joked that she needed credit because she was "constitutionally incapable of saving." Later, when asked about mortgages, she said:

> Mortgages scare me. I am constantly taking out credit. But a mortgage is totally different. I cannot understand how someone can take out a loan for twenty years. You have to be very daring. Today you are a prince, you have your own business, but tomorrow there is a crisis and you lose everything. Today you are living with your husband, tomorrow you fight and get divorced, whom will you rely on? It's a kabala. I mean, it's twenty thousand rubles a month! Right now I'm paying eight hundred rubles a month for a loan I took out to buy a TV. My mother says, "You are overpaying, three hundred a month is wasted on interest!" But I say that it's no problem. I can come up with eight hundred rubles a month for three years no matter what happens. Some people rush to pay it off faster, but what's the point of hurrying? You will just go shopping and take out a new loan!

As these examples illustrate, young Russians feel comfortable with credit as long as the monthly amount is modest, predictable, and short-term, and if the act of borrowing is tied to a retail experience rather than a visit to a bank. Borrowing to buy a home, on the other hand, is seen as a long-term risk and life-long obligation. The possibility of selling a mortgaged property or refinancing loan terms is rarely considered. The moral ranking of the virtue of debt is thus inverted compared to the United States: loans for small luxuries are normal and convenient, but a loan for a home is risky and imprudent. In this respect Russians resemble poor consumers in Brazil, who are averse to borrowing from banks, which "was equated with a lack of control, risk of insolvency, and failure." Credit cards and installment credit by contrast "were seen as resources and not as threats to stability and progress in life" (Mattoso and da Rocha 2008, 242).

Respondents with mortgages, aware of their stigma, described their circumstances as exceptional or their decisions as spontaneous. For example, Vladimir, who had taken out several mortgages and paid them off early, warned that they should be used only as short-term bridge loans; ordinary

Russians should avoid them because they will naively fall into a "pit of debt." Polina recalled that eviction from her rental apartment set the wheels in motion, and she just happened to be in the right place at the right time to find an affordable apartment and a low-interest loan. Yuri described his decision to get a mortgage as "spontaneous." He and his wife saw an advertisement for apartments in a new building next to their rental apartment. They went to look out of curiosity, and the sales manager who met them brought along a bank representative. While they were looking at the apartment and talking to the banker, they "suddenly realized that it was realistic for us to buy an apartment." Although most mortgages are initiated at banks, not inside apartments, this story reinforces Guseva's argument that lending at the point of purchase makes credit more palatable to Russians.

Mortgages as a Breach of the Social Contract

Many of Russians' objections to mortgages are instrumentally rational, based on calculating costs, benefits, and risks under conditions of financial uncertainty. But aversion to mortgage debt is moral as well as economic. The leaders of market transition claimed that capitalism would deliver higher living standards for everyone willing to work hard. Yet as chapter 5 demonstrated, most young Russians believe that an apartment was easier to "earn" in the Soviet period. Housing was distributed through the workplace and was a legal right for everyone who worked. The waiting period for a separate apartment was uncertain, but by the late Soviet era most people believed they would eventually get their own place. Today, although housing remains a constitutional right, affordable housing is not guaranteed in practice. Most respondents view housing conditions as a function of luck: the result of inheritance, a fortunate marriage, or happening to get rich by being in the right place at the right time.

New subsidies to make mortgages more affordable have backfired politically. After nearly two decades of state retrenchment from the housing sector, these subsidies reinforce the expectation that the government, and not the market or the individual, is ultimately responsible for ensuring that every family has its own apartment. Yet since a mortgage does not satisfy local definitions of ownership, a mortgage subsidy is not perceived as helpful. When asked what the government should do to make housing more affordable, most respondents proposed either some variant on the Soviet system of providing housing as an outright gift, or a quasi-mortgage program that would cap monthly payments at a relatively small proportion of income and be guaranteed even in case of unemployment and inability to pay.

This sense that practical (as opposed to juridical) ownership is a social right explains why Russians consider mortgage debt to be morally suspect. In *Credit Card Nation,* Robert Manning notes that American media accounts tend to blame borrowers' troubles on individual imprudence and youthful indiscretion, not the systemic overextension of credit. The kabala metaphor also assigns some personal responsibility to mortgage borrowers, because it suggests a voluntary choice to hang a yoke around one's neck. Yet Russians are far more critical of the banking system than they are of the people who use it. They tend to describe mortgagors as gullible rather than greedy. After kabala, the predominant metaphor for mortgage credit is *obman,* which means "scam." Mortgages are considered a scam in several senses. First, they create a false sense of ownership. Second, they are "unrealistic," with onerous monthly payments that at best make people "house poor": "You live in a house, but you have no life." Third, the high cumulative interest paid is called an "overpayment" (*pereplata*).

When speaking of small consumer loans, most respondents did not calculate the total amount of interest paid, focusing instead on the affordability of the monthly payment. With mortgages, on the other hand, they calculated and criticized the interest paid, especially in proportion to the original cost. For example, Evgeny complained, "If a person borrowed a certain amount, that's what he should have to pay back. A simple loan. But with a mortgage, a person has to pay back more than he borrowed. I don't want to play a game of chance with the government. I've taken out loans twice, but they were small loans for appliances. It's one thing to pay interest for a television, but we are speaking of housing!" Natasha echoed this sentiment that housing is special and should not be subject to interest. "It's one thing to use credit to pay for everyday needs, which people should handle themselves. But housing is fundamental: it's what you need simply to work, grow as a person, start a family, and have a normal life."

Many also lambasted the proportion of interest to principal in long-term loans. Valentina characterized mortgage interest as a scam: "You wind up in debt for the cost of two apartments, instead of for the one in which you are living. You have to overpay. It's a scam." This focus on the total interest over the life of a mortgage loan contrasts with the American case, in which self-amortization draws attention to the monthly payment. Although many mortgages are self-amortizing in Russia as well, few Russians have direct experience with them, which impedes the normalization of interest as a routine component of a fixed monthly payment.

The deepest sense of scam, however, is the broken promise that markets will reward hard work and provide prosperity. Alexei elaborated when explaining why mortgage programs for young families are a "lot of hot air": "In the Soviet epoch a young specialist could count on the fact that within a couple of years, he would receive an apartment, even if only a khrushchevka. At least they gave people some space of their own. Now, no matter how good of a specialist you are, you won't get anything. In general I prefer to live in our times, with a market based on supply and demand. But when it comes to housing, the government is obligated to build it and give it out, because the market doesn't work the way they promised. Just like under Yeltsin and Chernomyrdin, they thought everything would turn out better, but things have only gotten worse."

Responsibility for market failure, and the suffering that has ensued, lies with the government, according to most respondents. Maternity capital was a trick to encourage young Russians with children to take out mortgages, and leave them holding the bag when they could not pay. Likewise, the Young Family's Program, in Martha's words, "is a scheme for fools. They create a shortage so that people will run to get in line for the privilege of taking out a mortgage loan. It's a pyramid scam when you have to pay interest for a so-called subsidy, and wind up in a bottomless pit of debt." A sarcastic critique that appeared in the business media captures the widespread belief that policies to promote mortgages are a scam:

> They wanted to make things better: The head of the ARHML is simply being logical, as is Sberbank, by raising interest rates on "bad" loans. This "fee for risk" is appropriate under normal conditions, when the borrower is mainly to blame for his problems. But under conditions of crisis, those falling into the zone of risk include those who believed the words of [Finance Minister] Alexei Kudrin that Russia is "an island of stability," and they decided it was high time to have children in long-awaited housing, obtained with a mortgage. Undoubtedly, such people much be punished.[11]

Conclusion

A Market That Could Not Emerge

Transplanting American housing institutions to Russia failed both as housing policy and legitimation strategy, because the resultant housing order did not provide young families with a clear, fair path to attain a "separate apartment," the grounds for a normal family life. Desiring a separate apartment for the nuclear family is neither natural nor inevitable. For most of human history, people have lived with extended family. French social historian Philippe Aries (1962) dates the emergence of the nuclear family to the eighteenth century in Europe. Kenneth Jackson (1985) argues that the cultural shift toward the nuclear family only began in the mid-nineteenth century in the United States. There, most people lived in multigenerational households in 1850; such households had nearly vanished by 1960 (Ruggles 2007).

In Russia, the nuclear family did not become normative until the 1950s, a shift spurred by Khrushchev's promise to house each family in its own apartment. To this day, many families continue to live in extended households. Still, Soviet dispositions about normal housing for normal families have proven durable. Most Russians, even those too young to remember the Soviet epoch, believe that a separate apartment for the nuclear family is a need and a right. Conceptions of ownership remain rooted in the long-term usage rights of the Soviet epoch, as opposed to ideas about private property and homeownership transplanted from the United States.

Market failure was overdetermined by economic constraint and illiquidity on the one hand and cultural resistance on the other. Housing mobility for young families, which had been an entitlement, became a matter of fortune— gift or inheritance of a privatized property. At the same time, markets failed to produce opportunities for housing mobility through work. The result is the regime of property without markets, in which housing chances and mobility strategies depend mainly on networks of property relations within extended families. This regime, while apparently stable, is not fully legitimate. The government's attempt to instill a mortgage culture with maternity capital backfired, instead reinforcing citizens' claims on the state, while disappointing their expectations.

Is property without markets a transitory phenomenon, likely to fade when the current crisis eases? International institutions declared Russia's market transition complete a decade ago. In 2002, the European Union and the United States officially recognized Russia as having a "market economy," a milestone in Russia's bid for World Trade Organization membership (still pending as of this writing).[1] More recently, social scientists have begun to frame the transition as over. For example, Tova Höjdestrand, in her study of homelessness, opines that "'transition' has moved into the past tense" and the crisis of 2008–9 "will inscribe itself into history with a different name, be it 'post-transition,' 'the Putin period,' or something else." The concept of "post-Soviet" only makes sense "as long as the people we write about still identify with or relate to the Soviet past and as long as social scientists need them for historically informed studies" (2009, 4). Based on this criterion, housing, like homelessness, remained post-Soviet through 2009. Young Russians drew easily on discourses and even memories of the Soviet period, passed down by older generations, to interpret the post-Soviet housing order.

Primary data for this book were collected in 2009, raising the question of whether interviewees were overwrought due to a momentary financial crisis. Yet there was little talk of the most recent crisis in the interviews, except when speaking of fluctuations in prices, interest rates, and unemployment. More often, interviewees invoked crisis in ways consistent with Shevchenko's (2009) discourse of "permanent crisis." Although the 2009 crisis surely stood out for the minority of mortgage borrowers for whom job loss could mean foreclosure, for most Russians, the sense of crisis in the housing sector had never dissipated. Furthermore, most Russians doubted whether mortgages could solve Russia's housing woes even before the American subprime meltdown began. Confidence in mortgages hit a low point in 2009, when just 9 percent of the population said they would consider a mortgage—indicating some sensitivity of attitudes to macroeconomic fluctuations. But even at the peak of Russia's mini-mortgage boom in 2007, only 22 percent of Russians said they would consider one (FOM 2009a).

Mortgages seem unlikely to rebound when the economy recovers in light of profound ambivalence toward markets among both young and educated Russians. During the first decade of capitalist transition, supporters of market reform portrayed critics as nostalgic and maladjusted to change. The younger generation, particularly college-educated youth, were expected to embrace capitalism. And in some respects they did, especially in the practices of everyday consumption, from clothing fashions to credit cards (Gurova 2008; Guseva 2008). Yet, according to opinion polls, Russians under thirty-five remained at best ambivalent toward markets. In a 2005 survey on nostalgia, indicators of nostalgia, which did increase with age, were also remarkably high among Russians with no adult memories of the pre-Gorbachev era. And nostalgia actually increased with education (Munro 2006). A 2007 opinion poll asked whether modern Russian society is fairer than Soviet society of the 1970s and 1980s. Among eighteen- to thirty-five-year-olds, 23 percent agreed, 30 percent disagreed, and 46 percent had difficulty answering. Responses were similar for a question on whether freeing prices in 1992 was the right thing to do (FOM 2007b). Likewise, in qualitative interviews in Kaluga in 2009, more than 90 percent agreed that the government should control housing prices and interest rates on housing loans.

Although this book concentrates on the cultural causes and consequences of market failure, I do not deny the importance of material constraints and systemic instability. Politico-economic impediments to market development have been widely studied and are documented in part I of this book. Economic conditions could also help to explain variation in development of mortgage markets across the post-Soviet region, which share a similar Soviet cultural and infrastructural inheritance.[2] My intention is to advance understanding of culture as a mechanism that connects macroeconomic conditions with individuals' dispositions and practices (what Bourdieu would call the correspondence between social structures and mental structures).

Material and cultural factors are complementary and not competing explanations. Rather than trying to identify a single cause—material conditions or cultural dispositions—for market failure, it is more productive to think in terms of necessary and sufficient conditions. Most analysts attribute the problem to high prices and interest rates (about 12 percent). Affordability is of course essential to get a mortgage market off the ground, but is insufficient to explain market success or failure. Most Russians who could afford a mortgage do not want one; whereas Americans readily took out mortgages at similar terms in the 1980s. A cultural approach furthers our understanding of why mortgage markets have failed to emerge.

What would happen if salaries and mortgage terms were to become more stable and more Russians could qualify for loans? Would they want them? Perhaps new conditions would produce a new culture; however interview results give reason to be skeptical. We asked respondents whether mortgages could make housing more affordable in Russia. Two-thirds of respondents with higher education agreed mortgages could work in theory; two-thirds of respondents without higher education did not.

However, if we probe the reasoning behind these responses, Russians' prognoses for American-style mortgages appear overwhelmingly negative. First, about 20 percent of respondents asserted that Western mortgages could only work in Western contexts, where the market is civilized. Russia, they argued, is too disordered or corrupt to support a mortgage economy. Second, the mortgages that many envisioned could work for Russia are not really mortgages at all. Most proposed variants of installment loans, including monthly payments pegged to construction costs and consumer incomes, limits on profit from sale and interest on loans, and a government guarantee that consumers could not lose their homes due to unemployment, disability, or otherwise inability to pay. These proposals are far from the transplanted American mortgage: they combine elements of Soviet housing loans for cooperative apartments, the construction savings associations of Germany (Bausparkassen), and "Islamic mortgage" instruments to assuage ethical qualms about usury (Maurer 2006; Polterovich and Starkov 2007).

In short, the moral taint on mortgages in Russia will make it difficult to translate demand for housing into demand for credit, even after the current crisis lifts. If and when mortgages become more affordable, demand will not follow as long as Russians mistrust markets and pin their hopes on the state to solve the housing question. This does not mean, however, that misgivings will foment organized resistance. There is a difference between nostalgia, or wanting to return to the past, and reaction, or taking action to return to the past (Munro 2006). There is no apparent "social volcano" (Whyte 2010a) in Russia, even though perceptions of injustice are widespread. Dissent is disorganized; as of this writing it was unclear if electoral protests in December 2011 would spark more systematic protest about social policy and inequality. The stability of the Russian state rests mainly on negative legitimacy, or, as Reutov (2006) puts it, "inertial" or "forced" legitimacy. Modern political systems function best when legitimacy is positive, that is, when it entails belief not just in the *fact* of but in the *right* of rule.

Studying the illegitimacy of mortgages in Russia illuminates legitimation in established mortgage cultures. In his book on French housing markets, Pierre Bourdieu (2005) describes extensive coordination of interests in misrecognized form. Policies that privilege mortgage-based homeownership are "invariably expressed (or betrayed) in unrecognizable form" in the interactions between realtors and clients (149). The structure of supply and the structure of demand are homologous because of the matched social characteristics of buyers and realtors, which "underpins a whole series of strategic effects which are in the main involuntary and semi-unconscious" (73). Advertising "panders to pre-existing dispositions in order the better to exploit them" and has "poetic" effects that "evoke lived experience" by mobilizing "words or images capable of summoning up the experiences associated with houses . . . [which] are shared in as much as they owe something to cultural tradition, and, in particular, to inherited cognitive structures" (23). The final act in the purchase of a home is the process of settling, via the "long series of justifications one often garners when one enquires into the history of successive dwellings ('but at least you're in your own home'), which are the product of the immense *work of mourning* that must be accomplished (so as to manage to *content themselves* with what they have)" (173). In Russia, the work of mourning, required to match one's circumstances with one's aspirations, does not lead to resolution, but to a sense of loss of one's proper (Soviet) inheritance, and of foreboding about one's prospects for a normal family, in a normal home, in a normal country.[3]

The study of housing market failure in Russia also generates a comparative research agenda by denaturalizing the cultural dispositions that support the American housing system. Chapter 9 uses the case of failed institutional transplant from the United States to Russia to develop a theory of what mortgages mean to Americans. Russian reactions to mortgages render American dispositions puzzling and in need of explanation. There is nothing natural about equating mortgage debt with homeownership, or about the state abdicating responsibility for providing secure housing. I suspect that, if we were to expand the comparative study of cultural conceptions of debt and ownership beyond Russia, we would find further confirmation that the American equation of debt with ownership is unusual, a product of specific political, economic, and cultural conditions in the United States during the twentieth century. However, the perception among supporters of the Washington Consensus that this cultural equation is natural, rational, and universal explains the trajectory of post-Soviet housing policy—that is, entrenched commitment to the American model of homeownership based on securitized mortgages—despite persistent market failure domestically and dramatic market failure since 2007 in the United States.

These findings about Russia suggest some hypotheses about potential effects of housing crisis in the United States. Russians' expectations that the state should control the market are not exceptional, despite the socialist legacy of state responsibility for housing the populace. Actors in market societies also turn to government whenever accumulated individual losses produce a collective sense of unfairness and instability. Russia's troubles in establishing housing markets highlight how extensively states intervene in the housing sector even in market economies, whether via tax credits for homeowners, public housing for the poor, or rent controls in cities. When housing markets visibly fail, people turn to the state to demand social protection from suffering (Polanyi [1944] 2001). In such times, state regulation of the market, normally taken for granted, becomes a subject of open debate—whether over redistribution for "Main Street" versus "Wall Street" in the United States, or compensation for unequal inheritance and unjust salaries in Russia. The crux of legitimacy is not just who gets what, but whether the logic of inequality is seen as fair and predictable rather than arbitrary and unstable.

In light of the findings on Russia, should we expect the subprime crisis to destabilize the moral foundations of mortgages in the United States? Will American consumers also question the relationship between owing and owning? Surely the spike in foreclosures has made many Americans less sanguine about debt-financed homeownership. Less clear is whether insecurity will translate into new modes of action. News stories in the American press in 2009–10 told of consumers who "walk away" from their mortgage debt and rent a similar house for a fraction of what they had been paying to "own."[4] But many Americans consider so-called strategic default to be immoral, making them reluctant to abandon their loans even when it is in their long-term financial interests to do so (White 2010a, 2010b). Ambivalence about responsibility to repay debt during a crisis could change the moral and financial calculations consumers make about whether and how to become and remain homeowners. The slogan "Main Street versus Wall Street" also suggests that, at least in policy discourse, the morality of the system, and not just of the individuals who participate in it, has been called into question. However, in contrast to Russians, I do not expect American consumers to come to see homeownership as a social right—rather, it will remain a part of the American Dream, a dream that suddenly seems more fraught with moral hazard and more difficult to achieve.

APPENDIX

Table A.1. Characteristics of interviewees cited in text

Name	Age	Education	Occupation	Marital Status	Number of Children	Housing Tenure	Extended Family Members	Number of Rooms	Layout
Women									
Anastasia	23	Primary	Sales clerk	Married (husband in jail)	1	Extended family	Mother	2	Standard soviet
Anna	22	Secondary	Sales clerk	Single	0	Owner	Parents	1	Khrushchevka
Aurika	22	Secondary	Maternity leave	Married	1	Extended family	Parents	3	Stalinka
Darya	35	Higher	Teacher	Divorced	1	Extended family	Mother, sister, 2 nieces	2	Standard soviet
Diana	24	Secondary	Bookkeeper	Single	0	Extended family	Parents, brother	1	Better soviet
Emma	23	Higher (incomplete)	Student	Single	0	Extended family	Sister	2	Standard soviet
Faina	29	Higher	Accountant	Single	1	Extended family	Parents	2	Converted barrack
Flora	30	Higher	Lawyer	Married	0	Owner	Parents	2	Post-soviet
Galina	30	Higher	Teacher	Married	1	Extended family	Parents	3	Stalinka
Inga	24	Higher	Maternity leave	Married	1	Extended family	Parents, grand-mother, aunt, sister	4	Private house (old)
Irina	28	Higher	Market researcher	Married	1	Owner		2	Khrushchevka
Kira	35	Secondary	Sales clerk	Married	1	Renter		2	Hostel
Klara	30	Higher	Journalist	Married	1	Owner		2	Khrushchevka
Ksenya	24	Technical	Homemaker	Married	1	Extended family	Husband's grandfather	2	Khrushchevka
Larisa	34	Higher	Bank manager	Married	1	Mortgagor		3	Standard soviet
Lena	28	Technical	Medical technician	Divorced	1	Extended family	Mother, grand-mother	2	Standard soviet
Lucia	30	Higher	Advertising agent	Cohabitating	0	Renter		1	Khrushchevka
Ludmila	26	Higher	Senior accountant	Married	1	Extended family	Mother	2	Standard soviet

Name	Age	Education	Occupation	Marital status		Tenure	Household		Housing type
Lyuba	30	Secondary	Sales clerk	Divorced	1	Owner		1	Standard soviet
Margarita	26	Higher	Consultant	Cohabitating	0	Renter		1	Standard soviet
Maria	29	Higher	Museum administrator	Single	0	Mortgagor		1	Khrushchevka
Marianna	35	Higher	Company director	Married	1	Owner		3	Standard soviet
Marina	24	Higher	Teacher	Married	0	Renter		2	Khrushchevka
Martha	30	Secondary	Sales clerk	Single	1	Extended family	Mother, grandmother, brother	2	Khrushchevka
Natasha	25	Higher	Unemployed	Cohabitating	0	Renter		1	Post-Soviet
Nelly	32	Higher	Professor	Married	1	Extended family	Parents	3	Khrushchevka
Nika	24	Technical	Maternity leave	Single	3	Renter			Better soviet
Nina	30	Secondary	Salon owner	Married	1	Renter		2	Better soviet
Olga	33	Secondary	Seamstress	Divorced	1	Extended family	Mother, grandmother	2	Standard soviet
Olesia	29	Higher	Economist	Married	2	Renter		2	Standard soviet
Polina	35	Higher	Advertising executive	Married	2	Mortgagor		3	Hostel
Raisa	22	Higher	Pharmacist	Married	1	Renter		1	Hostel
Regina	30	Secondary	Homemaker	Married	1	Owner		1	Khrushchevka
Rosa	21	Technical (incomplete)	Maternity leave	Cohabitating	1	Owner		2	Hostel
Roxana	26	Technical	Midwife	Married	0	Renter			Private house (old)
Sofia	25	Higher	Civil servant	Married	0	Renter			
Svetlana	33	Higher	Librarian	Divorced	1	Extended family	Mother, father, grandmother	4	Hostel
Tamara	30	Higher	Interior decorator	Single	1	Renter		1	Dormitory
Tatyana	30	Higher	Curator	Cohabitating	0	Renter		1	Khrushchevka
Valentina	22	Technical	Unemployed	Single	0	Renter		1	Khrushchevka
Vera	32	Higher	Maternity leave	Married	2	Mortgagor		2	

(continued)

Table A.1. (*Continued*)

Name	Age	Education	Occupation	Marital Status	Number of Children	Housing Tenure	Extended Family Members	Number of Rooms	Layout
Veronica	25	Secondary	Clerk	Cohabitating	0	Owner		1	Hostel
Yana	28	Higher	Telephone operator	Married	1	Owner		2	Better soviet
Zhanna	30	Higher	Accountant	Single	0	Mortgagor		1	Post-soviet
Zina	22	Higher (incomplete)	Student	Single	0	Extended family	Parents	3	Stalinka
Zoya	33	Secondary	Homemaker	Married	3	Owner		5	Elite post-soviet
Men									
Albert	25	Secondary	Construction worker	Married	2	Owner		2	Better soviet
Alexei	30	Higher	Civil servant	Married	1	Owner		2	Better soviet
Arkady	34	Secondary	Entrepreneur	Married	3	Owner		4	Elite post-soviet
Boris	25	Technical	Prison guard	Married	0	Renter		1	Post-soviet
Dennis	31	Technical	Driver	Single	0	Extended family	Mother, 2 sisters	3	Khrushchevka
Dmitri	30	Higher	Computer programmer	Married	1	Extended family	Aunt	3	Standard soviet
Eduard	32	Secondary	Mechanic	Married	1	Renter		1	Khrushchevka
Evgeny	34	Technical	Machinist	Divorced	1	Owner		2	Better soviet
Georgy	26	Higher	Systems administrator	Married		Renter		1	Khrushchevka
Igor	29	Higher	Teacher	Single	0	Extended family	Mother	4	Khrushchevka
Ippolit	29	Secondary	Courier	Married	1	Extended family	Mother	2	Better soviet
Ivan	35	Secondary	Factory worker	Divorced	1	Renter		1	Hostel
Max	31	Incomplete higher	Student	Single	0	Renter		1	Room in stalinka
Mikhail	29	Secondary	Sales manager	Single	0	Extended family	Mother	2	Khrushchevka

Pavel	35	Higher	Construction engineer	Married	1	Renter		2	Private home
Roman	26	Higher	Scientist	Married	0	Owner		1	Standard soviet
Ruslan	36	Higher	Consultant	Married	1	Extended family	Parents	3	Standard soviet
Vadim	33	Higher	Civil servant	Single	0	Renter		1	Khrushchevka
Vitalii	31	Higher	Manager of retail business	Married	0	Owner		1	Post-soviet
Vladimir	30	Higher	Manager of construction firm	Married	1	Mortgagor		2	Post-soviet
Yuri	30	Higher	Engineer	Married	1	Mortgagor		1	Khrushchevka

Notes: There were a total of 130 interviews. This table lists only those who were referenced as case studies and examples in the text of the book. The full data set was coded and used for drawing conclusions about response patterns. Extended family members refers to anyone with whom the respondent lives other than the respondent's spouse/partner, or respondent's children.

 **Notes**

Introduction

1. PNP, "Proizvodstvo stroimaterialov—kliuchevoe uslovie realizatsii zhilishchnogo natsproekta," September 25, 2007, http://www.rost.ru/news/2007/09/251607_10947.shtml; PNP, "Vyderzhki iz stenogrammy vystupleniia Pervogo zamestitelia Predsedatelia Pravitel'stva RF Dmitriia Medvedeva na zasedanii prezidiuma Soveta pri Prezidente RF po realizatsii prioritetnykh natsional'nykh proektov i demograficheskoi politike," November 27, 2007, http://www.rost.ru/official/2007/11/270000_11813.shtml.

2. PNP, "Dmitrii Medvedev: 'Proiskhodit revoliutsiia v soznanii nashikh grazhdan—liudi uchatsia zhit' v kredit,'" March 29, 2006, http://www.rost.ru/themes/2006/03/292042_2078.shtml.

3. This will be the subject of my next major study, tentatively titled *To Owe Is to Own: The Culture of American Mortgages.*

4. Russians count all rooms, not just the number of bedrooms, when describing an apartment's size.

5. Literally, *khrushcheba,* a play on *trushchoba,* the word for slum.

6. Third Party Program of the Communist Party of the Soviet Union, as translated by Harris (2003, 60).

7. Statistics are based on the author's calculations from the Russian Longitudinal Monitoring Survey, unless otherwise noted.

8. Vladimir Putin, "Opening Address at the State Council Presidium Session on Housing Policy," January 19, 2007, http://archive.kremlin.ru/eng/text/speeches/2007/01/19/2356_type82912type82913_116943.shtml.

9. Bread, the most mundane of daily purchases, also retains this almost magical quality and is one of the few consumer goods for which the Russian government has not freed prices. See Zavisca (2004).

10. In quantitative analysis of mobility and fertility patterns, I extend the upper age limit to forty, for consistency with the demographic literature.

11. A chapter on the organization of home interiors will appear in the book *Home—Place—Community: Sociological Studies in Europe and America,* edited by Margarethe Kusenbach, Krista E. Paulsen, and Melinda M. Milligan (Frankfurt: Peter Lang), under contract.

12. Fred Weir, "Global Crisis Aside, Foreign Carmakers Flock to Russia," *Christian Science Monitor,* March 10, 2009, http://www.csmonitor.com/Business/2009/0310/global-crisis-aside-foreign-carmakers-flock-to-russia.

13. According to the Case-Shiller index of housing prices, prices began their steepest rate of ascent in San Diego in 2002, in Las Vegas in 2003, and in Phoenix

in 2004. Data were retrieved from the Standard & Poor's website at http://
www.standardandpoors.com/indices/sp-case-shiller-home-price-indices/en/us/
?indexId=spusa-cashpidff--p-us----.

Chapter 1

1. For memoirs of upward and downward mobility into communal apartments,
see chapters 5, 10, and 18 of Fitzpatrick and Slezkine (2000).

2. Passports were denied to rural inhabitants, who could only migrate as tem-
porary workers.

3. Joseph Stalin, "Speech at the First All-Union Conference of Stakhanovites,"
November 17, 1935, http://www.marxists.org/reference/archive/stalin/works/1935/
11/17.htm.

4. Stalin, "Speech at the First All-Union Conference of Stakhanovites."

5. This assumption created a hardship for the millions of elderly residents who
occupy fifth-floor walkups to this day.

6. Henceforth I will use the term "parlor" for what is typically called a "living
room" in English, to avoid conflating the American concept of "living room" with
the Soviet concept of "living space."

7. "Polozhenie rabochikh v strankh kapitala ukhudshaetsia," *Pravda,* October
5, 1961.

8. "Better to See Once," *Time,* August 3, 1959, http://www.time.com/time/
magazine/article/0,9171,825793,00.html.

9. See, for example, "Khoroshie veshchi v nash byt," *Pravda,* January 27, 1962, p. 1.

10. *Pravda,* March 14, 1957, p. 1.

11. For examples, see Daniel (1985), Kulu (2003), and the special issue of *International Journal of Urban and Regional Research* published in March 1987.

12. Note that the GSS-USSR questionnaire asks respondents to report the "living space" (*zhilaia ploshchad'*) occupied by their family, not the total "floor space"
(*obshchaia ploshchad'*).

13. Full results are available from the author on request.

14. Based on my calculations from the GSS-USSR and the American Housing
Survey of 1991, the coefficient of variation (a variable's mean divided by its variance)
for housing space per capita was twice as high in the United States (1.16) as in the
USSR (0.62). Likewise, the Gini coefficient, another common measure of inequality,
stood at 0.41 in the United States versus 0.29 in the USSR.

15. A dacha is a small plot of land for summer gardening and leisure. The
Soviet government began distributing these plots en masse in the 1960s. See Zavisca
(2003).

16. "Ot vsego serdtsa," *Pravda,* August 6, 1959, p. 6, http://dlib.eastview.com/
browse/doc/21546223.

17. "Nasha ulitsa, nashe zhilishche," *Znamia,* May 30, 1984.

18. "Portret potrebitelia," *Ogonek,* June 1976.

19. "Pod krishei doma svoego," *Znamia,* January 11, 1984.

20. "Report to the Plenary Session of the CPSU Central Committee," *Pravda,*
January 27, 1987.

Chapter 2

1. Mints (2000, 54) also attributes American consultants' aversion to specialized housing banks to the fallout from the savings and loan scandal in the United States.

2. The government announced a deadline for free privatization in 2004. Eligible housing not privatized by 2007 would revert to a permanent public housing stock. However, the deadline was deferred until 2010, and then again until 2013.

3. In this context, "rent" means maintenance fees that the government charges for both privatized and unprivatized apartments in buildings it maintains.

4. Constitution of the Russian Federation, Article 40, http://www.constitution.ru/en/10003000-03.htm.

5. Despite their risks, installment loans were still more popular than mortgages through 2009. See chapter 9.

6. Delta Capital was purchased by Societe Generale in 2006. In 2008 the US-Russian Investment Fund was transformed into a think tank.

7. USAID, "Russia: FY 2001 Program Description and Activity Data Sheets," 2002.

8. The index, developed by the IUE, is a based on a standard United Nations index, but modified for data available in Russia (Kosareva and Tumanov 2008). Means are used instead of medians for income and prices because Rosstat does not report median values; this likely skews the index downward to overestimate housing affordability. Home prices are estimated based on the average cost for fifty-four square meters of housing space (the federal norm for a family of three), rather than on actual housing prices, again due to data limitations. To adjust for limited access to credit, the official subsistence minimum for two adults and one child is deducted from average income.

9. Demographia, "6th Annual Demographia International Housing Affordability Survey: 2010 Ratings for Metropolitan Markets," http://www.demographia.com/dhi.pdf; Rosstroi, "Federal'naia tselevaia programma 'zhilishche' na 2002–2010 gody," http://www.fcpdom.ru/prog.php.

10. "New Russian Housing Law Allows Eviction of Non-Payers, Promises Targeted Aid," *BBC Monitoring,* April 23, 2003; "Kaluga: 173 milliona rublei sostavliaiut dolgi za kvartplatu," *Regions.ru News,* October 12, 2003.

11. "ROMIR: Russians Mostly Dislike Gov't Initiative," *RIA RosBusinessConsulting,* June 2, 2004.

12. "Housing, Monopolies Subsidies Must End, Says Putin," *EIU: Country Economic News,* May 30, 2001; "Housing Provision to People to be One of Putin's Trumps in the Election Campaign," *WPS: The Russian Finance Report,* March 7, 2003; "Putin on System of Social Benefits," *RBC News,* March 19, 2004.

13. Vladimir Putin, "Annual Address to the Federal Assembly of the Russian Federation," May 26, 2004, http://archive.kremlin.ru/eng/speeches/2004/05/26/1309_type70029type82912_71650.shtml.

14. European Mortgage Federation, Hypostat Database, http://www.hypo.org.

15. AHML, "Rynok zhil'ia i ipotechnogo kreditovaniia: itogi 2009 goda," April 2010, http://ahml.ru/common/img/uploaded/files/agency/reporting/quarterly/report4q2009.pdf.

16. Vladimir Putin, "Opening Remarks at a Meeting of the State Council on the Development of Mortgage and Other Measures to Stimulate Housing Construction," February 27, 2003, http://archive.kremlin.ru/eng/text/speeches/2003/02/27/0000_type82912type82913_158679.shtml.

17. PNP, "Ob"emy stroitel'stva zhil'ia v Rossii v 2010 godu prevysiat luchshie pokazateli sovetskikh let," February 19, 2007, http://www.rost.ru/news/2007/02/190000_8007.shtml; PNP, "V Poslanii Federal'nomu Sobraniiu Vladimir Putin proanaliziroval khod realizatsii chetyrekh natsional'nykh proektov," April 26, 2007, http://www.rost.ru/themes/2007/04/261530_8953.shtml; PNP, "Proizvodstvo stroimaterialov—kliuchevoe uslovie realizatsii zhilishchnogo natsproekta," September 25, 2007, http://www.rost.ru/news/2007/09/251607_10947.shtml; PNP, "Dmitrii Medvedev: v zhilishchnom stroitel'stve v poslednie gody kraine ne khvatalo novykh idei," June 6, 2007, http://www.rost.ru/themes/2007/07/061548_9921.shtml; PNP, "Agenstvo po ipotechnomu zhilishchnomu kreditovaniiu i regiony dolzhny smelee vvodit' novye ipotechnye produkty," April 3, 2007, http://www.rost.ru/themes/2007/04/031351_8593.shtml.

18. PFRF, "Pensionnyi fond Rossii prinimaet zaiavleniia na pogashenie ipotechnykh kreditov sredstvami materinskogo kapitala," January 13, 2009, http://www.pfrf.ru/press_center/315.html.

19. PNP, "Materinskii kapital zhenshchiny predpochtut potratit' na priobretenie zhil'ia," April 24, 2008, http://www.rost.ru/news/2008/04/242008_13817.shtml; PFRF, "Kak uspet' rasporiadit'sia materinskim kapitalom v 2010 godu," April 19, 2010, http://www.pfrf.ru/index.php?chapter_id=486&data_id=15726&do= view_single; PFRF, "V 2010 godu PFR planiruet vyplatit' 102 mlrd. rublei materinskogo kapitala," January 18, 2010, http://www.pfrf.ru/index.php?chapter_id=4650&data_id=12202&do=view_single.

20. "Opening Address at the State Council Presidium Session on Housing Policy," January 19, 2007, http://archive.kremlin.ru/eng/text/speeches/2007/01/19/2356_type82912type82913_116943.shtml; "Opening Remarks at the Session of the Council for the Implementation of Priority National Projects and Demographic Policy," September 13, 2007, http://archive.kremlin.ru/eng/speeches/2007/09/13/1633_type82912type82913_143955.shtml.

21. "Opening Address at the State Council Presidium Session on Housing Policy," 2007.

22. For histories of Russian housing law in English, see Mashkina et al. (2007) and Guseva (2009). The former summarizes developments in Russian housing law through 2005, based mainly on Kosareva (2007). The latter analyzes mortgage legislation and juridical practice through mid-2009.

23. Heather Timmons, "Trouble at Fannie Mae and Freddie Mac Stirs Concern Abroad," *New York Times,* July 21, 2008.

24. The requirements for life and disability insurance were waived in July 2009 after courts ruled that they conflicted with antimonopoly law. Most borrowers still took the insurance. Natal'ia Biianova and Tat'iana Grishina, "Ipotechnye zaemshchiki vybiraiut zhizn'," *Kommersant,* October 21, 2009.

25. AHML, "Ipotechnye tsennye bumagi," http://www.ahml.ru/ru/investors/hypothecary_securities/.

26. Ian Art, "Russkaia ipoteka na pereput'e," *FIS News,* November 8, 2007; "Current Mortgage Crisis in West Won't Affect Russian Banking," *Interfax,* October 19, 2007.

27. AHML, "Rynok zhil'ia i ipotechnogo kreditovaniia," 2010.

28. Andrew E. Kramer, "Russia Approves $36 Billion Loan Plan," *New York Times,* October 8, 2010; Mikhail Doronkin, "Square Meter's Back," *Kommersant,* June 10, 2010; "Prime Minister Vladimir Putin Addressed 11th Congress of United Russia Party," *State News Service,* November 21, 2009.

29. Joe Nocera, "From Treasury to Banks, an Ultimatum on Mortgage Relief," *New York Times,* July 10, 2009; Sahien Nasiripous and Arthur Delaney, "Extend and Pretend: The Obama Administration's Failed Foreclosure Program," *Huffington Post,* August 4, 2010, http://www.huffingtonpost.com/2010/08/04/extend-and-pretend-the-ob_n_668609.html.

30. "Russian Government Takes Measures to Help Mortgage Holders, Banks (NTV)," *BBC Monitoring: Former Soviet Union,* December 6, 2009; Anna Lialiakina, "Dolzhniki po ipoteke poluchat vtoroi shans," *Trud,* November 3, 2009; Faina Filina, "Restrukturizatsii kreditov nevygodny chastnym zaemshchikam bankov," *Finans,* July 14, 2009; Olga Senatorova, "Kak rabotaet skhema pomoshchi ipotechnym zaemshchikam," *Kvadratnyi metr,* September 30, 2009; "Government Fails to Deliver on Promises in Downturn—Russian Liberal Daily (Nezavisimaia Gazeta)," *BBC Monitoring: Former Soviet Union,* February 13, 2009.

31. In April 2010 AHML also announced lower interest rates for holders of maternity capital and participants in military mortgage bank savings programs. However, few of the banks with whom AHML works were participating in these programs as of this writing in June 2010. http://www.ahml.ru/ru/borrower/ipProg/voendom/.

32. "Strategiia razvitiia ipotechnogo zhilishchnogo kreditovaniia v Rossiiskoi Federatsii do 2030." Utverzhdena rasporiazheniem Pravitel'stva Rossiiskoi Federatsii ot 19 iulia 2010 g. No. 1201-p.

33. PFRF, "V 2010 godu PFR planiruet vyplatit 102 mlrd. rublei materinskogo kapitala," 2010.

34. "Pogashenie ipoteki materinskim kapitalom," *Govorit Moskva,* April 21, 2009.

Chapter 3

1. Maternity capital can also be applied toward the child's education or toward the mother's pension fund. However housing has been and is expected to remain the favored application. See chapter 2.

2. Based on policy documents from the respective countries and UNECE data on average wages for 2007.

3. See chapter 1 for a review of Soviet pronatalist housing policy. For an overview of Soviet pronatalism beyond the context of housing, see Rivkin-Fish (2010).

4. "Russian TV Reports on Putin-Medvedev Meeting With Duma Leaders," *BBC Monitoring: Former Soviet Union,* March 12, 2008.

5. I collected 267 textual documents and 54 visual images from the following federal sources: the offices of the President (kremlin.ru), the Prime Minister

(premier.gov.ru), the Priority National Projects (rost.ru), and the Pension Fund (pfrf.ru). All these organizations maintain online archives of relevant materials.

6. For analyses of nonstate discourse on demography in general and the birthrate in particular, see the work of Michele Rivkin-Fish.

7. The federal government also exercises tight discursive control over regional governments. I looked at several dozen texts from the Kaluga region and found that they closely resembled federal sources.

8. Human Fertility Database, Max Planck Institute for Demographic Research (Germany) and Vienna Institute of Demography (Austria), http://www.humanfertility.org.

9. The TFR, the most common measure of fertility, does not take into account "tempo effects"—women waiting to have children until they are older. An adjusted measure suggests that the dip in 1999 was transitory, caused by women postponing childbearing (especially of a second child) after the 1998 ruble crisis (Goldstein et al. 2009).

10. PNP, "Dmitrii Medvedev predlozhil riad effectivnykh mer po resheniiu demograficheskoi problemy," March 7, 2007. http://www.rost.ru/themes/2007/03/071905_8273.shtml.

11. PNP, "Demografiia—eto megaproekt, kotoryi ob"edinit chetyre prior-itetnykh natsional'nykh proekta," May 15, 2006, http://www.rost.ru/news/2006/05/151335_3110.shtml; PNP, "Vpervye sredi prioritetov biudzhetnoi politiki Rossii—reshenie demograficheskikh problem," June 22, 2006, http://www.rost.ru/news/2006/06/221655_3918.shtml; Vladimir Putin, "Annual Address to the Federal Assembly," May 10, 2006, http://archive.kremlin.ru/eng/speeches/2006/05/10/1823_type70029type82912_105566.shtml; PNP, "Materinskii (semeinyi) kapi-tal," August 7, 2007, http://www.rost.ru/projects/health/p07/p71/a71.shtml.

12. Vladimir Putin, "Vystuplenie na vstreche s chlenami Pravitel'stva, rukovods-vtom Federal'nogo Sobraniia i chlenami prezidiuma Gosudarstvennogo soveta," September 5, 2005, http://archive.kremlin.ru/text/appears/2005/09/93296.shtml; "Annual Address to the Federal Assembly," 2006.

13. I also noticed little talk of ethnic threat in interviews with young Russians in Kaluga in 2009; by contrast, I encountered ethno-nationalist discourses frequently during fieldwork in the same city in 2002.

14. Regional advertisements for maternity capital sometimes represent other, locally predominant ethnic groups.

15. "Annual Address to the Federal Assembly," 2006; "Prime Minister Vladimir Putin Chairs a Meeting of the Presidium of the Presidential Council on National Priority Projects and Demographic Policy," April 23, 2010, http://www.premier.gov.ru/eng/events/news/10315.

16. PNP, "Vyderzhki iz stenogrammy vystupleniia Pervogo zamestitelia Predse-datelia Pravitel'stva RF Dmitriia Medvedeva na zasedanii Soveta pri Prezidente Ros-sii po realizatsii prioritetnykh natsional'nykh proektov i demograficheskoi politike," March 7, 2007, http://www.rost.ru/official/2007/03/070000_8275.shtml.

17. "Annual Address to the Federal Assembly," 2006.

18. For more detailed description of these policies, see Rotkirch et al. (2007).

19. "Conversation with Vladimir Putin," December 4, 2008, http://www.premier.gov.ru/eng/events/news/2638/.

20. The birthrate tripled around June 12, creating a nightmare at maternity wards. Yasha Levine, "Incentivized Birth: How Russia's Baby-Boosting Policies Are Hurting the Population," *Slate,* July 10, 2008, http://www.slate.com/id/2195133.

21. "Interv"iu zamestitelia predsedatelia Pensionnogo Fonda RF Lilii Chizhik o vonovedeniiakh v ispol'zovanii materinskogo kapitala," *Radio Govorit Moskva,* February 11, 2009.

22. "A Conversation with Vladimir Putin: To Be Continued," December 3, 2009, http://www.premier.gov.ru/eng/events/news/8412/; "Putin Reports on Social Programs to State Duma," *SKRIN Market and Corporate News,* April 21, 2010.

23. Vladimir Putin, "Transcript of Meeting With Participants in the Third Meeting of the Valdai Discussion Club," September 9, 2006, http://archive.kremlin.ru/eng/text/speeches/2006/09/09/1209_type82917type84779_111165.shtml; PNP, "Agenstvo po ipotechnomu zhilishchnomu kreditovaniiu i regiony dolzhny smelee vvodit' novye ipotechnye produkty," April 3, 2007, http://www.rost.ru/themes/2007/04/031351_8593.shtml.

24. "Prime Minister Vladimir Putin Chairs a Meeting," April 23, 2010; "Putin Holds Meeting of Presidium of Council on National Priority Projects," *SKRIN Market and Corporate News,* July 5, 2010.

25. "Remarks by Russian President Dmitri Medvedev and Trans-Baikal Regional Governor Ravil Geniatulin," OKINB, February 19, 2009; PFRF, "V Kazluzhskoi Otdelenii PFR proshla press-konferentsiia, temoi kotoroi stal materinskii kapital," February 18, 2009, http://www.pfrf.ru/ot_kalug/pr_releases/4473.html.

26. "Prime Minister Vladimir Putin Chairs a Meeting of the Presidium of the Presidential Council for Priority National Projects and Demographic Policy," February 26, 2010, http://www.premier.gov.ru/eng/events/news/9525/; Mikhail Doronkin, "Square Meter's Back," *Kommersant,* June 10, 2010; State News Service, "Prime Minister Vladimir Putin Addressed Eleventh Congress of United Russia Party," 2009.

27. "Press Conference with Yekaterina Lakhova, Chair of the State Duma Committee on Women, Family and Children," OKINB, May 16, 2006.

28. "Housing Provision to People to be One of Putin's Trumps in the Election Campaign," *WPS: The Russian Finance Report,* March 7, 2003; OKINB, "Interview With Vice Premier Alexander Zhukov," June 24, 2006.

29. "Vyskazyvaniia T.A. Golikovoi informatsionnym agenstvam," February 19, 2007, http://www.minfin.ru.

30. "Conversation with Vladimir Putin," 2008, http://www.premier.gov.ru/eng/events/1338.html; "Vladimir Putin Addressed Eleventh Congress," 2009.

Chapter 4

1. This is a lower-bound estimate of extended family arrangements, due to potential measurement error deriving from the RLMS definition of a household as "people living together and sharing a common budget." If related people have separate budgets and consider themselves to be separate households residing at one address, one of these households is randomly sampled in the RLMS. Such cases are unfortunately impossible to identify, so it may appear that a household lives in a separate apartment

as a nuclear family, when in fact there are other relatives living in the same housing unit. However, if households report splitting in later rounds, it is possible to distinguish whether a portion of the former household actually moved, or just separated budgets. Less than 1 percent of households report splits within housing units in subsequent waves, suggesting that this is a minor issue in the data.

2. The coefficient of variation is the ratio of the standard deviation to the mean. The Gini coefficient measures the extent to which a distribution differs from a hypothetical distribution in which each person receives an identical share, by comparing the average difference between all pairs of individuals to the mean. The index varies between 0 and 1, with 0 indicating absolute equality, and 1 indicating absolute inequality.

3. See Fehérváry (2002) for a fascinating qualitative study of the status connotations of "American kitchens" in postsocialist Hungary.

4. Similar results obtain for alternative measurements of income and for comparisons across occupational status groups.

5. Regression results are available from the author on request.

6. The prospective design of the RLMS, in which the same people are interviewed repeatedly, contains more detailed and accurate data over time than do retrospective studies that rely on recall. There is a tradeoff, however, in the potential for sampling-related bias due to attrition and censoring. A working paper is available from the author that addresses these issues. In sum, attrition does not appear to be biased with respect to transitions to housing autonomy. As a sensitivity check for the effects of left-censoring, models were fit to a restricted sample of respondents under age twenty-five at the time of entry. Results are substantively similar to those for the full sample.

7. Semiautonomous cases living in dormitories or rentals are dropped from the analysis. Most Russians consider rentals to be insecure and overpriced. While rentals provide a degree of independence from the extended family, renters themselves typically feel very insecure about their housing rights and do not consider renting equivalent to having a separate apartment of one's own. Although some Russians live in dormitories long term due to lack of alternatives, conditions are poor and they do not provide the privacy of a separate apartment. Roommates are almost all students renting rooms; long-term roommates are rare in Russia. Ideally I would perform a competing risks analysis for these semiautonomous destinations (Goldscheider and DaVanzo 1986), but sample sizes are insufficient.

8. Income of the extended family was also included in the model; similarly, the odds of transitioning were not higher even for the wealthiest quintile, compared with the bottom quintile. Sensitivity analyses for other functional forms for income were also tried (linear, quadratic, logarithmic, and spline effects of both percentile and real values), as were alternative income measures (expenditures, individual versus nuclear family income), with similar results.

9. Full models with time interactions are available from the author.

10. The size of this effect is impressive given that, as a proxy for inheritance, it is attenuated by measurement error. We are only able to measure "in-place" inheritances, since the RLMS does not identify whether moves to new addresses are due to inheritance. Given that monetary resources do not explain these moves, it is likely that unobserved inheritances and gifts account for many of them.

11. Igor Berezin, "Doma, v kotorykh my zhivem," ROMIR report, 2007, http://www.romir.ru/news/analitika/houses/. This report is based on a February 2007 national survey conducted by ROMIR, one of Russia's leading market research firms.

Chapter 5

1. FOM, "Natsional'nye proekty skvoz' prizmu obshchestvennogo mneniia," 2007a; Levada Center, "Zhilishchnyi vopros i vozmozhnost' ipotechnogo kreditovaniia sredi zhitelei krupnykh gorodov strany," March 28, 2006, www.levada. ru/press/2006032801.html; Igor' Berezin, "V blizhaishie dva goda rossiiane gotovy vziat' 1.5–2.5 milliona ipotechnykh kreditov," 2008, http://www.romir.ru/news/analitika/ipoteka/.

2. For an analysis of discourses on agricultural versus leisurely uses of Russian urban gardens, see my article in *Slavic Review* (2003).

3. ISSP Research Group, International Social Survey Programme (ISSP): Social Inequality III, 1999.

4. "A 15-Hour Day for the Sake of Russia's Resurgence," *OKINB,* September 29, 1992.

5. PNP, "Dmitrii Medvedev: Zhil'e budet dostupnym, esli stroit' mnogo," March 5, 2007, http://www.rost.ru/news/2007/03/050000_8234.shtml.

Chapter 6

1. In apartments without utility meters, rates are based on square footage and the number of persons registered at the address. Therefore registering nonresidents can be costly for primary residents.

Chapter 7

1. Vladimir Putin, "Annual Address to the Federal Assembly of the Russian Federation," May 26, 2004, http://archive.kremlin.ru/eng/speeches/2004/05/26/1309_type70029type82912_71650.shtml.

2. Maleva and Siniavskaia (2006) provide descriptive statistics on the association between rooms per capita and the number of children, but they do not formally test for the effect in a multivariate, longitudinal model.

3. I will be fielding a new Survey of Housing Experiences in Russia in 2012 (with Ted Gerber, supported by the National Science Foundation). This survey will provide unprecedented retrospective data that will allow us to rigorously test for causal effects of housing on childbearing decisions, as well as a range of other outcomes.

4. Perelli-Harris's 2006 study also uses the RLMS, but there are two main differences between our work. First, she does not consider the effects of housing on fertility. Second, her analysis does not take full advantage of the RLMS's longitudinal design (at the time she designed her study, RLMS had only just begun to track movers). As with any longitudinal survey, attrition can introduce bias. Bias would be a problem if movers were both more likely to drop out, and more likely to experience changes in either housing conditions or fertility. Previous researchers have found that attrition in the RLMS and related surveys does not introduce serious bias into measures of household structure, fertility, education, employment, wages, or expenditures (Swafford and Kosolapov 2002; Falaris 2003). With respect to housing, attrition may introduce bias into my analysis if movers are both more likely to drop out, and more likely to experience changes in either housing conditions or fertility. Fortunately, RLMS follow up of movers has been quite aggressive,

especially since 2001, and refusals and absences are much more common reasons for attrition than moving. I further find that attrition is not biased on housing transitions in the RLMS. Perelli-Harris (2006) also finds no attrition bias on the desire for additional children.

5. Relevant attributes of male partners could be included in the models of women's trajectories. I tested models that included men's employment status and education, but dropped these variables from the final model because they either had no noticeable effect, or were highly correlated with women's attributes.

6. In a sensitivity analysis, I tried distinguishing owners from renters to test for the importance of secure tenure versus living separately from the nuclear family. Sample sizes for renters were too small to make valid inferences.

7. A total of 5,523 person-year periods are present in the long-form of the data set (in which a separate observation represents each study year for which each person in the analysis still has only one child at the beginning of the time interval).

8. Age is treated as a categorical variable (in five-year increments) to avoid excessive collinearity with years since the previous birth. Education is a dummy variable indicating whether the respondent had a university degree or was enrolled in university when they were last interviewed. Income variables are transformed into percentiles for a given year to control for inflation and real increases in average income.

9. I also ran a similar model on the combined dataset with appropriate interaction terms, but present the separate models here for ease of interpretation.

Chapter 8

1. In this chapter I only analyze discourses about the *housing* application of maternity capital. There was also some talk about possible uses toward education or the mother's pension, but these were subordinate discourses in the interviews and are not a focus of this book.

2. Unless otherwise noted, references to focus groups and national surveys in this chapter are drawn from FOM research reports on studies of the PNP (e.g., FOM2006b, FOM2007a, and others available at http://bd.fom.ru).

3. Michele Rivkin-Fish identifies a similar public discourse, which she labels "instrumentalist" critiques, in Russian media and academic journals (2010, 717–19).

Chapter 9

1. Vladimir Putin, "Opening Remarks at a Meeting of the State Council on the Development of Mortgage and Other Measures to Stimulate Housing Construction," February 27, 2003, http://archive.kremlin.ru/eng/text/speeches/2003/02/27/0000_type82912type82913_158679.shtml.

2. "Use It or Lose It," *My First Place,* Home and Garden Television Network, Season 8, episode HMFP-801H, 2008.

3. See http://makinghomeaffordable.gov. For examples of pre-subprime crisis policy discourse equating mortgages with ownership, see Basolo (2007, 99–101).

4. The legal status of a mortgage varies by state in the United States. A minority of states employs "title theory," in which the lender holds the title until the loan is paid off (Jennings 2010).

5. English text of the convention can be found at "Supplementary Convention on the Abolition of Slavery, the Slave Trade, and Institutions and Practices Similar to Slavery, 226 U.N.T.S.3," University of Minnesota Human Rights Library, http://www1.umn.edu/humanrts/instree/f3scas.htm. The Russian translation is at the entry for *dolgovaia kabala* at http://www.pravoteka.ru/enc/1931.html.

6. For example: "Ipoteka: kabala ili vykhod iz zhilishchnoi bezyskhodsnosti?" *Trud*, March 29, 2007; "Ipotechnyi kredit: blago ili kabala?" *Komsomol'skaia pravda*, September 25, 2007; "Ipoteka. Mozhno li sdelat' 'kabalu' chut' miagche?" *Lichnyie den'gi*, June 20, 2007.

7. "Polozhenie rabochikh v strankakh kapitala ukhudshaetsia," *Pravda*, October 5, 1961.

8. Natal'ia Biianova and Tat'iana Grishina, "Ipotechnye zaemshchiki vybiraiut zhizn'," *Kommersant*, October 21, 2009, http://www.kommersant.ru/doc/1259534.

9. Most Russians are aware of an ongoing international financial crisis, and most also believe that the global crisis is negatively influencing Russia's economy. According to a 2009 survey, they were evenly split on whether Russia's crisis had internal origins, or if it arrived from other countries (FOM 2009b).

10. Bondarenko (2009); FOM (2009b, 2010); ROMIR (2009).

11. Vladislav Seregin and Elena Gosteva, "Defolt s fizicheskim litsom: priznaki bankrotstva," *RBK.Kredit*, May 12, 2009, http://www.rusipoteka.ru/pressreview/2009/priznaki_bankrotstva/.

Conclusion

1. "Time to Trade: The European Union and America Say Russia Is a Market Economy. Yet Membership of the World Trade Organisation Is Still Some Way Off," *Economist*, June 13, 2002, http://www.economist.com/node/1182451; "Russia's WTO Membership Bid Backed by the European Union," *BBC News*, December 8, 2010, http://www.bbc.co.uk/news/business-11944053.

2. For example, as of 2008, Ukraine had a 10 percent mortgage-to-GDP ratio, versus Russia's 3 percent. Although this is still very low compared with Western Europe and the United States, differences in loan affordability may account for variation in the extent of mortgage borrowing within the post-Soviet region.

3. For a superb account of the perpetual "work of mourning" endemic to the post-Soviet epoch, see Oushakine (2009).

4. Daniel Gross, "Default Nation: If Billionaires Don't Feel Guilty about Walking Away from Their Debts, Should Homeowners?" *Newsweek*, December 21, 2009; Roger Lowenstein, "Walk Away from Your Mortgage!" *New York Times*, January 7, 2010.

◣ WORKS CITED

Aassve, Arnstein, Francesco C. Billari, Stefano Mazzuco, and Fausta Ongaro. 2002. Leaving Home: A Comparative Analysis of ECHP Data. *Journal of European Social Policy* 12 (4): 259–75.

Alexeev, Michael. 1988. The Effect of Housing Allocation on Social Inequality: A Soviet Perspective. *Journal of Comparative Economics* 12 (2): 228–34. http://dx.doi.org/10.1016/0147-5967(88)90005-4.

———. 1990. Distribution of Housing Subsidies in the USSR, with Some Soviet-Hungarian Comparisons. *Comparative Economic Studies* 32 (3): 138–57.

Andrienko, Yuri, and Sergei Guriev. 2004. Determinants of Interregional Mobility in Russia: Evidence from Panel Data. *Economics of Transition* 12 (1): 1–27. http://dx.doi.org/10.1111/j.0967-0750.2004.00170.x.

Andrusz, Gregory D. 1984. *Housing and Urban Development in the USSR.* London: Macmillan.

———. 1987. The Built Environment in Soviet Theory and Practice. *International Journal of Urban and Regional Research* 11 (4): 478–99. http://dx.doi.org/10.1111/j.1468-2427.1987.tb00063.x.

———. 1990a. A Note on the Financing of Housing in the Soviet Union. *Soviet Studies* 42 (3): 555–70. http://dx.doi.org/10.1080/09668139008411886.

———. 1990b. "Housing Policy in the Soviet Union." In *Housing Policies in Eastern Europe and the Soviet Union,* edited by John Sillince, 228–329. London: Routledge.

———. 1990c. "The Market as Distributor of Housing under Socialism: Its Virtues and Vices." In *Social Change and Social Issues in the Former USSR,* edited by Walter Joyce, 1–26. New York: St Martin's Press.

———. 1992. Housing Co-operatives in the Soviet Union. *Housing Studies* 7 (2): 138–53. http://dx.doi.org/10.1080/02673039208720730.

———. 2002. "Cooperatives and the Legacy of State Socialism." In *The Legacy of State Socialism and the Future of Transformation,* edited by David Lane, 127–46. Lanham, MD: Rowman and Littlefield.

Aries, Phillipe. 1962. *Centuries of Childhood: A Social History of Family Life.* Translated by Robert Baldick. New York: Knopf.

Arku, Godwin, and Richard Harris. 2005. Housing as a Tool of Economic Development since 1929. *International Journal of Urban and Regional Research* 29 (4): 895–915. http://dx.doi.org/10.1111/j.1468-2427.2005.00627.x.

Attwood, Lynne. 2004. "Housing in the Khrushchev Era." In *Women in the Khrushchev Era,* edited by Melanie Ilič, Susan E. Reid, and Lynne Attwood, 177–202. New York: Palgrave Macmillan.

Balter, Michael. 2006. The Baby Deficit. *Science.* June 30.

Baranskaya, Natalya. 1989. *Nedelia kak nedelia = Just Another Week.* Edited by Lora Paperno, Natalie Roklina, and Richard Leed. Columbus, OH: Slavica.

Basolo, Victoria. 2007. Explaining the Support for Homeownership Policy in US Cities: A Political Economy Perspective. *Housing Studies* 22 (1): 99–119. http://dx.doi.org/10.1080/02673030601024648.

Benford, Robert D., and David A. Snow. 2000. Framing Processes and Social Movements: An Overview and Assessment. *Annual Review of Sociology* 26: 611–39. http://dx.doi.org/10.1146/annurev.soc.26.1.611.

Berezin, Igor'. 2007. Doma, v kotorykh my zhivem. http://www.romir.ru/news/analitika/houses.

Berkowitz, Daniel, Katharina Pistor, and Jean-Francois Richard. 2003. The Transplant Effect. *American Journal of Comparative Law* 51 (1): 163–203. http://dx.doi.org/10.2307/3649143.

Bigulov, V. Kh., A. O. Kryshtanovskii, and A. S. Michurin. 1984. Material'noe blagosostoianie i sotsial'noe blagopoluchie: opyt postroeniia indeksov i analiz vzaimosviazi. *Sotsiologicheskie issledovaniia* 11 (4): 88–94.

Billari, Francesco C., Dimiter Philipov, and Pau Baizán. 2001. Leaving Home in Europe: The Experience of Cohorts Born Around 1960. *International Journal of Population Geography* 7 (5): 339–56. http://dx.doi.org/10.1002/ijpg.231.

Birenbaum-Carmeli, Daphna. 2003. Reproductive Policy in Context: Implications on Women's Rights in Israel, 1945–2000. *Policy Studies* 24 (2–3): 101–13. http://dx.doi.org/10.1080/0144287032000170993.

Blitz, Brad K. 2007. Decentralisation, Citizenship, and Mobility: Residency Restrictions and Skilled Migration in Moscow. *Citizenship Studies* 11 (4): 383–404. http://dx.doi.org/10.1080/13621020701476277.

Blossfeld, Hans Peter, Erik Klijzing, Melinda Mills, and Karin Kurz, eds. 2005. *Globalization, Uncertainty, and Youth in Society: The Losers in a Globalizing World.* London: Routledge.

Bollen, Kenneth A., Jennifer L. Glanville, and Guy Stecklov. 2002. Economic Status Proxies in Studies of Fertility in Developing Countries: Does the Measure Matter? *Population Studies* 56 (1): 81–96. http://dx.doi.org/10.1080/00324720213796.

Bondarenko, Natal'ia. 2002. Tipologiia lichnogo potrebleniia naseleniia Rossii. *Monitoring obshchestvennogo mneniia* 57 (1): 34–44.

——. 2009. Krizis i problemy potrebitel'skogo kreditovaniia. Krizis: samochuvstvie i povedenie potrebitelei (conference sponsored by the Levada Center), February 13.

Bonnell, Victoria E. 1993. The Peasant Woman in Stalinist Political Art of the 1930s. *American Historical Review* 98 (1): 55–82. http://dx.doi.org/10.2307/2166382.

Bourdieu, Pierre. 1984. *Distinction: A Social Critique of the Judgment of Taste.* Cambridge, MA: Harvard University Press.

——. 1991. *Language and Symbolic Power.* Cambridge, MA: Harvard University Press.

——. 2005. *The Social Structures of the Economy.* Cambridge, UK: Polity Press.

Boym, Svetlana. 1994. *Common Places: Mythologies of Everyday Life in Russia.* Cambridge, MA: Harvard University Press.

Breslauer, George W. 1982. *Khrushchev and Brezhnev as Leaders: Building Authority in Soviet Politics.* London: Allen and Unwin.

Brown, Jessica Autumn, and Myra Marx Ferree. 2005. Close Your Eyes and Think of England: Pronatalism in the British Print Media. *Gender and Society* 19 (1): 5–24. http://dx.doi.org/10.1177/0891243204271222.

Buchli, Victor. 1997. Khrushchev, Modernism, and the Fight against *Petit-bourgeois* Consciousness in the Soviet Home. *Journal of Design History* 10 (2): 161–76. http: //dx.doi.org/10.1093/jdh/10.2.161.

Buckley, Cynthia. 1995. The Myth of Managed Migration: Migration Control and the Market in the Soviet Period. *Slavic Review* 54 (4): 896–916. http: //dx.doi. org/10.2307/2501398.

Buckley, Robert M., and Eugene N. Gurenko. 1997. Housing and Income Distribution in Russia: Zhivago's Legacy. *World Bank Research Observer* 12 (1): 19–32. http: //www.jstor.org/stable/3986355.

Buckley, Robert M., and Sasha Tsenkova. 2001. Housing Market Systems in Reforming Socialist Economies: Comparative Indicators of Performance and Policy. *European Journal of Housing Policy* 1 (2): 257–89. http: //dx.doi.org/ 10.1080/14616710110083669.

Burawoy, Michael, Pavel Krotov, and T. Lytkina. 1999. *Ot dereviannogo Parizha k panel'noi orbite: model' zhilishchnykh klassov Syktyvkara.* Syktyvkar: Institut regional'nykh sotsial'nykh issledovanii Respubliki Komi.

Burawoy, Michael, and János Lucáks. 1992. *The Radiant Past: Ideology and Reality in Hungary's Road to Capitalism.* Chicago: University of Chicago Press.

Cairney, John, and Michael H. Boyle. 2004. Home Ownership, Mortgages and Psychological Distress. *Housing Studies* 19 (2): 161–74. http://dx.doi.org/10.1080/ 0267303032000168577.

Calder, Lendol Glen. 1999. *Financing the American Dream: A Cultural History of Consumer Credit.* Princeton, NJ: Princeton University Press.

Carrozzo, Peter. 2004. Marketing the American Mortgage: The Emergency Home Finance Act of 1970, Standardization and the Secondary Market Revolution. *Real Property, Probate and Trust Journal* 39: 765–804.

Carruthers, Bruce G., and Laura Ariovich. 2010. *Money and Credit: A Sociological Approach.* Cambridge, UK: Polity Press.

Carruthers, Bruce G., and Arthur L. Stinchcombe. 1999. The Social Structure of Liquidity: Flexibility, Markets, and States. *Theory and Society* 28 (3): 353–82. http: //dx.doi.org/10.1023/A:1006903103304.

Chan, Cheris Shun-ching. 2009. Creating a Market in the Presence of Cultural Resistance: The Case of Life Insurance in China. *Theory and Society* 38 (3): 271–305. http: //dx.doi.org/10.1007/s11186-008-9081-1.

Chernykh, Alla I. 1995. Zhilishchnyi peredel: Politika 20-kh godov v sfere zhil'ia. *Sotsiologicheskie issledovaniia* 22 (10): 71–78.

Communist Party of the Soviet Union (CPSU). 1961. The 1919 Lenin Program of the CPSU (Bolsheviks). *International Socialist Review* 22 (4): 115–24.

Conley, Dalton, and Brian Gifford. 2006. Home Ownership, Social Insurance, and the Welfare State. *Sociological Forum* 21 (1): 55–82. http: //www.jstor.org/stable/4540927.

Cook, Linda J. 1993. *The Soviet Social Contract and Why It Failed: Welfare Policy and Workers' Politics from Brezhnev to Yeltsin.* Cambridge, MA: Harvard University Press.

———. 2007. *Postcommunist Welfare States: Reform Politics in Russia and Eastern Europe.* Ithaca, NY: Cornell University Press.

Cook, Nicole, Susan J. Smith, and Beverley A. Searle. 2009. Mortgage Markets and Cultures of Consumption. *Consumption, Markets and Culture* 12 (2): 133–54. http: //dx.doi.org/10.1080/10253860902840958.

Crowder, Kyle, Scott J. South, and Erick Chavez. 2006. Wealth, Race, and Inter-Neighborhood Migration. *American Sociological Review* 71 (1): 72–94. http: // dx.doi.org/10.1177/000312240607100104.

Daniel, Zsuzsa. 1985. The Effect of Housing Allocation on Social Inequality in Hungary. *Journal of Comparative Economics* 9 (4): 391–409. http: //dx.doi.org/10.1016/0147-5967(85)90019-8.

Daniell, Jennifer, and Raymond J. Struyk. 1994. Housing Privatization in Moscow: Who Privatizes and Why. *International Journal of Urban and Regional Research* 18 (3): 510–25. http: //dx.doi.org/10.1111/j.1468-2427.1994.tb00281.x.

Davis, Deborah S. 2003. "From Welfare Benefit to Capitalized Asset: The Re-commodification of Residential Space in Urban China." In *Housing and Social Change: East-West Perspectives,* edited by Ray Forrest and James Lee, 183–98. London: Routledge.

———. 2004. "Talking About Property in the New Chinese Domestic Property Regime." In *The Sociology of the Economy,* edited by Frank Dobbin, 288–307. New York: Russell Sage.

———. 2010. Who Gets the House? Renegotiating Property Rights in Post-Socialist Urban China. *Modern China* 36 (5): 463–92. http: //dx.doi.org/10.1177/0097700410373265.

Davis, Deborah S., and Wang Feng, eds. 2008. *Creating Wealth and Poverty in Postsocialist China.* Stanford, CA: Stanford University Press.

De Grazia, Victoria. 1992. *How Fascism Ruled Women: Italy, 1922–1945.* Berkeley: University of California Press.

Demeny, Paul. 2007. A Clouded View of Europe's Demographic Future. *Vienna Yearbook of Population Research:* 27–35. http: //dx.doi.org/10.1553/populationyearbook2007s27.

Dolgova, L. V., V. V. Osipov, and O. B. Pavolotskaia. 1993. Otnoshenie naseleniia k protsessu privatizatsii zhil'ia. *Sotsiologicheskie issledovaniia* 20 (10): 40–47.

Dölling, Irene, Daphne Hahn, and Sylka Scholz. 2000. "Birth Strike in the New Federal States: Is Sterilization an Act of Resistance?" In *Reproducing Gender: Politics, Publics, and Everyday Life after Socialism,* edited by Susan Gal and Gail Kligman, 118–48. Princeton, NJ: Princeton University Press.

Dübel, Hans Joachim, W. Jan Brzeski, and Ellen Hamilton. 2006. Rental Choice and Housing Policy Realignment in Transition: Post-Privatization Challenges in the Europe and Central Asia Region. World Bank Policy Research Working Paper 3884. Washington, DC: World Bank Infrastructure Department, Europe and Central Asia Region. http: //go.worldbank.org/V192521E80.

Dunham, Vera S. 1990. *In Stalin's Time: Middleclass Values in Soviet Fiction.* 2nd ed. Durham, NC: Duke University Press.

Evans, Alfred B., Jr. 1977. Developed Socialism in Soviet Ideology. *Soviet Studies* 29 (3): 409–28. http: //dx.doi.org/10.1080/09668137708411136.

Falaris, Evangelos M. 2003. The Effect of Survey Attrition in Longitudinal Surveys: Evidence From Peru, Côte D'Ivoire and Vietnam. *Journal of Development Economics* 70 (1): 133–57. http: //dx.doi.org/10.1016/S0304-3878(02)00079-2.

Fargues, Philippe. 2000. Protracted National Conflict and Fertility Change: Palestinians and Israelis in the Twentieth Century. *Population and Development Review* 26 (3): 441–82. http: //dx.doi.org/10.1111/j.1728-4457.2000.00441.x.

Fehérváry, Krisztina. 2002. American Kitchens, Luxury Bathrooms, and the Search for a 'Normal Life' in Postsocialist Hungary. *Ethnos* 67 (3): 369–400. http: // dx.doi.org/10.1080/0014184022000031211.

Ferree, Myra Marx, William Anthony Gamson, Jürgen Gerhards, and Dieter Rucht. 2002. *Shaping Abortion Discourse: Democracy and the Public Sphere in Germany and the United States.* Cambridge, UK: Cambridge University Press.

Field, Deborah A. 2007. *Private Life and Communist Morality in Khrushchev's Russia.* New York: Peter Lang.

Fischer, Claude S., and Michael Hout. 2006. *Century of Difference: How America Changed in the Last One Hundred Years.* New York: Russell Sage Foundation.

Fitch Ratings. 2007. Mortgage Market and RMBS: Comparison of Mexico and Russia. *Structured Finance,* October 26.

Fitzpatrick, Sheila. 1992. *The Cultural Front: Power and Culture in Revolutionary Russia.* Ithaca, NY: Cornell University Press.

Fitzpatrick, Sheila, and Yuri Slezkine, eds. 2000. *In the Shadow of Revolution: Life Stories of Russian Women from 1917 to the Second World War.* Princeton, NJ: Princeton University Press.

FOM. 2006a. Ipoteka i problema dostupnosti zhil'ia. August 10. http: //bd.fom.ru/ report/cat/home_fam/hosehom/hom_ipo/dd063123.

———. 2006b. Analiticheskii otchet. Volna 1. Sotsiologicheskii monitoring natsional'nykh proektov. Dokument 4, seriia 1, vypusk 2. April. http: //bd.fom.ru/pdf/np_ cg_02.pdf.

———. 2007a. Natsional'nye proekty skvoz' prizmu obshchestvennogo mneniia. Sotsiologicheskii monitoring natsional'nykh proektov. Dokument 19, seriia 1, vypusk 8. April. http: //bd.fom.ru/pdf/np_cg_08.pdf.

———. 2007b. Shto takoe spravedlivoe obshchesvto? http: //bd.fom.ru/report/cat/ busienss/ec_ref/d074523.

———. 2007c. Zhil'e dlia molodykh semei. May 31. http: //bd.fom.ru/report/map/ d072223.

———. 2008. Zhilishchnyi vopros: polozhenie del. March 27. http: //bd.fom.ru/report/ map/d081221.

———. 2009a. Zhil'e i ipoteka. April 30. http: //bd.fom.ru/report/cat/home_fam/ hosehom/hom_ipo/d091714.

———. 2009b. Godovshchina krizisa. November 5. http: //bd.fom.ru/pdf/d44god.pdf.

———. 2010. Kredity: praktiki i otnoshenie. August 12. http: //bd.fom.ru/pdf/ d31kpo10.pdf.

Frejka, Tomas. 1980. Fertility Trends and Policies: Czechoslovakia in the 1970s. *Population and Development Review* 6 (1): 65–93. http: //dx.doi.org/10.2307/1972658.

Friedman, Debra, Michael Hechter, and Satoshi Kanazawa. 1994. A Theory of the Value of Children. *Demography* 31 (3): 375–401. http: //dx.doi.org/10.2307/ 2061749.

Furstenberg, Frank F., ed. 2002. *Early Adulthood in Cross-National Perspective.* Thousand Oaks, CA: Sage.

Gal, Susan, and Gail Kligman. 2000. *The Politics of Gender after Socialism: A Comparative-Historical Essay.* Princeton, NJ: Princeton University Press.

Galster, George, Dave E. Marcotte, Marvin B. Mandell, Hal Wolman, and Nancy Augustine. 2007. The Impact of Parental Homeownership on Children's

Outcomes during Early Adulthood. *Housing Policy Debate* 18 (4): 785–827. http://dx.doi.org/10.1080/10511482.2007.9521621.

Gauthier, Anne Hélène. 1996. *The State and the Family: A Comparative Analysis of Family Policies in Industrialized Countries.* Oxford: Clarendon Press.

Gelpi, Rosa-Maria, and Francois Julien-Labruyère. 2000. *The History of Consumer Credit: Doctrines and Practices.* Translated by Liam Gavin. New York: St. Martin's Press.

Gerasimova, Katerina. 1999. "The Soviet Communal Apartment." In *Beyond the Limits: The Concept of Space in Russian History and Culture,* edited by Jeremy Smith, 107–30. Helsinki: Suomen Historiallinen Seura (SHS).

——. 2002. "Public Privacy in the Soviet Communal Apartment." In *Socialist Spaces: Sites of Everyday Life in the Eastern Bloc,* edited by David Crowley and Susan E. Reid, 207–30. Oxford: Berg.

——. 2003. "Public Spaces in the Communal Apartment." In *Public Spheres in Soviet-Type Societies: Between the Great Show of the Party-State and Religious Counter-Cultures,* edited by Gábor Tamás Rittersporn, Malte Rolf, and Jan C. Behrends, 165–93. New York: Peter Lang.

Gerber, Theodore P., and Michael Hout. 1998. More Shock Than Therapy: Market Transition, Employment, and Income in Russia, 1991–1995. *American Journal of Sociology* 104 (1): 1–50. http://dx.doi.org/10.1086/210001.

Giddens, Anthony. 1981. *A Contemporary Critique of Historical Materialism.* Vol. 1. London: Macmillan.

Gilbert, Alan. 2002. Power, Ideology and the Washington Consensus: The Development and Spread of Chilean Housing Policy. *Housing Studies* 17 (2): 305–24. http://dx.doi.org/10.1080/02673030220123243.

Gilroy, Rose. 2005. The Role of Housing Space in Determining Freedom and Flourishing in Older People. *Social Indicators Research* 74 (1): 141–58. http://dx.doi.org/10.1007/s11205-005-6520-5.

Goldscheider, Frances, and Julie DaVanzo. 1985. Living Arrangements and the Transition to Adulthood. *Demography* 22 (4): 545–63. http://dx.doi.org/10.2307/2061587.

——. 1986. Semiautonomy and Leaving Home in Early Adulthood. *Social Forces* 65 (1): 187–201. http://dx.doi.org/10.2307/2578942.

Goldstein, Joshua R., Tomáš Sobotka, and Aiva Jasilioniene. 2009. The End of "Lowest-Low" Fertility? *Population and Development Review* 35 (4): 663–99. http://dx.doi.org/10.1111/padr.2009.35.issue-4.

Goskomstat. 1987. *Narodnoe khoziaistvo SSSR za 70 let: iubileinyi statisticheskii ezhegodnik.* Moscow: Financy i statistika.

——. 1991. *Narodnoe khoziaistvo SSSR v 1990 g.: statisticheskii ezhegodnik.* Moscow: Financy i statistika.

——. 2000. *Russian Statistical Yearbook.* Moscow: Goskomstat.

Green, Richard K., and Susan M. Wachter. 2005. The American Mortgage in Historical and International Context. *Journal of Economic Perspectives* 19 (4): 93–114. http://dx.doi.org/10.1257/089533005775196660.

——. 2010. "The Housing Finance Revolution." In *The Blackwell Companion to the Economics of Housing: The Housing Wealth of Nations,* edited by Susan J. Smith and Beverley A. Searle, 414–46. Oxford, UK: Wiley-Blackwell. http://dx.doi.org/10.1002/9781444317978.ch18.

Grishin, Petr, and Maxim Raskosnov. 2007. *Russia's Mortgage Market: Squeeze? What Squeeze?* Renaissance Capital.

Gronow, Jukka. 2003. *Caviar with Champagne: Common Luxury and the Ideals of the Good Life in Stalin's Russia.* Oxford: Berg.

Guiso, Luigi, and Tullio Jappelli. 2002. Private Transfers, Borrowing Constraints, and the Timing of Homeownership. *Journal of Money, Credit, and Banking* 34 (2): 315–39. http: //dx.doi.org/10.1353/mcb.2002.0039.

Gurova, Olga. 2008. Fast Fashion: bystro shit', bystro prodat', bystro vybrosit'. Kontseptsiia mody i potreblenie veshchei v sovremennom rossiiskom obshchestve. *Ekonomicheskaia sotsiologiia* 9 (5): 56–67.

Guseva, Alya. 2008. *Into the Red: The Birth of the Credit Card Market in Postcommunist Russia.* Stanford, CA: Stanford University Press.

Guseva, Yuliya. 2009. Russian Mortgage Finance and Legal Reforms in Times of Financial Crises: Transplanting American Law Models. *Columbia Journal of East European Law* 3 (1): 75–144.

Guzanova, Alla K. 1998. The Housing Market in the Russian Federation: Privatization and Its Implications for Market Development. World Bank Policy Research Paper 1891. Washington, DC: World Bank. http: //go.worldbank.org/OR00IPU2U0.

Hamnett, Chris. 1991. A Nation of Inheritors? Housing Inheritance, Wealth, and Inequality in Britain. *Journal of Social Policy* 20 (4): 509–36. http: //dx.doi.org/10.1017/S0047279400019784.

Harris, Steven E. 2003. Moving to the Separate Apartment: Building, Distributing, Furnishing, and Living in Urban Housing in Soviet Russia, 1950s–1960s. Ph.D. diss., University of Chicago.

——. 2005. In Search of "Ordinary" Russia: Everyday Life in the NEP, the Thaw, and the Communal Apartment. *Kritika: Explorations in Russian and Eurasian History* 6 (3): 583–614. http: //dx.doi.org/10.1353/kri.2005.0038.

Harvey, David. 2010. *The Enigma of Capital and the Crises of Capitalism.* Oxford: Oxford University Press.

Hauslohner, Peter. 1987. Gorbachev's Social Contract. *Soviet Economy* 3 (1): 54–89.

Healy, Kieran. 2006. *Last Best Gifts: Altruism and the Market for Human Blood and Organs.* Chicago: University of Chicago Press.

Helderman, Amanda, and Clara Mulder. 2007. Intergenerational Transmission of Homeownership: The Roles of Gifts and Continuities in Housing Market Characteristics. *Urban Studies* 44 (2): 231–47. http: //dx.doi.org/10.1080/00420980601075018.

Herman, Leon M. 1971. Urbanization and New Housing Construction in the Soviet Union. *American Journal of Economics and Sociology* 30 (2): 203–20. http: //dx.doi.org/10.1111/j.1536-7150.1971.tb02959.x.

Hoffmann, David L. 2000. Mothers in the Motherland: Stalinist Pronatalism in Its Pan-European Context. *Journal of Social History* 34 (1): 35–54. http: //dx.doi.org/10.1353/jsh.2000.0108.

Höjdestrand, Tova. 2009. *Needed by Nobody: Homelessness and Humanness in Post-Socialist Russia.* Ithaca, NY: Cornell University Press.

Holdsworth, Clare. 2000. Leaving Home in Britain and Spain. *European Sociological Review* 16 (2): 201–22. http: //dx.doi.org/10.1093/esr/16.2.201.

Humphrey, Caroline. 1998. The Villas of the "New Russians": A Sketch of Con-
    sumption and Identity in Post-Soviet Landscapes. *Focaal: Globalization / Local-
    ization: Paradoxes of Cultural Identity* 30–31: 85–106.
——. 2005. Ideology in Infrastructure: Architecture and Soviet Imagination. *Journal
    of the Royal Anthropological Institute* 11 (1): 39–58. http: //dx.doi.org/10.1111/
    j.1467-9655.2005.00225.x.
Iacovou, Maria. 2001. Leaving Home in the European Union. ISER Working Papers,
    no. 2001–18, Institute of Social and Economic Research, Essex, UK. http: //
    www.iser.essex.ac.uk/publications/working-papers/iser/2001-18.pdf.
Institute for Urban Economics (IUE). 2007. *Annual Report.* Moscow: Institute for
    Urban Economics.
Izmozik, Vladlen S., and Natal'ia B. Lebina. 2001. Zhilishchnyi vopros v bytu len-
    ingradskoi partiino-sovetskoi nomenklatury 1920–1930-kh godov. *Voprosy
    istorii,* no. 4: 98–110.
Jackson, Kenneth T. 1985. *Crabgrass Frontier: The Suburbanization of the United States.*
    New York: Oxford University Press.
Jarvis, Helen. 2008. "Doing Deals on the House" in a "Post-Welfare" Society: Evi-
    dence of Micro-Market Practices from Britain and the USA. *Housing Studies*
    23 (2): 213–31. http: //dx.doi.org/10.1080/02673030801893149.
Jennings, Marianne M. 2010. *Real Estate Law.* Mason, OH: South-Western Cengage
    Learning.
Johnson, Juliet. 2000. *A Fistful of Rubles: The Rise and Fall of the Russian Banking
    System.* Ithaca, NY: Cornell University Press.
Jones, Gareth A., and Kavita Datta. 2000. Enabling Markets to Work? Housing Policy
    in the "New" South Africa. *International Planning Studies* 5 (3): 393–416. http: //
    dx.doi.org/10.1080/713672861.
Katanian, Konstantin. 1998. The Propiska and the Constitutional Court. *East Euro-
    pean Constitutional Review* 7 (2): 52–57. http: //www1.law.nyu.edu/eecr/
    vol7num2/special/propiska.html.
Keister, Lisa A. 2000. *Wealth in America: Trends in Wealth Inequality.* Cambridge, UK:
    Cambridge University Press.
Kelley, Jonathan, and M.D.R. Evans. 2009. "Economic Development Reduces Tol-
    erance for Inequality: A Comparative Analysis of Thirty Nations." In *The
    International Social Survey Programme 1984–2009: Charting the Globe,* edited
    by Max Haller, Roger Jowell, and Tom W. Smith, 49–71. Abingdon, UK:
    Routledge.
Kelley, Jonathan, and Krzysztof Zagorski. 2005. Economic Change and the Legiti-
    mation of Inequality: The Transition from Socialism to the Free Market in
    Central-East Europe. *Research in Social Stratification and Mobility* 22: 319–64.
    http: //dx.doi.org/10.1016/S0276-5624(04)22011-X.
Kelly, Catriona. 1999. "*Kul'turnost'* in the Soviet Union: Ideal and Reality." In *Rein-
    terpreting Russia,* edited by Geoffrey A. Hosking and Robert Service, 198–213.
    London: Arnold.
——. 2001. *Refining Russia: Advice Literature, Polite Culture, and Gender from Catherine
    to Yeltsin.* Oxford: Oxford University Press.
Kenworthy, Lane. 2007. Inequality and Sociology. *American Behavioral Scientist* 50 (5):
    584–602. http: //dx.doi.org/10.1177/0002764206295008.

Khrushchev, Nikita S. 1955. On Wide-Scale Introduction of Industrial Methods, Improving the Quality and Reducing the Cost of Construction. *Current Digest of the Russian Press* 52 (6): 7–33.

King, Leslie. 1998. "France Needs Children": Pronatalism, Nationalism and Women's Equity. *Sociological Quarterly* 39 (1): 33–52. http: //dx.doi.org/10.1111/j.1533-8525.1998.tb02348.x.

——. 2002. Demographic Trends, Pronatalism, and National Ideologies in the Late Twentieth Century. *Ethnic and Racial Studies* 25 (3): 367–89.

Kligman, Gail. 1992. The Politics of Reproduction in Ceausescu's Romania: A Case Study in Political Culture. *East European Politics and Societies* 6 (3): 364–418. http: //dx.doi.org/10.1177/0888325492006003010.

Kluegel, James R., and Davis S. Mason. 2004. Fairness Matters: Social Justice and Political Legitimacy in Post-Communist Europe. *Europe-Asia Studies* 56 (4): 813–34. http: //dx.doi.org/10.1080/0966813042000258051.

Kohler, Hans-Peter, Francesco C. Billari, and José Antonio Ortega. 2002. The Emergence of Lowest-Low Fertility in Europe during the 1990s. *Population and Development Review* 28 (4): 641–80. http: //dx.doi.org/10.1111/j.1728-4457.2002.00641.x.

Kohler, Hans-Peter, and Iliana Kohler. 2002. Fertility Decline in Russia in the Early and Mid 1990s: The Role of Economic Uncertainty and Labour Market Crises. *European Journal of Population* 18 (3): 233–62. http: //dx.doi.org/10.1023/A:1019701812709.

Konrád, György, and Iván Szelényi. 1979. *The Intellectuals on the Road to Class Power.* New York: Harcourt Brace Jovanovich.

Kosareva, Nadezhda B., ed. 2007. *Osnovy ipotechnogo kreditovaniia.* Moscow: Institut ekonomiki goroda.

Kosareva, Nadezhda B., and Raymond J. Struyk. 1993. Housing Privatization in the Russian Federation. *Housing Policy Debate* 4 (1): 81–100. http: //dx.doi.org/10.1080/10511482.1993.9521125.

Kosareva, Nadezhda B., Andrei Tkachenko, and Raymond J. Struyk. 2000. "Russia: Dramatic Shift to Demand-Side Assistance." In *Homeownership and Housing Finance Policy in the Former Soviet Bloc: Costly Populism,* edited by Raymond J. Struyk, 151–215. Washington, DC: Urban Institute.

Kosareva, Nadezhda B., and Andrei Tumanov. 2008. Assessing Housing Affordability in Russia. *Problems of Economic Transition* 50 (10): 6–29. http: //dx.doi.org/10.2753/PET1061-1991501001.

Kotkin, Stephen. 1995. *Magnetic Mountain: Stalinism as a Civilization.* Berkeley: University of California Press.

Krause, Elizabeth L. 2001. "Empty Cradles" and the Quiet Revolution: Demographic Discourse and Cultural Struggles of Gender, Race, and Class in Italy. *Cultural Anthropology* 16(4): 576–611. http: //dx.doi.org/10.1525/can.2001.16.4.576.

Krause, Elizabeth L., and Milena Marchesi. 2007. Fertility Politics as "Social Viagra": Reproducing Boundaries, Social Cohesion, and Modernity in Italy. *American Anthropologist* 109 (2): 350–62. http://dx.doi.org/10.1525/aa.2007.109.2.350.

Kulu, Hill. 2003. Housing Differences in the Late Soviet City: The Case of Tartu, Estonia. *International Journal of Urban and Regional Research* 27 (4): 897–911. http: //dx.doi.org/10.1111/j.0309-1317.2003.00490.x.

Kulu, Hill, and Andres Vikat. 2007. Fertility Differences by Housing Type: The Effect of Housing Conditions or of Selective Moves? *Demographic Research* 17: 775–802. http://dx.doi.org/10.4054/DemRes.2007.17.26.

Kurz, Karin. 2004. Labour Market Position, Intergenerational Transfers and Home-ownership: A Longitudinal Analysis for West German Birth Cohorts. *European Sociological Review* 20 (2): 141–59. http://dx.doi.org/10.1093/esr/jch009.

Lakoff, George. 1993. "The Contemporary Theory of Metaphor." In *Metaphor and Thought,* edited by Anthony Ortony, 202–51. Cambridge, MA: Cambridge University Press.

Lane, Robert E. 1986. Market Justice, Political Justice. *American Political Science Review* 80 (2): 383–402. http://dx.doi.org/10.2307/1958264.

Langley, Paul. 2008. Sub-Prime Mortgage Lending: A Cultural Economy. *Economy and Society* 37 (4): 469–94. http://dx.doi.org/10.1080/03085140802357893.

Lapidus, Gail Warshofsky. 1982. *Women, Work, and Family in the Soviet Union.* Armonk, NY: M.E. Sharpe.

Lauster, Nathanael T. 2008. Better Homes and Families: Housing Markets and Young Couple Stability in Sweden. *Journal of Marriage and Family* 70 (4): 891–903. http://dx.doi.org/10.1111/j.1741-3737.2008.00534.x.

———. 2010. Housing and the Proper Performance of American Motherhood, 1940–2005. *Housing Studies* 25 (4): 543–57. http://dx.doi.org/ 10.1080/ 02673031003711485.

Lauster, Nathanael T., and Urban Fransson. 2006. Of Marriages and Mortgages: The Second Demographic Transition and the Relationship Between Marriage and Homeownership in Sweden. *Housing Studies* 21 (6): 909–27. http://dx.doi. org/10.1080/02673030600917826.

Lee, Ching Kwan. 2008. "From Inequality to Inequity: Popular Conceptions of Social (In)justice in Beijing." In *Creating Wealth and Poverty in Postsocialist China,* edited by Deborah S. Davis and Wang Feng, 213–31. Stanford, CA: Stanford University Press.

Levada Center. 2010. O reproduktivnom povedenii rossiian. August 19. http:// www.levada.ru/press/2010081900.html.

———. 2011. Rossiiane o bankovskikh kartakh i schetakh. February 28. http://www. levada.ru/press/2011022802.html.

Lovell, Stephen. 2003. *Summerfolk: A History of the Dacha, 1710–2000.* Ithaca, NY: Cornell University Press.

Lux, Martin. 2003. Efficiency and Effectiveness of Housing Policies in the Central and Eastern Europe Countries. *European Journal of Housing Policy* 3 (3): 243–65. http://dx.doi.org/10.1080/14616710310001603712.

Lykova, Tatiana, Ekaterina Petrova, Sergei Sivaev, and Raymond J. Struyk. 2004. Participation in a Decentralised Housing Allowance Programme in a Transition Economy. *Housing Studies* 19 (4): 617–34. http://dx.doi.org/10.1080/02673 03042000221990.

Maier, V. F. 1988. *Planirovanie sotsial'nogo razvitiia i povysheniia urovnia zhizni naroda.* Moscow: Izdatel'stvo MGU.

Maleva, T. M., and O. V. Siniavskaia. 2006. Sotsial'no-ekonomicheskie faktory rozhdaemosti v Rossii: empericheskie izmereniia i vyzovy sotsial'noi politike. *SPERO: Sotsial'naia politika: ekspertiza, rekomendatsii, obrazy,* no. 5: 70–97.

Mandić, Srna. 2001. Residential Mobility versus "In-place" Adjustments in Slovenia: Viewpoint from a Society "in Transition." *Housing Studies* 16 (1): 53–73. http://dx.doi.org/10.1080/02673030020015128.

——. 2008. Home-Leaving and its Structural Determinants in Western and Eastern Europe: An Exploratory Study. *Housing Studies* 23 (4): 615–37. http://dx.doi.org/10.1080/02673030802112754.

Mandić, Srna, and David Clapham. 1996. The Meaning of Home Ownership in the Transition from Socialism: The Example of Slovenia. *Urban Studies* 33 (1): 83–97. http://dx.doi.org/10.1080/00420989650012130.

Manning, Robert D. 2000. *Credit Card Nation: The Consequences of America's Addiction to Credit.* New York: Basic Books.

Marx, Karl. [1875] 1977. "Critique of the Gotha Program." In *Karl Marx: Selected Writings,* edited by David McLellan, 564–70. New York: W. W. Norton.

Mashkina, Olga, Piia Heliste, and Riitta Kosonen. 2007. *The Emerging Mortgage Market in Russia: An Overview with Local and Foreign Perspectives.* Helsinki: Helsinki School of Economics. http://hsepubl.lib.hse.fi/pdf/hseother/b82.pdf.

Matthews, Mervyn. 1978. *Privilege in the Soviet Union: A Study of Elite Life-Styles under Communism.* London: Allen and Unwin.

——. 1979. "Social Dimensions in Soviet Urban Housing." In *The Socialist City: Spatial Structure and Urban Policy,* edited by R. A. French and F. E. Ian Hamilton, 105–18. Chichester, West Sussex, UK: John Wiley and Sons.

——. 1993. *The Passport Society: Controlling Movement in Russia and the USSR.* Boulder, CO: Westview Press.

Mattoso, Cecília Lima do Queirós, and Angela da Rocha. 2008. Building, Losing, and Reconstructing Social Identities: An Investigation into the Symbolic Use of Credit by Poor Consumers in Brazil. *Latin American Business Review* 9 (3/4): 227–55. http://dx.doi.org/10.1080/10978520902754310.

Maurer, Bill. 2006. *Pious Property: Islamic Mortgages in the United States.* New York: Russell Sage Foundation.

McCoy, Patricia A., and Elizabeth Renuart. 2008. "The Legal Infrastructure of Subprime and Nontraditional Home Mortgages." In *Borrowing to Live: Consumer and Mortgage Credit Revisited,* edited by Nicolas P. Retsinas and Eric S. Belsky, 110–137. Washington DC: Brookings Institution Press.

McDonald, Peter. 2000. Gender Equity in Theories of Fertility Transition. *Population and Development Review* 26 (3): 427–39. http://dx.doi.org/10.1111/j.1728-4457.2000.00427.x.

——. 2006. Low Fertility and the State: The Efficacy of Policy. *Population and Development Review* 32 (3): 485–510. http://dx.doi.org/10.1111/j.1728-4457.2006.00134.x.

McIntosh, C. Alison. 1986. Recent Pronatalist Policies in Western Europe. *Population and Development Review* 12: 318–34. http://dx.doi.org/10.2307/2807915.

McIntyre, Robert J. 1975. Pronatalist Programmes in Eastern Europe. *Soviet Studies* 27 (3): 366–80. http://www.jstor.org/stable/150442.

——. 1982. On Demographic Policy Debates in the USSR. *Population and Development Review* 8 (2): 363–64. http://dx.doi.org/10.2307/1972991.

Meerovich, Mark G. 2003. *Ocherki istorii zhilishchnoi politiki v SSSR i ee realizatsii v arkhitekturnom proektirovanii (1917–1941 gg.).* Irkutsk: Izdatel'stvo Irkutskogo gosudarstvennogo tekhnicheskogo universiteta.

Mendelson, Sarah, and Theodore P. Gerber. 2008. Young Russian Women on Procreation, Trafficking, and Prostitution: Myths, Reality, and Policy Implications. Presentation to the Carnegie Moscow Center, Russia, July 23.

Mints, Victor. 2000. Selecting a Housing Finance System for Russia. *Housing Finance International* 15 (2): 49–57.

Moore, Barrington. 1954. *Terror and Progress in the USSR: Some Sources of Change and Stability in the Soviet Dictatorship.* Cambridge, MA: Harvard University Press.

Moskoff, William. 1984. *Labour and Leisure in the Soviet Union: The Conflict between Public and Private Decision-Making in a Planned Economy.* London: Macmillan.

Mroz, T. A., L. Henderson, M. A. Bontch-Osmolovskii, and B. M. Popkin. 2004. Monitoring Economic Conditions in the Russian Federation: The Russian Longitudinal Monitoring Survey 1992–2003. Report Submitted to USAID. Chapel Hill, NC: University of North Carolina at Chapel Hill.

Mukhija, Vinit. 2004. The Contradictions in Enabling Private Developers of Affordable Housing: A Cautionary Case From Ahmedabad, India. *Urban Studies* 41 (11): 2231–44. http://dx.doi.org/10.1080/0042098042000268438.

Mulder, Clara H. 2006a. Home-Ownership and Family Formation. *Journal of Housing and the Built Environment* 21 (3): 281–98. http://dx.doi.org/10.1007/s10901-006-9050-9.

———. 2006b. Population and Housing: A Two-Sided Relationship. *Demographic Research* 15: 401–12. http://dx.doi.org/10.4054/DemRes.2006.15.13.

Mulder, Clara H., and Francesco C. Billari. 2010. Homeownership Regimes and Low Fertility. *Housing Studies* 25 (4): 527–41. http://dx.doi.org/10.1080/02673031003711469.

Mulder, Clara H., and Nathanael T. Lauster. 2010. Housing and Family: An Introduction. *Housing Studies* 25 (4): 433–40. http://dx.doi.org/10.1080/02673031003771109.

Mulder, Clara, H., and Michael Wagner. 2001. The Connections between Family Formation and First-time Home Ownership in the Context of West Germany and the Netherlands. *European Journal of Population* 17 (2): 137–64. http://dx.doi.org/10.1023/A:1010706308868.

Munro, Neil. 2006. Russia's Persistent Communist Legacy: Nostalgia, Reaction, and Reactionary Expectations. *Post-Soviet Affairs* 22 (4): 289–313. http://dx.doi.org/10.2747/1060-586X.22.4.289.

Murrell, Peter. 1993. What Is Shock Therapy? What Did It Do in Poland and Russia? *Post-Soviet Affairs* 9 (2): 111–40.

Myrdal, Alva, and Gunnar Myrdal. 1934. *Kris i befolkningsfragan.* Stokholm: Bonnier.

Neary, Rebecca Balmas. 1999. Mothering Socialist Society: The Wife-Activists' Movement and the Soviet Culture of Daily Life, 1934–41. *Russian Review* 58 (3): 396–412. http://dx.doi.org/10.1111/0036-0341.00081.

Nee, Victor, and Yang Cao. 2002. Postsocialist Inequalities: The Causes of Continuity and Discontinuity. *Research in Social Stratification and Mobility* 19: 3–39. http://dx.doi.org/10.1016/S0276-5624(02)80035-X.

Newman, Sandra J. 2008. Does Housing Matter for Poor Families? A Critical Summary of Research and Issues Still to be Resolved. *Journal of Policy Analysis and Management* 27 (4): 895–925. http://dx.doi.org/10.1002/pam.20381.

Osberg, Lars, and Timothy Smeeding. 2006. "Fair" Inequality? Attitudes toward Pay Differentials: The United States in Comparative Perspective. *American Sociological Review* 71 (3): 450–73. http://dx.doi.org/10.1177/000312240607100305.

Osokina, Elena A. 1997. *Ierarkhiia potrebleniia: o zhizni liudei v usloviiakh stalinskogo snabzheniia, 1928–1935 gg.* Moscow: Izdatel'stvo MGOU.

Oushakine, Serguei Alex. 2009. *The Patriotism of Despair: Nation, War, and Loss in Russia.* Ithaca, NY: Cornell University Press.

PDR. 2006. Vladimir Putin on Raising Russia's Birth Rate. *Population and Development Review* 32 (2): 385–89. http://dx.doi.org/10.1111/j.1728-4457.2006.00126.x.

Perelli-Harris, Brienna. 2005. The Path to Lowest-Low Fertility in Ukraine. *Population Studies* 59 (1): 55–70. http://dx.doi.org/10.1080/0032472052000332700.

———. 2006. The Influence of Informal Work and Subjective Well-Being on Childbearing in Post-Soviet Russia. *Population and Development Review* 32 (4): 729–53. http://dx.doi.org/10.1111/j.1728-4457.2006.00148.x.

Perelli-Harris, Brienna, and Theodore P. Gerber. 2011. Nonmarital Childbearing in Russia: Second Demographic Transition or Pattern of Disadvantage? *Demography* 48 (1): 317–342.

Petrova, A. S. 2003. Khochu zhit' kak belyi chelovek. July 7. http://bd.fom.ru/report/map/of032904.

Philipov, Dimiter, and Aiva Jasilioniene. 2008. Union Formation and Fertility in Bulgaria and Russia: A Life Table Description of Recent Trends. *Demographic Research* 19: 2057–112. http://dx.doi.org/10.4054/DemRes.2008.19.62.

Pickvance, C. G. 1994. Housing Privatization and Housing Protest in the Transition From State Socialism: A Comparative Study of Budapest and Moscow. *International Journal of Urban and Regional Research* 18 (3): 433–50. http://dx.doi.org/10.1111/j.1468-2427.1994.tb00277.x.

Polanyi, Karl. [1944] 2001. *The Great Transformation: The Political and Economic Origins of Our Time.* Boston: Beacon Press.

Polterovich, V. M., and O. Iu. Starkov. 2007. Strategiia formirovaniia ipotechnogo rynka v Rossii. *Ekonomika i matematicheskie metody* 43 (4): 3–22.

Popov, Valerii P. 1996. Pasportnaia sistema sovetskogo krepostnichestva. *Novyi Mir,* no. 6. http://magazines.russ.ru/novyi_mi/1996/6/popov.html.

Powell, Mark. 1999. The Pronatalist Undercurrent of the $500-per-Child Tax Credit. *Population and Environment* 20 (5): 455–65. http://dx.doi.org/10.1023/A:1023313103035.

Reid, Susan E. 2002. Cold War in the Kitchen: Gender and the De-Stalinization of Consumer Taste in the Soviet Union under Khrushchev. *Slavic Review* 61 (2): 211–52. http://dx.doi.org/10.2307/2697116.

———. 2005. The Khrushchev Kitchen: Domesticating the Scientific-Technological Revolution. *Journal of Contemporary History* 40 (2): 289–316. http://dx.doi.org/10.1177/0022009405051554.

———. 2008. Who Will Beat Whom? Soviet Popular Reception of the American National Exhibition in Moscow, 1959. *Kritika: Explorations in Russian and Eurasian History* 9 (4): 855–904. http://dx.doi.org/10.1353/kri.0.0030.

———. 2009. Communist Comfort: Socialist Modernism and the Making of Cosy Homes in the Khrushchev Era. *Gender and History* 21 (3): 465–98. http://dx.doi.org/10.1111/j.1468-0424.2009.01564.x.

Reutov, Evgenii Viktorovich. 2006. Obshchestvo i vlast': krizis legitimnosti? *Sotsiologicheskie issledovaniia* 32: 82–88.

Rex, John A. 1968. "The Sociology of a Zone of Transition." In *Readings in Urban Sociology,* edited by R. E. Pahl, 211–31. London: Pergamon Press.

Ries, Nancy. 1997. *Russian Talk: Culture and Conversation during Perestroika.* Ithaca, NY: Cornell University Press.

Rivkin-Fish, Michele. 2003. Anthropology, Demography, and the Search for a Critical Analysis of Fertility: Insights from Russia. *American Anthropologist* 105 (2): 289–301. http: //dx.doi.org/10.1525/aa.2003.105.2.289.

——. 2010. Pronatalism, Gender Politics, and the Renewal of Family Support in Russia: Toward a Feminist Anthropology of "Maternity Capital." *Slavic Review* 69 (3): 701–24.

Roberts, Ken, Galina I. Osadchaya, Khasan V. Dsuzev, Victor G. Gorodyanenko, and Jochen Tholen. 2003. Economic Conditions, and the Family and Housing Transitions of Young Adults in Russia and Ukraine. *Journal of Youth Studies* 6 (1): 71–88.

Rojas, Eduardo. 2001. The Long Road to Housing Sector Reform: Lessons from the Chilean Housing Experience. *Housing Studies* 16 (4): 461–83. http: //dx.doi. org/10.1080/02673030120066554.

ROMIR. 2009. Dve treti rossiian, esli im srochno ponadobiatsia den'gi, budut brat' ikh v kredit. http://romir.ru/about/newsletter_July09.html.

Roshchina, Ia. M. 2006. Modelirovanie faktorov sklonnosti sem'i k rozhdeniiu rebenka v Rossii. *SPERO: Sotsial'naia politika: ekspertiza, rekomendatsii, obrazy,* no. 5: 98–133.

Rossi, Giovanna. 1997. The Nestlings: Why Young Adults Stay at Home Longer: The Italian Case. *Journal of Family Issues* 18 (6): 627–44. http: //dx.doi.org/10.1177/019251397018006004.

Rosstat. Federal'naia sluzhba gosudarstvennoi statistiki. http: //www.gks.ru.

——. 2007. *Zhilishchnoe khoziaistvo i bytovoe obsluzhivanie naseleniia v Rossii.* Federal'naia sluzhba gosudarstvennoi statistiki.

Roth-Ey, Kristin. 2007. Finding a Home for Television in the USSR, 1950–1970. *Slavic Review* 66 (2): 278–306. http: //dx.doi.org/10.2307/20060221.

Rotkirch, Anna, Anna Temkina, and Elena Zdravomyslova. 2007. Who Helps the Degraded Housewife? Comments on Vladimir Putin's Demographic Speech. *European Journal of Women's Studies* 14 (4): 349–57. http: //dx.doi. org/10.1177/1350506807081884.

Roy, Friedemann. 2008. Mortgage Markets in Central and Eastern Europe: A Review of Past Experiences and Future Perspectives. *European Journal of Housing Policy* 8 (2): 133–60. http: //dx.doi.org/10.1080/14616710802061953.

Ruble, Blair A. 1993. "From *Khrushcheby* to *Korobki.*" In *Russian Housing in the Modern Age: Design and Social History,* edited by William Craft Brumfield and Blair A. Ruble, 232–70. Washington, DC: Woodrow Wilson Center Press.

Ruggles, Steven. 2007. The Decline of Intergenerational Coresidence in the United States, 1850 to 2000. *American Sociological Review* 72 (6): 964–89. http: //dx.doi. org/10.1177/000312240707200606.

Saunders, Peter. 1984. Beyond Housing Classes: The Sociological Significance of Private Property Rights in Means of Consumption. *International Journal of Urban and Regional Research* 8 (2): 202–27. http: //dx.doi.org/10.1111/j.1468-2427.1984.tb00608.x.

Schaible, Damian. S. 2001. Life in Russia's "Closed City": Moscow's Movement Restrictions and the Rule of Law. *New York University Law Review* 76 (1): 344–73.

Schwartz, Harry. 1965. *The Soviet Economy since Stalin*. Philadelphia: Lippincott.

Schwartz, Herman, and Leonard Seabrooke. 2008. Varieties of Residential Capitalism in the International Political Economy: Old Welfare States and the New Politics of Housing. *Comparative European Politics* 6 (3): 237–61. http://dx.doi.org/10.1057/cep.2008.10.

Semenova, Victoria. 2004. "Equality in Poverty: The Symbolic Meaning of *Kommunalki* in the 1930s–50s." In *On Living through Soviet Russia*, edited by Daniel Bertaux, Paul Thompson, and Anna Rotkirch, 53–66. London: Routledge.

Sheptulina, N.N. 1982. "Protection of Female Labor." In *Women, Work, and Family in the Soviet Union*, edited by Gail Warshofsky Lapidus. Armonk, NY: M.E. Sharpe.

Shevchenko, Olga. 2009. *Crisis and the Everyday in Postsocialist Moscow*. Bloomington: Indiana University Press.

Shlapentokh, Vladimir. 1999. Social Inequality in Post-communist Russia: The Attitudes of the Political Elite and the Masses (1991–1998). *Europe-Asia Studies* 51 (7): 1167–81. http://dx.doi.org/10.1080/09668139998480.

Sidorov, Dmitry A. 1992. Variations in Perceived Level of Prestige of Residential Areas in the Former USSR. *Urban Geography* 13 (4): 355–73. http://dx.doi.org/10.2747/0272-3638.13.4.355.

Siegelbaum, Lewis H. 1998. "Dear Comrade, You Ask What We Need": Socialist Paternalism and Soviet Rural "Notables" in the mid-1930s. *Slavic Review* 57 (1): 107–32. http://dx.doi.org/10.2307/2502055.

Simpson, Alfred William Brian. 1986. *A History of the Land Law*. 2nd ed. Oxford: Clarendon Press.

Skyner, Louis. 2005. Rehousing and Refinancing Russia: Creating Access to Affordable Mortgaging. *Europe-Asia Studies* 57 (4): 561–81. http://dx.doi.org/10.1080/09668130500105126.

Slavnikova, N. I., et al. 2000. "Speeches by Stakhanovites." In *In the Shadow of Revolution: Life Stories of Russian Women from 1917 to the Second World War*, edited by Sheila Fitzpatrick and Yuri Slezkine, 331–41. Princeton, NJ: Princeton University Press.

Smith, Susan J., M. Munro, J. Ford, and R. Davis. 2002. *A Review of Flexible Mortgages*. London: Council of Mortgage Lenders.

Spilerman, Seymour. 2000. Wealth and Stratification Processes. *Annual Review of Sociology* 26: 497–524. http://dx.doi.org/10.1146/annurev.soc.26.1.497.

———. 2004. The Impact of Parental Wealth on Early Living Standards in Israel. *American Journal of Sociology* 110 (1): 92–122. http://dx.doi.org/10.1086/424943.

Stark, Laura, and Hans-Peter Kohler. 2002. The Debate over Low Fertility in the Popular Press: A Cross-National Comparison, 1998–1999. *Population Research and Policy Review* 21 (6): 535–74. http://dx.doi.org/10.1023/A:1022990905200.

———. 2004. The Popular Debate about Low Fertility: An Analysis of the German Press, 1993–2001. *European Journal of Population* 20 (4): 293–321. http://dx.doi.org/10.1007/s10680-004-1695-z.

Stephenson, Svetlana. 2006. *Crossing the Line: Vagrancy, Homelessness and Social Displacement in Russia*. Aldershot, Hampshire, UK: Ashgate.

Stiglitz, Joseph E. 2008. "Is There a Post-Washington Consensus Consensus?" In *The Washington Consensus Reconsidered: Towards a New Global Governance,* edited by Narcis Serra and Joseph E. Stiglitz, 41–56. Oxford: Oxford University Press.

Ström, Sara. 2010. Housing and First Births in Sweden, 1972–2005. *Housing Studies* 25 (4): 509–26. http://dx.doi.org/10.1080/02673031003711519.

Struyk, Raymond J. 1997. *Housing Sector Reform Project I: Final Report.* Washington DC: Urban Institute.

——. 1998. *Housing Sector Reform Project II: Final Report.* Washington DC: Urban Institute.

——, ed. 2000. *Homeownership and Housing Finance Policy in the Former Soviet Bloc: Costly Populism.* Washington, DC: Urban Institute.

Struyk, Raymond J., Alexander S. Puzanov, and Lisa A. Lee. 1997. Monitoring Russia's Experience with Housing Allowances. *Urban Studies* 34 (11): 1789–818. http://dx.doi.org/10.1080/0042098975259.

Stryker, Robin. 2000. Legitimacy Processes as Institutional Politics: Implications for Theory and Research in the Sociology of Organizations. *Research in the Sociology of Organizations* 17: 179–223. http://dx.doi.org/10.1016/S0733-558X(00)17006-5.

Sun, Shirley Hsiao-Li. 2012. *Population Policy and Reproduction in Singapore: Making Future Citizens.* London: Routledge.

Sutela, Pekka. 1994. Insider Privatisation in Russia: Speculations on Systemic Change. *Europe-Asia Studies* 46 (3): 417–35. http://dx.doi.org/10.1080/09668139408412171.

Swafford, Michael, and Mikhail Kosolapov. 2002. Sample Design, Response Rates, and Weights in the Russian Longitudinal Monitoring Survey, Rounds 5 to 10: An Abbreviated Description. Institute of Sociology, Russian Academy of Sciences, unpublished working paper.

Swafford, Michael, Polina Kozyreva, Mikhail Kosolapov, Gennady Denisovsky, and Alfiya Nizamova. 1995. General Social Survey of the European USSR, April-May 1991. [Computer file]. ICPSR06500-v1. Ann Arbor, MI: Inter-university Consortium for Political and Social Research [distributor]. http://dx.doi.org/10.3886/ICPSR06500.

Szelényi, Iván. 1983. *Urban Inequalities under State Socialism.* Oxford: Oxford University Press.

Tikhonova, Nataliya. 2004. "Social Exclusion in Russia." In *Poverty and Social Exclusion in the New Russia,* edited by Nick Manning and Nataliya Tikhonova, 109–46. Burlington, VT: Ashgate.

Timasheff, Nicholas S. 1946. *The Great Retreat: The Growth and Decline of Communism in Russia.* New York: E.P. Dutton.

Tran, Hoai Anh, and Elisabeth Dalholm. 2005. Favoured Owners, Neglected Tenants: Privatisation of State Owned Housing in Hanoi. *Housing Studies* 20 (6): 897–929. http://dx.doi.org/10.1080/02673030500291066.

Trifonov, Yury. 1973. *The Exchange.* In *The Long Goodbye: Three Novellas,* 17–97. New York: Harper and Row.

United Nations. 2008. *World Population Policies 2007.* New York: Department of Economic and Social Affairs. http://www.un.org/esa/population/publications/wpp2007/Publication_index.htm.

United Nations Economic Commission for Europe (UNECE). 2004. Country Profile on the Housing Sector: Russian Federation. http://www.unece.org/hlm/prgm/cph/countries/russia/welcome.html.

———. 2005. *Housing Finance Systems for Countries in Transition: Principles and Examples.* New York: United Nations.

United Nations in Russia. 2008. Demographic Policy in Russia: From Reflection to Action. http://www.undp.ru/download.php?749.

Utekhin, Il'ia. 2004. *Ocherki kommunal'nogo byta.* Moscow: OGI.

van de Kaa, Dirk J. 1987. Europe's Second Demographic Transition. *Population Bulletin* 42 (1): 1–59.

Varga-Harris, Christine. 2008. Homemaking and the Aesthetic and Moral Perimeters of the Soviet Home during the Khrushchev Era. *Journal of Social History* 41 (3): 561–89. http://dx.doi.org/10.1353/jsh.2008.0051.

Verdery, Katherine. 1996. *What Was Socialism, and What Comes Next?* Princeton, NJ: Princeton University Press.

Verhoeven, Willem-Jan, Wim Jansen, and Jos Dessens. 2005. Income Attainment during Transformation Processes: A Meta-Analysis of the Market Transition Theory. *European Sociological Review* 21 (3): 201–26. http://dx.doi.org/10.1093/esr/jci020.

Vishnevskii, A. G., E. M. Andreev, and A. I. Treivish. 2004. Prospects for Russia's Development: The Role of the Demographic Factor. *Problems of Economic Transition* 46 (11): 6–95.

Vlasovskaia, A.V., et al. 2000. "Speeches by Stakhanovites' Wives." In *In the Shadow of Revolution: Life Stories of Russian Women from 1917 to the Second World War,* edited by Sheila Fitzpatrick and Yuri Slezkine, 359–66. Princeton, NJ: Princeton University Press.

Volkonskaia, Sofia. 2000. "The Way of Bitterness." In *In the Shadow of Revolution: Life Stories of Russian Women from 1917 to the Second World War,* edited by Sheila Fitzpatrick and Yuri Slezkine, 140–65. Princeton, NJ: Princeton University Press.

Volkov, A.G. 1982. "Changes in the Status of Women and the Demographic Development of the Family." In *Women, Work, and Family in the Soviet Union,* edited by Gail Warshofsky Lapidus, 218–30. Armonk, NY: M. E. Sharpe.

Volkov, Vadim. 2000. "The Concept of Kul'turnost': Notes on the Stalinist Civilizing Process." In *Stalinism: New Directions,* edited by Sheila Fitzpatrick, 210–30. London: Routledge.

Walker, Charles. 2010. Space, Kinship Networks and Youth Transition in Provincial Russia: Negotiating Urban-Rural and Inter-Regional Migration. *Europe-Asia Studies* 62 (4): 647–69. http://dx.doi.org/10.1080/09668131003736995.

Weber, Max. 1978. *Economy and Society: An Outline of Interpretive Sociology.* Edited by Guenther Roth and Claus Wittich. Berkeley: University of California Press.

White, Anne. 1990. *De-Stalinization and the House of Culture: Declining State Control over Leisure in the USSR, Poland, and Hungary, 1953–89.* London: Routledge.

White, Brent T. 2010a. The Morality of Strategic Default. *UCLA Law Review Discourse* 58: 155–64.

White, Brent T. 2010b. Underwater and Not Walking Away: Shame, Fear, and the Social Management of the Housing Crisis. *Wake Forest Law Review* 45: 971–1023.

Whittington, Leslie A., James Alm, and H. Elizabeth Peters. 1990. Fertility and the Personal Exemption: Implicit Pronatalist Policy in the United States. *American Economic Review* 80 (3): 545–56. http://www.jstor.org/stable/2006683.

Whyte, Martin King. 2010a. *Myth of the Social Volcano: Perceptions of Inequality and Distributive Injustice in Contemporary China.* Stanford, CA: Stanford University Press.

——. 2010b. "Fair versus Unfair: How Do Chinese Citizens View Current Inequalities?" In *Growing Pains: Tensions and Opportunity in China's Transformation,* edited by Jean Chun Oi, Scott Rozelle, and Xueguang Zhou, 305–32. Stanford, CA: Shorenstein Asia-Pacific Research Center.

Williamson, John. 1990. "What Washington Means by Policy Reform." In *Latin American Adjustment: How Much Has Happened?,* edited by John Williamson, 7–40. Washington, DC: Institute for International Economics.

Wolchik, Sharon L. 2000. "Reproductive Policies in the Czech and Slovak Republics." In *Reproducing Gender: Politics, Publics, and Everyday Life after Socialism,* edited by Susan Gal and Gail Kligman, 58–91. Princeton, NJ: Princeton University Press.

World Bank. 1993. *Housing: Enabling Markets to Work.* Washington, DC: World Bank. http://go.worldbank.org/NEGGR70NK0.

Yemtsov, Ruslan. 2008. "Housing Privatization and Household Wealth in Transition." In *Personal Wealth from a Global Perspective,* edited by James B. Davies, 312–33. Oxford: Oxford University Press.

Yurchak, Alexei. 2003. Soviet Hegemony of Form: Everything Was Forever, Until It Was No More. *Comparative Studies in Society and History* 45 (3): 480–510. http://dx.doi.org/10.1017/S0010417503000239.

Zakharov, Sergei. 2008. Russian Federation: From the First to Second Demographic Transition. *Demographic Research* 19: 907–72. http://dx.doi.org/10.4054/DemRes.2008.19.24.

Zaslavsky, Victor. 1980. Socioeconomic Inequality and Changes in Soviet Ideology. *Theory and Society* 9 (2): 383–407. http://dx.doi.org/10.1007/BF00207283.

Zavisca, Jane R. 2003. Contesting Capitalism at the Post-Soviet Dacha: The Meaning of Food Cultivation for Urban Russians. *Slavic Review* 62 (4): 786–810. http://dx.doi.org/10.2307/3185655.

——. 2004. Consumer Inequalities and Regime Legitimacy in Late Soviet and Post-Soviet Russia. Ph.D. diss., University of California, Berkeley.

——. 2008. Property without Markets: Housing Policy and Politics in Post-Soviet Russia, 1992–2007. *Comparative European Politics* 6: 365–386. http://dx.doi.org/10.1057/cep.2008.16.

Zelizer, Viviana A. 2005. *The Purchase of Intimacy.* Princeton, NJ: Princeton University Press.

Zhou, Xueguang, and Olga Suhomlinova. 2001. Redistribution under State Socialism: A USSR and PRC Comparison. *Research in Social Stratification and Mobility* 18: 163–204. http://dx.doi.org/10.1016/S0276-5624(01)80026-3.

Zubrzycki, Geneviève. 2007. "The Cross, the Madonna, and the Jew: Persistent Symbolic Representations of the Nation in Poland." In *Nationalism in a Global Era: The Persistence of Nations,* edited by Mitchell Young, Eric Zuelow, and Andreas Sturm, 118–40. Abingdon, UK: Routledge.

◼ INDEX

affordability
  housing purchase, 16–18, 55–61, 119–28,
    145
  mortgages, 1–2, 60–61, 66–67, 83–84,
    175, 184–85
  rentals, 111–12, 152
AHML (Agency for Home Mortgage
  Lending), 53–54, 64–67
apartments. *See* khrushchevkas; separate
  apartments
aspirations. *See* dream houses; satisfaction;
  separate apartments
autonomy
  concept, 87, 90–91, 114
  control over space, 108–9, 154
  preference for, 105–13, 154
  See also under ownership

banks, 62–67, 180–83, 188–93
  See also mortgages
Bausparkassen (German housing banks),
  50, 197
birthrate, 72, 85
  maternity capital, effect on, 68, 85, 163,
    165–72
  See also fertility decline
Bourdieu, Pierre, 7–9, 178, 185, 198
Brezhnev, Leonid, 34, 45
builders. *See* construction

childbearing
  education and, 94, 148–49, 151, 154–62,
    167–68
  first vs. second child, 8, 149, 150–53,
    157, 168
  housing and, 58, 93–98, 113–15, 145,
    149–54, 157–62
  morality of, 168–72
  work/employment and, 146–50, 153, 162
  See also fertility decline

children, preferred number, 8, 116, 145,
  149–54, 157, 162, 165–66, 168
children's rooms, 3–4, 46, 106, 108, 115–16,
  144, 149–50, 153–56
China, 5, 105, 132–33
civilization discourse
  popular, 155–56, 174, 197
  state, 1–2, 7–8, 28, 60, 64
class. *See* housing classes; inequality
Cold War, 32, 44–47, 181
commodification of housing, 6, 85–88, 92,
  100
communal apartments, 13, 24–25, 28–29,
  33, 43
construction
  attitudes toward, 117, 122–23, 127–28, 197
  Soviet, 24, 29–35, 40–41, 47–48
  trends, 1, 16–19, 51–55, 60–62, 70,
    80–81, 86–88, 160
consumer credit, 1–2, 9–11, 176–81, 186–
  92, 196–97
  See also mortgages
consumerism, 26–29, 41–46, 78, 164, 170–
  72, 178–79
consumption, 3, 10, 32–33, 86, 104
control. *See* autonomy
corruption
  banks/builders, 122–24, 192–93, 197
  Soviet, 35, 121
  state, 57–58, 127–28, 166, 173–74
cost of housing. *See* affordability
credit, consumer, 1–2, 9–11, 176–81, 186–
  92, 196–97
  See also mortgages
crisis, demographic, 7, 61, 74–78, 82, 164
  See also fertility decline
crisis, housing as symbol of, 2, 8, 19, 103,
  128
crisis, permanent, 19, 180–82, 186–90, 193,
  195–96

crisis of 2008–2010, 19, 62–63, 66–68,
    80–81, 198–99
crowding, 3–4, 46, 88–89, 112, 139–42,
    151–56
    See also extended family, living with; hostels

dachas, 45
Davis, Deborah, 5–6, 132–33
demographic crisis, 7, 61, 74–78, 82, 164
    See also fertility decline
dependence. *See* extended family, living with
detached homes. *See* dream houses; elite
    housing
distributive justice, 103–5, 118–26, 174
divorce, 35, 45, 115, 132, 140–42, 173, 190
domesticity, 108–14, 154
dormitories. *See* hostels
dream houses, 106–7, 114–18, 153–54

education
    attitudes toward markets and, 105, 128,
        196–97
    childbearing and, 94, 148–49, 151, 154–
        62, 167–68
    housing inequality and, 97–99
    housing preferences and, 93–94, 114–18,
        146
    perceptions of justice and, 103, 105,
        119–20, 122, 125–26, 128
elite housing, 54–55, 90, 115–17, 120,
    184–85, 188
employment. *See* work/employment
entitlement reform, 52–54, 57–58
entitlement to housing. *See* right to housing
Europe/West, compared to Russia
    household structure, 93–95, 99–100, 194
    housing markets, 50–51, 57, 60–61, 65–66
    pronatalism, 69, 72–74, 76–78
    stability, 156, 178, 186, 188, 197
    style, 114–17
extended family
    gift/inheritance from, 60, 110, 114–19,
        132, 135–42, 155, 169, 195
    inequality within, 109, 115, 135–42
    living with, 3–4, 90–97, 107–15, 131–32,
        136–38, 145, 150–51
    See also autonomy; separate apartments

fairness, 103–5, 118–26, 174
family. *See* children; divorce; extended fam-
    ily; marriage; nuclear family; single
    mothers; singles
Fannie Mae, 53, 66
fate, 117–19, 122, 125, 191
    See also hope and hopelessness

fertility decline
    comparative perspective, 72–74
    consumerism and, 45–46, 78
    crisis of, 7, 61, 74–78, 82, 164
    housing/economy and, 8, 145–50,
        162–68, 172
    second demographic transition and,
        155–56, 167–68
    See also birthrate; childbearing; maternity
        capital; pronatalism
fertility rate. *See* birthrate
foreclosure, 4, 66–67, 153, 180–83
    See also mortgage law
furniture
    in rentals, 113–14
    Soviet, 27–28, 30–33, 41–43, 46
    style, 108–10, 117

Gaidar, Yegor, 124
gender issues
    inequality, 72–73, 93, 140
    paternalism, 69–71, 81–82, 171–73
    reproductive decisions, 150–51
    See also pronatalism
generations, 11–12, 196
    See also children; extended family
Germany, 50, 78, 188, 197
Giddens, Anthony, 5
government-sponsored enterprises (GSEs),
    50, 53–54, 64–67
Guseva, Alya, 10, 176, 189–91
Guseva, Yulia, 65, 134, 177, 210n22

Harris, Steven, 13, 27–30, 43
Harvey, David, 7
home improvement, 89–90, 114, 117, 155
homelessness, 13, 36, 113, 125
    See also propiskas
home ownership. *See* ownership; separate
    apartments
hope and hopelessness, 117, 125, 127, 139,
    142, 164–65
    Soviet vs. post-Soviet, 3–4, 33, 107, 115,
        122, 152
hostels
    living in, 113, 122, 139, 152, 156, 165
    prevalence of, 25, 91–92
households. *See* extended family; nuclear
    family; single mothers; singles
houses. *See* elite housing
housing classes, 8–9, 36–37, 86–87,
    147–48
    See also inequality, housing
housing finance. *See* mortgages
housing inequality. *See* inequality, housing

housing markets. *See* market failure; market
reform
housing mobility. *See* mobility
housing policy. *See name of policy,* e.g. maternity capital, Young Families Program
housing subsidies. *See* subsidies, housing
HSRP (Housing Sector Reform Project), 1,
49–54, 86–87, 104

income
distributive injustice and, 104–5, 123–24,
187
housing status and, 92–100
See also affordability; work/employment
independence. *See* autonomy
inequality, housing
concept of, 8–9, 86–87
determinants of, 88–90, 92–100
ideology on, 6, 26–27, 34, 70, 82–87
intra-family, 12, 135–38, 140
legitimacy of, 84, 103–5, 119–25
Soviet, 26–29, 34–41, 47, 89f, 94–95
See also housing classes; mobility patterns
inheritance
fairness of, 6, 119–20, 123–26, 191, 199
and inequality, 37, 88, 90–94, 98–99, 105,
118, 169
mobility and, 60, 110, 114–19, 132,
135–42, 155, 169, 195
in-laws. *See* extended family
instability. *See* stability and instability
installment loans, 10, 53, 55, 130, 176,
188–90, 197
See also mortgages
Institute for Urban Economics (IUE), 53
interiors, 30–31, 89–90, 108, 113–17, 134
See also furniture
Irony of Fate (film), 42–43
Islamic mortgages, 197

jobs. *See* work/employment
justice, distributive, 103–5, 118–26, 174

Kaluga, 13–19, 52, 55, 61–62, 111–12, 116,
127–28
Khrushchev, Nikita, 23, 29–34, 43, 144,
181, 194
khrushchevkas (Soviet apartments)
design/quality, 15, 17f, 30–31, 56
living in, 3–4, 43, 46, 154, 184–85
Kitchen Debate (Khrushchev/Nixon), 32, 181
kitchens
renovated, 89–90
Soviet, 30–33, 40–41
two women in, 108–9, 112–13

Kosareva, Nadezhda, 51–53, 209n8, 210n22
Kotkin, Stephen, 25
kottedzhy. *See* dream houses; elite housing

labor. *See* work/employment
law, mortgage, 53–54, 64–65, 134–35,
142–43
law on privatization, 51–52, 109, 134
leaving parental home. *See* autonomy;
extended family; separate apartments
legitimacy
inequality, 84, 103–5, 119–25
market reform, 2, 6, 8, 57–59, 120, 122–
28, 192–97
mortgages, 10–11, 163–64, 176–79, 196–99
Lenin, Vladimir, 23–24, 26
living space norm
and eligibility for subsidies, 58, 62,
139–40
Soviet origins, 24–26, 29–31, 44
loans. *See* installment loans; mortgages
luck, 117–19, 122, 125, 191
See also hope and hopelessness
luxury housing. *See* elite housing

Manning, Robert, 178–79, 186, 189, 192
market, control of. *See* state control of
market
market failure, 2–3, 6–8, 54–58, 99–100,
122, 175–77, 192–95
See also property without markets
market reform, 51–54, 57–59, 61–68
legitimacy of, 2, 6–8, 57–59, 105, 120,
122–28, 192–99
See also HSRP; privatization; United
States, influence in Russia; Washington
Consensus
marriage and housing, 4, 35–40, 62, 93–94,
115, 140–42, 151–52
See also divorce
Marx, Karl, 26, 34, 36–37
maternity capital, 1
attitudes toward, 151, 165–72, 193
effect on birthrate, 68, 85, 163, 165–72
as housing market stimulus, 7, 62–63,
69–71, 79–81
inequality and, 82–84
as legitimation strategy, 68, 85, 163–64,
172–74
as pronatalist stimulus, 78–79, 82, 144–45
See also pronatalism
Medvedev, Dmitri, 1–2, 61, 75, 77, 80–82, 127
methodology, 11–15, 71, 96–97, 157–60
middle-class identity, 28, 79–84, 99, 168–70
See also normalcy

mobility patterns, 56–57, 89–92, 118
  See also inequality, housing
mobility strategies, 114–19, 127–28, 135–
  42, 155, 182–83, 191
money, social meaning of, 10–11, 178–79
mortgage law, 53–54, 64–65, 134–35, 142–43
mortgages
  affordability, 1–2, 60–61, 66–67, 83–84,
    175, 184–85
  demand, 10–11, 175–76, 189, 195–97
  property rights, 2–3, 135–36, 181–86
  securitization, 50, 53–54, 62–67
  state discourse on, 1–2, 58–64, 77–78,
    81, 175
  subsidies, 61–63, 80–81, 139–40, 191
  terms and trends, 59–60, 62, 64–67, 175
  See also installment loans; maternity
    capital; United States; Young Families
    Program
mortgages, perceptions of
  debt bondage (kabala), 4, 176, 179–83,
    186–93
  legitimacy, 10–11, 163–64, 176–79,
    196–99
  ownership and, 2–4, 6, 12, 176–78,
    181–86, 198
mortgagors, 110–11, 119, 153, 166, 183–85,
  190–91
Moscow, 16–18, 35–36, 57–58, 61, 133–34
multiuse rooms, 30–32

neoliberalism. *See* Washington Consensus
normalcy and abnormalcy
  of mortgages, 180–83, 190, 192–93
  of nuclear family, 45–46, 58, 114, 169–
    70, 194
  of postsocialism, 105, 117, 124, 126, 156,
    172–74, 187, 198
  of separate apartment, 4–5, 8, 41–47, 85,
    110, 113, 132, 142–45, 148–55, 162,
    165
nostalgia, 8, 196–97
  See also socialism and postsocialism
nuclear family, 4–5, 28–29, 45–46, 106, 132,
  169, 194
  See also autonomy; normalcy, nuclear
    family

Oushakine, Serguei, 76, 217n3
ownership
  autonomy and, 12, 87, 106–11, 131, 145
  mortgages and, 2–4, 6, 12, 176–78,
    181–86, 198
  privatization and, 88, 92, 99–100, 134,
    138–40

security and, 5–6, 9, 12, 111–14, 135–38,
  140–42, 152–53, 194
Soviet sense of, 41, 43–47, 121, 123, 131
See also property rights; propiskas; separate apartments

Perelli-Harris, Brienna, 93, 148–49, 177–78
perestroika, 6, 47–48
permanent crisis, 19, 180–82, 186–90, 193,
  195–96
placemaking. *See* domesticity
policy. *See name of policy*, e.g. maternity
  capital, Young Families Program
postsocialism. *See under* normalcy and
  abnormalcy; socialism and postsocialism
poverty. *See* inequality
preferences in housing
  for autonomy, 105–13, 154
  education and, 93–94, 114–18, 146
  for separate apartments, 4, 8, 93, 105–18,
    123, 145, 184
  See also dream houses
preferred number of children, 8, 116, 145,
  149–54, 157, 162, 165–66, 168
price controls, 11, 123–24, 128, 196
prices. *See* affordability
Priority National Projects, 61–64, 72,
  75–77, 85, 127–28
  See also maternity capital; Young Families
    Program
privacy. *See* autonomy; domesticity
privatization
  attitudes toward, 5, 123–24, 131, 169–72
  effects on inequality, 51, 88, 99, 124
  effects on market, 56–57, 100, 130, 139
  law, 51–52, 109, 134
  ownership and, 92, 134, 138–40
pronatalism
  attitudes toward, 164–72
  housing and, 69, 144–45
  nationalism and, 72–75, 82
  paternalism of, 45–46, 78–79
  See also maternity capital; Soviet housing,
    pronatalism and property rights
  concept, 5–6, 12, 91, 132–33
  de facto vs. de jure, 109, 134–35, 148,
    191–92
  intrafamilial inequalities, 109, 115,
    135–42
  mortgages, 2–3, 135–36, 181–86
  rentals, 112–13, 134–35
  Soviet, 5–6, 35–37, 48, 121, 132, 136
  unprivatized housing, 115, 135, 139–40
  See also ownership; propiskas

property without markets, 6, 87–90, 98–99, 195
propiskas (residency permits)
  post-Soviet, 65, 112, 129, 131–42
  Soviet, 25–26, 34–36, 47, 133
purchase of housing, 16–18, 55–61, 119–28, 145
Putin, Vladimir
  on market reform, 7–8, 57–59, 64
  on maternity capital, 70, 75–81, 84–85, 145
  on mortgages, 58–64, 77–78, 81, 175

registration of residence. See propiskas
Reid, Susan, 32, 41, 43, 181
renovation. See home improvement
rentals, 91–92, 111–14, 150–53, 168, 183
right to housing
  legal, 52, 133–34, 191
  perceptions of, 6, 9–11, 103, 122–26, 177–78, 191–92, 194, 198
  Soviet, 6, 31–32, 34, 45–47
  state discourse on, 58, 80, 82
  See also property rights
Rivkin-Fish, Michele, 45–46, 69–71, 73, 76, 81, 85
rooms
  children's, 3–4, 46, 106, 108, 115–16, 144, 149–50, 153–56
  concept of, 30–31, 160, 207n4
  within extended family, 107, 108f, 112
  kitchens, 30–33, 40–41, 89–90, 108–9, 112–13
  living (parlor), 30, 106, 208n6
  multiuse, 30–32
Russian Longitudinal Monitoring Survey (RLMS), 13, 97, 157

satisfaction with housing, 103, 107–18, 145, 150–56, 184–85
Saunders, Peter, 5–6
saving for housing
  impossibility of, 55–56, 130, 138
  vs. mortgage, 2, 184
SDT (second demographic transition), 72–73, 75, 148
  education and, 93–95, 155–56, 167–68
secondary housing market, 56–57
securitization, 50, 53–54, 62–67
security. See ownership; property rights; separate apartments
separate apartments
  meaning of, 12–13, 91
  preference for, 4, 8, 93, 105–18, 123, 145, 184

prevalence of, 5, 88–91
  See also under normalcy
Shevchenko, Olga, 19, 128, 187, 195–96
shock therapy, 51–53, 124
  See also privatization
single-family homes. See dream houses; elite housing
single mothers, 3–4, 107, 109, 113, 149–50, 154, 169, 173
singles, 33, 42, 62, 94–98, 107–8, 114–15, 150–51
socialism and postsocialism
  hope and hopelessness, 3–4, 33, 107, 115, 122, 152–53
  nostalgia, 8, 196–97
  paths to housing, 5–6, 103, 107–15, 119–26, 191, 193
social meaning of money, 10–11, 178–79
sociology, 3, 5–11.86, 178–79
Soviet housing
  communal apartments, 13, 24–25, 28–29, 33, 43
  construction, 24, 29–35, 40–41, 47–48
  inequality, 26–29, 34–41, 47, 89f, 94–95
  living space norm, 24–26, 29–32, 44
  ownership, sense of, 41, 43–47, 121, 123, 131
  perestroika and, 6, 47–48
  pronatalism and, 27–28, 33, 45–46, 70–72, 82, 171–72
  property rights, 5–6, 35–37, 48, 132, 136
  See also khrushchevkas; propiskas; separate apartments
space. See crowding; living space norm
stability and instability, 4, 6, 119, 156, 178–83, 186–90, 193
  See also crisis
Stalin, Josef, 25–29, 74
Stalinka, 114, 136
state control of market
  attitudes toward, 103, 122–28, 164–67, 191, 196–97
  policies, 7–8, 60–67
stratification
  See inequality; housing classes; mobility
Struyk, Raymond, 51, 53–54, 58, 104
style. See interiors
subsidies, housing, 51–52, 57–58, 61–62, 70, 84–85
  attitudes toward, 118, 123–28, 139–40, 164–67, 182, 191
  See also maternity capital; mortgages, subsidies; Young Families Program
Szelenyi, Ivan, 36–37

tenure, 12–13, 91–92
  See also extended family; mortgages; rent-
    als; separate apartments
transplant effect, 2–3, 7–9, 49–54, 64–67,
    70, 132–33, 177–79, 194
trust and distrust
  of credit, 1–2, 9–10, 176
  within extended family, 138–39
  of government, 173–74, 187, 197
  See also corruption

United States
  influence in Russia, 1–3, 7, 49–54, 64–67,
    86–87, 132, 194–97 (*See also* HSRP)
  mortgage culture, 9, 177–79, 186
  subprime crisis, 66, 198–99
  See also Europe/West
USAID, 49–54, 86–87, 104

Washington Consensus, 49–53, 64, 70,
    86–87, 99–100, 104, 198–99
Weber, Max, 36, 87
Week Like Any Other (novel), 44, 171
West. *See* Europe/West
work/employment
  and childbearing, 146–50, 153, 162
  and housing status, 92, 94–100
  as path to mobility, 4, 118–22, 125, 128,
    138–39
  See also affordability
World Bank, 49–50, 70

Yeltsin, Boris, 49–54, 57, 193
Young Families Program (YFP), 61–63,
    127–28, 139–40, 182, 193
  See also mortgages, subsidies; Priority
    National Projects